Paraverbal Communication in Psychotherapy

Paraverbal Communication in Psychotherapy

Beyond the Words

James M. Donovan,
Kristin A. R. Osborn,
Susan Rice

ROWMAN & LITTLEFIELD
New York • London

Published by Rowman & Littlefield
A wholly owned subsidiary of The Rowman & Littlefield Publishing Group, Inc.
4501 Forbes Boulevard, Suite 200, Lanham, Maryland 20706
www.rowman.com

Unit A, Whitacre Mews, 26-34 Stannary Street, London SE11 4AB

British Library Cataloguing in Publication Information Available

Library of Congress Cataloging-in-Publication Data

Names: Donovan, James M. (James Montgomery), 1943- author. | Osborn, Kristin A. R.,
author. | Rice, Susan (Susan S.), author.
Title: Paraverbal communication in psychotherapy : beyond the words / James M.
Donovan, Kristin A.R. Osborn, and Susan Rice.
Description: Lanham : Rowman & Littlefield, [2017] | Includes bibliographical
references and index.
Identifiers: LCCN 2016037533 (print) | LCCN 2016038659 (ebook) |
ISBN 9781442246737 (cloth : alk. paper) | ISBN 9781442246751 (pbk. : alk. paper) |
ISBN 9781442246744 (electronic)
Subjects: | MESH: Psychotherapeutic Processes | Nonverbal Communication–psychology |
Health Communication | Professional-Patient Relations
Classification: LCC RC480.5 (print) | LCC RC480.5 (ebook) | NLM WM 420 |
DDC 616.89/14—dc23
LC record available at https://lccn.loc.gov/2016037533

♾™ The paper used in this publication meets the minimum requirements of American
National Standard for Information Sciences—Permanence of Paper for Printed Library
Materials, ANSI/NISO Z39.48-1992.

Printed in the United States of America

To Liz, Abbie, Brian and Bette, you have taught me so much about communication. I love you. Dad/Jim

To Jeremy and Isaiah, with gratitude and love, Kristin

To Chris and to Chris, my loves, Susan

In loving memory of Leigh McCullough

Contents

Preface

Three Paraverbal Puzzles

"Take away the words and you find all the adornments that surround them. Body language, gestures, the story of the eyes."—Gail Caldwell, *Let's Take The Long Way Home* (2010, p. 140)

CASE #1—MARVIN AND ANN—DISMISSIVE ANGER

One week ago, this professional Caucasian couple in their late 50s, married 30 years, both biologists, come for their sixth visit which, like the first five, does not get very far. Ann reports that Marvin is disputatious, negative, and often loses his temper with family members, with her, and with strangers. The prescription for an antidepressant and the sleep apnea intervention have helped him a little with self-regulation, but as our latest frustrating session nears its close, we still cannot grasp what makes him so truculent.

As is my wont, at the close of this session, I hand him a note on which I list the new learning of today's meeting for the couple to review, if they wish, before our next appointment.

Marvin: (loud, sharp, derogatory, almost insolent tone) Didn't I tell you these scraps of paper are of no use to me?

Jim: I'm sorry I forgot. What would help you between meetings?

Marvin: (very loud, derisive inflection, glares at me) Nothing, I don't think you know what you're doing.

Jim: (calm, keeping eye contact) Funny I've done this a long time. (neutral tone)

Marvin: (very loud, insulting edge now, leans forward, almost menacingly) You're a fraud and a charlatan! (furious critical delivery)

Jim: (annoyed myself now, direct eye contact, more powerful inflection) Why would you return to someone so inept? (posing a paradox)

Marvin: My wife Ann thinks it helps. I think it's useless, and you're useless. (dismissively)

Jim: (more neutrally) It's time to stop. Shall we keep the next appointment? What do you think?

Ann: Yes, let's. I think it's valuable to me. I'm at the end of my rope. (tone of despair)

Jim: Okay. (more optimistic inflection, more relaxed body posture) Ann gets up to leave; Marvin stalks after her. I sit dazed, feeling abused, angry, and a little frightened of Marvin's sudden outburst. Why does he act with such virulence? Does this treatment have a future?

CASE #2—PAT—NO WORDS

I've treated Pat, a 24-year-old white, single, male veterinary student for two years, weekly or bi-weekly. One day he begins to reminisce about his German shepherd dog from his teenage years. They were very close. When he did his homework, the dog often sat by. His pet seemed the only member of the family with whom Pat felt a bond. In the middle of his adolescence, the parents decided to move to a condo that would not accept large animals. They left the dog at the old house and returned to feed and walk him daily. Pat feels overwhelmed with guilt, convinced he should have stayed in the former home to care for his pal. The dog died a few months later.

I try to explain that adolescents have limited autonomy. When his parents refused his request, he had few options.

Pat, who formerly has taken a friendly and engaged tone with me, now glares and will not speak for the rest of this hour. He's entirely mute for the next six sessions and will not respond to any of my questions or attempts to connect. I share my helplessness but still no response from Pat. During this period, he arrives and leaves on time but remains absolutely silent and looks down at his feet with a tight, apparently angry jaw. I'm mostly confused but also a little worried that he might act self-destructively after he leaves the appointment, since he's obviously so upset. I do not sense any physical threat from him toward myself. The rage seems internal. What is my next move?

CASE #3—PAMELA AND FRED—A SMILE

Pamela, a 55-year-old, white, college-educated, housewife, sculptress, and a quiet woman, arrives for perhaps her eighth monthly session with her 60-year-old husband Fred, a lawyer. They come so infrequently because they want "check in" appointments but not more intensive therapy. They're an economically successful couple with three adult daughters.

I've not seen them in three months, this time, due to their vacation and to the bad weather. Little has changed; they seem moderately stalemated as usual. Fred wants more interaction and affection. Pamela feels more ambivalent about both but also committed to Fred. Her husband is the more talkative and quickly becomes frustrated when Pamela responds to him with only a few words. He asks her about her plans for the upcoming summer break.

> *Pamela:* I'm writing in my journal. I want to work on my sculpting and my exercise—and my relationships—particularly with you— (a sweet, gentle smile crosses her lips—often she's nearly expressionless but not now.)

Fred doesn't seem to notice this smile and does not respond to her. I point it out, then he too smiles broadly. We continue the meeting talking about activities that they could do together at their summer house, a discussion that has some animation. Both seem more relaxed and a little more mutually engaged.

After each appointment, I try to watch my couples, as they walk down the hall away from my office, to gauge the impact of the session on their body language. She departs, and he catches up to her and puts his right arm around her shoulder. She puts her left arm around his waist. He asks her, "Are you doing this because Jim's watching?" I shout after them: "This looks suspiciously like affection. I'm turning into the waiting room now, and no one's observing anymore." What will the next session with Fred and Pamela bring?

Each of these scenarios unfolded at my clinic two in the last month, one ten years past. All felt complex and confusing certainly for the therapist and probably for the patients. The mystery begins because each of these encounters turn on paraverbal information—voice tones, bodily movements, facial expressions, radio silence, far more than on any spoken words. What moved Marvin to speak in so devaluing a way to me? How should I respond to him?

Why did Pat immediately, uncharacteristically, became angrily mute and stay that way, when remembering the death of his beloved pet? Should I try harder to help him break his isolation and if so how?

What is the meaning of Pamela's sudden warm smile? Why did Fred seem oblivious to it at first? Should I pursue further their smiling one after the other? What do these facial messages mean to each other? How important are they to the therapy? What is the meaning of their affectionate walk down the hall?

Paraverbal interplay regularly unfolds in our treatments. However, we usually don't call direct attention to it. As in these three scenarios, paradoxically, the extra-verbal relating seems often to carry crucial significance for the treatment. We'll unravel these three excerpts, more, by the end of Chapter 1.

We use them here to introduce our subject. We wrote this book to illustrate the central importance of extra-verbal communication in therapy, and in relationships in general, and to illustrate paths through which we might explore these phenomena more fully. We probably all agree that our knowledge of nonverbal relating lags our ability to respond to the verbal interchange. Given this challenge, studying a videotape on which we can run, and rerun, the important paraverbal exchanges, feels like a logical starting place.

Chapter One

The History of Dynamic Psychotherapy

Its Paraverbal World

THE NEW THERAPIST AND THE VIDEOTAPE

The universe of dynamic psychotherapy has undergone slow but ultimately dramatic changes since the 1970s. Now a new psychotherapist has taken up residence in the office. This book tells the story of what we found when we studied that new therapist directly, by watching her work, on videotape or through extended case excerpts. Here we learn that today's counselor's thoughts, words, and behaviors sharply set her in contrast to her counterparts of just 25 years earlier.

The videotape, for the first time, reveals to us not only the verbatim spoken exchanges but also the bodily messages: the tones of voice—the facial expressions—the gestures of patient *and* therapist as they choreograph their interaction. When we begin to examine the therapy participants as *embodied* speakers, at this moment, we find ourselves on the outskirts of mostly untrodden territory. We sense an evolutionary advance perhaps about to take place on the screen because we can now choose to study all the extra-verbal information, as well as the verbal, in the therapy interchange.

We write for an audience of professional therapists, junior or senior, and psychotherapy researchers, but all practicing clinicians. We have a proposition to test. If we examine and systematically score, line by line, the paraverbal behavior of the client and therapist on the video screen, we will discover a new layer of communicative bond unfolding between the participants, as seems likely in our three introductory cases so far.

When we start down this path, the therapist will find herself confronted with an entire range of fresh questions. How would I note, and perhaps

1

directly remark upon, the paraverbal messages sent by my client? How do I observe my own nonverbal participation? Might I shift my approach by including more emphatic extra-verbal messages from my side of the office, and how might I ascertain the reciprocal effect on my client?

We suggest, first, that the psychotherapy interaction already carries with it a universe of paraverbal data, which the participants continually exchange. We, the researchers, and our readers, need to learn much more about this information. Second, as she becomes more comfortable with the extra-verbal perspective, the therapist might want to change her mode of practice to make more full use, in specific ways, of these nonverbal currents that swirl around and through her and her client. The balance of our book will grapple with these two questions.

However, to grasp the meaning of this possibly imminent shift, as we may welcome paraverbal data into our psychotherapy scholarship, we must understand the history of the two psychodynamic evolutions that have preceded this third development. Also, others have touched on the issue of extra-verbal communication in therapy, and we need to review their contributions.

Finally, we must consider the mechanisms through which changes in outlook and practice actually take place in our field to prepare ourselves for this potential next evolutionary move. We can't, in other words, just begin to analyze videotapes and case vignettes from a paraverbal standpoint, without first grounding ourselves in the core issues of today's and yesterday's therapy world (Wachtel, 2014).

As our primary resource data, we'll study and score a total of four single-session videotapes from three clinicians who differ in gender, age, and theoretical approach, though all are very experienced therapists—Jim Donovan, Kristin Osborn, LMHC, and Paul Wachtel.

First, we need to review some important earlier developments, tracing how we arrived, as a field, clinically and theoretically, at our present position, vis a vis paraverbal communication now in 2016. We'll discover that at first the dominant momentum tended to banish the study of nonverbal data, but now that trend may have shifted toward a different emphasis.

DYNAMIC PSYCHOTHERAPY:
2015—THE RELATIONAL STANCE

All of us encountered the modern practitioner first in the literature, so, we'll start with that writing before we turn to any video or case history information. Unlike the situation in the late 1970s of a Kernberg (1975) or a Kohut (1971), no single figure has emerged in the past quarter century, whose individual ideas have radically shifted the arc of our field, so the recent developments we currently observe perhaps appear less pronounced. Rather, many have cooperated, at a lurching and stuttering pace, to construct the position we now call "Relational" psychotherapy, probably the predominant theme in our psychodynamic world of 2016.

For psychotherapy study, we cannot perceive exactly when a season shifts and the wind starts to come from a different direction. If, however, we leaf through a text from the 1960s or 1970s, even an outstanding one, Greenson (1967), for instance, or Kohut (1971), and then turn to today's, or to yesterday's, equally well-done piece, for example, Maroda (1991, 1999, 2010), Wishnie (2005), or Wachtel (2008), we're startled. The description of the therapist's voice and behavior, of the underlying theories of change and of the preferred therapeutic technique, don't just seem astoundingly different from 25 years before; they are shockingly different.

Somewhere in the volumes by Mitchell (1983, 1988, 1995), Casement (1985), Stolorow, Brandschaft and Atwood (1987), Maroda (1991, 1999, 2010), Wishnie (2005), Wallin (2007), or Wachtel (2008) or still others, we will find the emergence of that relational therapist at first appearing, then disappearing, but now here to stay. To study the modern clinician directly, we need to map, historically, the recent evolution of the field up to today, where we can get a glimpse of the paraverbal therapist who maybe just entering our landscape.

We'll pursue how each change in therapeutic approach arose and how new thinkers helped evolve one viewpoint into the next. We ask the reader to accompany us on this path, for a bit, because we need to understand how the paraverbal position might now start to unfold within our evolution at this particular time.

Only if we survey this road, more thoroughly and our present position on it, can we know what work we need to take on to integrate the next shift, perhaps one that includes an emphasis on extra-verbal relating. We are mindful, too, that psychotherapy schools, beyond the psychodynamic one, have continued to develop over the last two decades, in their understanding of patient/therapist interactions. In Chapter 2, we'll also catch up with the spectrum of these non-dynamic outlooks.

METHODS OF THERAPEUTIC INTERVENTION: SOME HISTORICAL PERSPECTIVE—THE LAST 45 YEARS

Martha Stark in *Modes of Therapeutic Action* (1999), has captured the subtle, though inexorable, evolution of the contemporary psychotherapist as clearly and thoroughly as anyone. Now in the very early 2000s, Stark explains that the modern dynamic therapist can assume one of three possible stances (or any combination thereof) toward her client.

She can, at Level 1, *interpret* the patient's unconscious life according to Freudian Drive Theory or, at Level 2, she can *provide* the client with the missing good object (following Kohut's self-psychology (1971) or Winnicott's "transitional object" position (1971) or, at Level 3, she may *enter into* an intimate fully relational interaction with the client to address, little by little, the damage wrought by childhood traumatic interchanges (Mitchell and Greenberg, 1983; Ehrenberg, 1992; Mitchell and Black, 1995; Aron 1996; Wishnie, 2005; Wachtel 2008).

We'll take time now to study these three possible therapeutic positions in some depth, since they bear directly on our research. What place does nonverbal communication have within any of these approaches? We'll revisit these stages of therapeutic advancement in historical and theoretical sequence. This survey will ultimately take us deeply into Level 3, relational work. Here we'll find a therapist just beginning to focus and practice with a paraverbal emphasis.

Level 1:

To understand our present location, we have to go back before we go forward. Let's retrace our steps. Prior to the 1970s, in Level 1 therapy (see Stark, 1999), interpretation of instinctual drive, ostensibly represented the primary accepted psychodynamic strategy. Psychoanalytic institutes and dynamic psychology training programs espoused this approach, as did the symbolic leaders of the field, originally Freud of course, but also the important contemporary figures of that time, Greenson (1967), for example.

When I (Jim) left my psychodynamic graduate school program in 1970, my peers and my teachers shared the idealized picture of an omniscient, older, white, male therapist–analyst, impeccably dressed, empathic but rather distant from, and ambiguous in personality to, his patient. He often sat out of sight and sent well formulated, carefully timed interpretations of oedipal strivings and transference wishes, across the gulf that he had constructed between himself and his client.

We practitioners in training identified with this complex caricature of the psychoanalyst. When we sought therapy ourselves, we often encountered that same formal, distant, interpretive, purportedly blank screen therapist greeting us, not very warmly, at the office door, caricature perhaps, but also a description of how real and respected practitioners, at that time, often did proceed.

This figure, of course, sent strong paraverbal messages of his own: ironically perhaps, emphasizing distance and propriety, but we rarely dared remark on this restrictive atmosphere in the room. He certainly never did. He seemed intent on reducing nonverbal communication, between patient and counselor, to a minimum. For him it appeared all about the spoken words. Over the next few pages, we'll see that the tide is now maybe beginning to flow in the opposite direction, toward studying more paraverbal connections.

EVOLUTION NUMBER 1: OBJECT
RELATIONS INTERVENTIONS

Though few of us held much inkling of such things in the late 1960s, ideas quite at odds with this stereotyped, Level 1, approach had already begun to bubble under the edges of the broad surface of our field. Visionaries like Ferenczi (1931), Reik (1948), Searles (1965), Racker (1968), Balint (1968, 1972), and Winnicott (1971) argued early on that the doctor must provide the client something far deeper and more human than a punctiliously crafted, rational, verbal interpretation of his unconscious conflict.

Their therapist, corresponding to Stark's Level 2 provider of today, made powerful *relationship offers*, some couched paraverbally, in addition to, and in tandem with, insight-oriented clarification. The crucial conceptual leap here is that the therapist represents the *missing good* object both theoretically and in clinical practice.

When we read Fairbairn (1952), Racker (1968), Balint (1968, 1972), and Winnicott (1971) in the original, we feel them reach toward us across time and space. We cannot miss the freshness and the authenticity of their words and actions, as they offer us their brilliant grasp of the therapeutic interchange, and of the corresponding therapeutic process, at its core. These remarkable thinkers sound as if they wrote in 2016, not five decades earlier.

If we return to our three introductory scenarios on page 1, we begin to realize that in each instance, our clients have offered us a paraverbal dilemma, that is, 24-year-old Pat won't speak. To respond productively, we're probably going to have to act strongly on some nonverbal, not just verbal dimension. These early object relationists gave us some hints on how to proceed.

For example, a young, adult, female patient, sometime in 1967 or 1968, crippled with uncertainty, complained once again to Michael Balint of her paralyzing inhibition and confessed that she could not even attempt a somersault as a child, although she badly wanted to try one. Balint suggested, "What about it now?" She got up, and to the amazement of both, did a perfect somersault across the office floor (recounted in Mitchell 1988, p. 154—originally in Balint 1968, pp. 128–129). These gymnastics marked a turning point in her treatment. Moreover, this new humanly available, unquestionably supportive, practitioner began to change our entire understanding of psychotherapy.

Here, Balint became the encouraging, giving parental object who accompanied his patient in her experiment to lift a deadening defense of self-censure. Any weak paragraphs we might add cannot define a Level 2 object relations therapist better than Balint's liberating offer to his patient—"What about it now?." Clearly, in this response to this client, a rational, carefully formulated interpretation would account for only part, maybe a small part, of the therapeutic leverage. For one of the first times historically, we cannot miss the *extra-verbal* dimension to Balint's intervention, a remarkable departure in technique. He suggests a somersault. We can see our subject of paraverbal relating now just entering the stage.

I remember the initial thrill of holding the books by Fairbairn (1952), Racker (1968), Balint (1968), and Winnicott (1971), and slowly reading through their pages. They seemed as startling as Technicolor. The therapist became personally alive. For me and for many others, these authors opened an entirely new vista into the process of psychotherapy to explore the relationship first of all and then, perhaps, the unconscious verbal meanings. As the 1970s closed and the 1980s started, this powerful current had begun to sweep us along in a fresh direction, although maybe not many of us realized it at the time.

We'll describe this first evolution in dynamic therapy in a bit more depth. Stark (1999) and Mitchell (1988) before her documented a developmental stage in our psychotherapeutic thought that we may often forget. We did not jump in one long stride from a drive-oriented, insight-oriented, interpretive orientation to the relational treatment we look at today. The object relations position provided the bridge between the two.

It arrived with the work of the original Level 2 therapists some of whom we've just named: Balint (1968), Winnicott (1971), Fairbairn (1952), Harry Guntrip (1969, 1975), Kohut (1971), and Massud Khan (1974). These thinkers not only realized that the client's core difficulty revolved around an empathic relationship missed in childhood, but they also concluded, in a next brilliant paradigm-changing step, that the treatment *must make good* on the childhood loss and provide, maybe for the first time, some aspects of the primary holding relationship, which the client could then take in as his or her own.

Balint (Balint, Ornstein and Balint, 1972), for example, offered us a landmark case in which he treated the Stationary Manufacturer, a middle-aged man, fighting off a paranoid decomposition, fueled by his obsession with his wife's possible prior sexual involvements. Balint volunteered nary one interpretation in his therapy but carefully allowed the Stationary Manufacturer to use him as "a sounding board"—the client's term.

In Balint's skillful 27-session therapy, carefully spaced across a two-year period, the client recovered his equilibrium and remained relatively symptom free thereafter. Psychotropics was undeveloped in 1970 but, in any case, Balint made no use of medications in the supportive treatment of this very distressed man. His intervention was about the interaction. We guess, but cannot know, that this patient/therapist exchange included paraverbal signs of calm understanding from Balint, perhaps a warm smile, a reassuring tone and hand gestures with an open palm. Unfortunately, he does not report directly about any of these behavioral offers.

This next sentence summarizes the thrust of Balint's case and the rationale of object relations dynamic psychotherapy. The therapist becomes the missing object and proffers a *relationship* (Level-2 intervention) and not only an *interpretation* (Level 1). The field had started to change forever. The pioneers showed that we could push away from Level 1 and move, in addition, toward a Level-2 approach, whenever appropriate (Stark, 1999). More paraverbal therapist involvement may well have accompanied this shift in therapist stance, but as noted, unfortunately, we have no direct evidence of this.

EVOLUTION NUMBER 2—RELATIONAL THERAPY

We need to pay careful attention to Stark's next distinction. Object relations theory might, and we think does, almost inevitably usher in the age of relational therapy in which we presently find ourselves ensconced in 2016. However, relational therapy differs so importantly from object relations treatment that this change represents another evolution. We'll take a moment now to spell out the architecture of that next major step.

To recapitulate, the object relationists and the self-psychologists, Stark's Level 2 therapists, focus on what the parent *did*, that is, acted as a harmful intrusive influence, or *did not do*, that is, failed to provide a caring holding relationship. The goal of therapy thus moves directly from making the *unconscious conscious* (Level 1) to *introducing a relationship* (Level 2) that the patient can internalize to begin the repair of his personality issues (Stark 1999, p. xvii).

However, as Stark observes, Level 2 therapy, although strongly empathetic, acts in only *one* direction. The therapist provides a holding interaction and understands her client in a way that she vitally requires. The counselor encourages the patient to use her for support and understanding, but the therapist does not participate as *another full human being*. If we study Kohut's case reports, for example, we consistently find the sympathetic, available listener ever alert for mirroring and idealizing transferences, but *we do not find* a fully present relational partner who freely allows many sides of his own self to enter the exchange.

The relational therapist assumes that the client requires a distinctively fuller, two-way interaction, to address his or her issues. If object relations treatment is a "one and a half person" therapy—the patient entirely there, coupled with some aspects of the therapist's personality fully in the office, relational therapy represents a complete "two-person" endeavor.

In this new relational mode, both participants are transparently present (Stark 1999, xxii). The personal feelings, memories, and spontaneous responses of the *therapist* potentially become part of the matrix cocreated by the client and by the practitioner (Maroda 1991, 1999, 2010; Wishnie 2005; Wachtel 2008). Moreover, a potentially paraverbal exchange now slides toward more central focus since both participants become more open to each other.

We can't move on, though, and leave insight and object relations behind as vestigial parts of the field. Stark reminds us that we need to draw on all three modes in constructive sequences. We try to impart to our client fresh self-knowledge (Level 1 therapy) and a holding, empathic, relationship experience, at Level 2, in each session.

When, as entire persons, we function at Level 3, we stay open to the patient's questions and misgivings about us, and we may share our own positive or conflicted feelings about that client, as well as something of our own personal histories and memories. We can laugh with, directly encourage and maybe even cry with, and get angry with, that patient. Note the nonverbal emphases in this last sentence "laugh," "cry," "get angry." When relational therapy moves toward center stage, paraverbal technique may soon follow.

The birth of relational therapy

Guntrip (1975) has provided us a unique view into the actual work of Fairbairn and of Winnicott. He participated sequentially in analysis with both. In Guntrip's monograph, we can observe the very beginnings of relational therapy, and we can see in detail how it evolves from the object relations position.

Fairbairn, one founder of the object relations theoretical school (1952), in practice, was actually quite distant from Guntrip his client. He sat impersonally behind his imposing desk and made object relations interpretations to Guntrip based on his understanding of his patient's particular oedipal dynamics.

On the other hand, Fairbairn also did offer Guntrip the experience of a generous accepting object because, off camera after the therapy sessions, or in written correspondence between meetings, Fairbairn became the "good human father" (Guntrip, 1975, p. 148) and engaged in coequal, collegial, theoretical discussions with Guntrip. Fairbairn now assumes a more open paraverbal position.

Despite these helpful personal offers from Fairbairn, Guntrip realized that he would not penetrate to his deepest, most repressed memories in this treatment. He phased out the therapy with Fairbairn in 1960. Fairbairn died at the end of 1964, but he had introduced Guntrip to Winnicott through the post in 1954.

Guntrip began an analysis with Winnicott in the mid-1960s. Now we meet Winnicott, face to face, in a rare verbatim record of his work. Guntrip, at different points, quotes him word for word. We encounter both the object relations and the relational therapist embedded within just a few paragraphs. For example, at the end of the first session with Guntrip, Winnicott offered "I've nothing particular to say yet, but if I don't say something, you may begin to feel I'm not here" (p. 152).

At the second session, with astounding insight, Winnicott continued:

> ... You know about me but I'm not a person to you yet. You may go away feeling alone and that I'm not real. ... (Guntrip, 1975, p. 152)

Here we see Winnicott offering himself as a deeply supportive present object and speaking in a very personal tone. At this moment, he's the embodiment of the Level 2 object relations therapist, providing the earlier parental support that Guntrip had so sorely missed growing up.

However, more followed. By the close of the treatment, Winnicott also transformed into the prototypic Level 3 relational therapist (circa 1969), who didn't formally begin to emerge in the literature for 15 more years. Now Guntrip returns to his highly energized "hard talking" in the therapy; Winnicott responds using his full self.

> "It's like you're giving birth to a baby with my help. You gave me half an hour of concentrated talk, rich in content. I felt *strained* listening and holding the situation for you. You had to know that I *could stand* you talking hard at me and my not being destroyed. I had to stand it while you were in labor being creative, not destructive, producing something rich in content. You are talking about object relating, using the object and finding you don't destroy it. I couldn't have made that interpretation five years ago. ...
> ... "You too have a good breast." You've always been able to give more than take. I'm good for you but *you're good for me.* Doing your analysis is almost the most *reassuring thing that happens to me.* The chap before you makes me feel I'm no good at all. You don't have to be good for me. I don't need it, and can cope without it but, in fact, you are good for me." (p. 153; all italics ours)

In this paragraph, Winnicott reveals many of his own feelings and needs as he enters into a full two-person relationship with Guntrip. "Here at last I had a good mother who could value her child so that I could cope with what was to come" (p. 153). Winnicott has now become more than a good object but an equal, when he tells Guntrip of his own dilemma with a patient whom he sees earlier in the day, and when he lets Guntrip know how nurturing, but not life sustaining, the relationship with Guntrip has become for Winnicott himself.

At the close of the therapy, Winnicott has clearly personified a two-person, Level 3 relational therapist. This moment, sometime in 1969, marks the birth of the Level 3 relational therapist.

Guntrip, 40 years ago, emphasized the difference in the physical positions his two analysts took in the office. Here we pick up the first hints of the paraverbal interaction that they arranged. Each posture sent a clear nonverbal message. He tells us that Fairbairn sat behind a gigantic desk in a large chair, by Guntrip's description, "in state." Winnicott sat next to the patient in a small chair so that the client, while prone on the analytic couch, could turn and see him. In addition, Winnicott's spoken words clearly include a transparent supportive tone, "You are good for me," not so Fairbairn. Winnicott sounds paraverbally connected—sitting close by, speaking gently. Guntrip feels far more free with Winnicott than with Fairbairn.

However, beyond these important contrasts in the office arrangement and the different voice inflections of the counselors, Guntrip rarely emphasizes further extra-verbal interventions, offered by Fairbairn or Winnicott, beyond their actual words. Nevertheless, for perhaps the first time in their literature, Guntrip's description of Winnicott communicates the consistently warm presence of the relational therapist.

Now we need a videotape ... we've arrived at the center of our subject

Regrettably we do not have the potential connecting link between Winnicott's relational therapy and our studies of paraverbal communication. Had we a video of Winnicott or of Balint, which we sorely miss, we might hear their bonding, open voice tones, slow supportive prosody, and observe their relaxed inviting, calming bodily positions that could well have contributed a great deal to their impact as therapists. We certainly have examples of Winnicott's inclusive engaged phrases—"You'll be afraid I'm not here," or from Balint "What about (a somersault) now?"

CURRENT DYNAMIC THERAPY

Extensive research evidence on psychotherapy supports the general position that a successful treatment likely includes a supportive self-object therapist and a positive, mutually caring and respectful, relational alliance. See, for example, Greenberg, Rice and Elliot (1993) and Bohart and Tallman, (1999).

In two comprehensive reviews, Wampold (2001) and Norcross et al. (2002, 2014) summarize the results of hundreds of outcome and process studies and argue that psychotherapy does not represent a purely Level 1, quasi-medical procedural treatment, in which only the experience and the technique, and not the person of the therapist, influence the success of the enterprise.

Rather, therapy apparently reflects a "contextual" undertaking in which the *personality* of the therapist and the *quality* of the personal alliance count for significant proportions of the variance in outcome. The personal characteristics of the well-trained vascular surgeon presumably make no difference in the success of his procedure. If that doctor and his or her clinical team have the skills, the patient usually successfully recovers, but undertaking psychotherapy evidently requires a deeper level of personal involvement by the practitioner.

After reading Greenberg et al. (1993), Bohart and Tallman (1999), and Norcross and Wampold, we can only come away with the "evidence-based" view that psychotherapy involves a technique but also a relationship (see, as well, Wachtel 2008, 2011) between two persons (and between their paraverbal selves?). Norcross and Wampold's studies support the Stark and Wachtel theoretical positions—successful therapy requires more than insight (Level 1) alone.

Now whither the field?

If we could chart our progress as psychotherapy scholars up to this point and then stop, our world would look something like this. We live and work in 2016; relational therapy seems here to stay. We need to continue to study this set of principles. How do the patient and the therapist cocreate an atmosphere in which the former can feel held by the therapist as a whole person, while he or she experiences and affectively works through previous relationship trauma? These issues have become increasingly important not only in relational psychotherapy therapy but in the affect-focused, nondirective, collaborative and cognitive behavioral approaches as well (Greenberg et al., 1993; Bohart and Tallman, 1999; Wachtel, 2014). Can we anticipate the next move?

A THIRD EVOLUTIONARY STEP?: THE MISSING PARAVERBAL DATA

If we review Stark's three modes of therapeutic action, we've already noticed that the therapist becomes more personally and bodily involved at each developmental step. This means that *paraverbal communication* also becomes more critically important at each succeeding level, whether or not this change in style draws any direct mention.

If the relational therapist is present as a full person—what does he or she actually communicate as an embodied person, as well as with his or her words. Here we refind the focus of our book. One can interpret affect and resistance and keep the exchange within the realm of verbal insight, but as soon as we become giving "self objects" or "relational partners," our *nonverbal selves*, and inevitably those of our clients too begin to take important focus. From page 1, recall Marvin's disdainful tone and body language toward me, and my irritated response back to him—much extra-verbal content here.

Empathic, Level 3 therapists often speak gently, look directly at their clients, perhaps sigh, and definitely smile. Their patients may return those gestures with grateful or relaxed looks, as they become recognized persons. Of course, either participant might also display sad or angry facial expressions, or frightened tones of voice or other troubled body language, at different points in a single hour or in a series of therapy sessions. We have to track all these nonverbal messages.

Relational therapists laugh, raise their voices, shrug their shoulders, and open their hands and arms in accepting gestures, but sometimes look upset or confused, all of which contribute markedly to the relationship and to the process of its continuing formation. Jacobs (1991), Beebe and Lachmann (2002), and Wishnie (2005) have begun to discuss the implications of this paraverbal world for psychotherapy, but as a general field, we've just started down this path of investigation. In sum, the realization begins to sneak up on us that a therapist, present as a full person is there in his or her complete body also, not just in her words, and so is his or her client (see also Ogden and Fisher, 2015).

Case summaries in the literature still report little about the patient's appearance, gestures, timbres, and rhythms of speech and rarely describe the therapist's paraverbal self: opened or closed hand gestures, smiles, or gentleness or flatness in vocal tone (see Allen, 2013).

Many powerful factors account for these omissions. For the most part, we simply haven't had the data, or haven't looked at much data that we did have, to explore the paraverbal aspects of psychotherapy. If it's relational, it means that, for both counselor and client, voice tone and rhythm, smiles, frowns, and bodily positions play a central role in the interaction; so where's the specific information? The answer is that we don't have much of it in any useable form, as yet. However, in Chapter 2, we'll review the important emerging research in the study of nonverbal messaging.

In 1991, Jacobs began to describe his patients" physical actions on the couch and the meanings those gestures seemed to have for the treatment. Ms. C, an apparently passive/aggressive female patient, for example, evidently angry, dropped into silence and turned to face the wall, but she never verbalized any of her feelings at that point. Simultaneously, Jacobs felt his own body tense, constrict, and move back from his client. The two engaged in an intense interchange but with not a word.

They later had a chance to discuss their interaction; the client directly revealed her previous anger at Jacobs. Jacobs closed by concluding that his contribution represented only the introduction to our topic, to the region of nonverbal communication in therapy. He assured us that further research projects would advance this knowledge (Jacobs, 1991).

In the intervening 25 years, with a few significant exceptions that we'll mention shortly, the field hasn't started this "further research." What happened, and what didn't happen? Why did we get deflected from the promising momentum to study paraverbal phenomena that Jacobs provided?

First, why were we so slow to pick up Jacob's challenge and study extra-verbal happenings in therapy? For one reason, we haven't had the paraverbal information available to us to research such areas—where would we find it? But even if we did have that data, we also lack a vocabulary to convey our observations about these phenomena in any sensible fashion.

How do you verbally communicate about the paraverbal? How do you describe a smile, a hand gesture, a grimace, a drop in speech tone or a slowing in its prosody? Our usual lexicon doesn't help us very much here at all. We're going to have to invent new phrases to capture these happenings and use these phrases deftly enough so that others will find our descriptions recognizable and useful.

Second, as Ekman (2001, 2003) has so frequently reported, many facial and bodily movements shift in microseconds. Malcolm Gladwell's popular science book Blink (2005) suggests, over and over, that paraverbal data registers so quickly that we're usually completely unaware of its great influence. Did the African-American man in the Bronx, facing the white police officers in a darkened doorway, take a gun, or a large set of keys, out of his pocket? This nonverbal, split second, perceptual moment carried life-threatening significance for all the participants (Gladwell, 2005). Evidently, we have to remain very alert to paraverbal messaging or it will slip by us.

Third, we can pretty easily grasp that if we're going to study extra-verbal happenings in psychotherapy, we require an actual visual record of events to study slowly and carefully. We're going to need videotape data, information not easily obtained. Moreover, we must find some way of organizing and scoring that material to capture the rapidity and complexity with which it unfolds.

This book is about what happens when you study videotapes or detailed case reports of psychotherapy and analyze the paraverbal communication, which you can observe. Later in this chapter, we'll return to our strategy for gathering and codifying that taped information.

PARAVERBAL DATA IN PSYCHOTHERAPY—TWO
SECTORS OF PROBABLE CLINICAL DISCOVERY

Two areas powerfully illustrate the importance of paraverbal nuance for our work, but we've perhaps overlooked their significance in this respect so far: (1) the mother–infant research reports and (2) the treatment of patients with nonpsychotic personality disorder. Developments in both spheres begin to confront us with the role of nonverbal communication in therapy.

A. The Mother–Infant Communication Studies

From the late 1980s, psychoanalytic scholars studied and wrote about the relational aspects of therapy more and more closely. Meanwhile another series of research reports, from an entirely different group, began to emerge, which carried great meaning for our work in psychotherapy, and in fact, for all investigations of interpersonal relationships—the mother–infant communication studies.

Stern et al. (1985, 1998), Lyons-Ruth (1998, 2005), Beebe et al. (2002, 2005), and Tronick (2007) pursued ingenious methods of observing and describing the mother–infant exchange, by definition a (partially) paraverbal phenomenon, since one participant could not talk, although it turns out that the baby sure does communicate. This research exclusively used the microanalysis of videotaped material. Very few, if any, psychotherapy studies, even now in 2016, focus on this kind of second-by-second visual research design.

What did Stern, Beebe, and Tronick discover?

Beyond words, how do two people interchange? How do they recognize each other's feelings and respond to them? How can they know if they remain in touch with each other, if they cannot express this verbally? As we ponder these nonverbal questions, we realize we're now approaching basic issues about the epicenter of human relatedness. How do we achieve real intimacy with another person, with or without words? We're also inevitably engaging with what happens at the heart of the psychotherapy exchange.

We'll review the specific mother–infant communication research findings at length in Chapter 2. In briefest summary, Stern, Beebe, and their colleagues concluded that the mother and infant interacted in a complex choreography to sooth, regulate, and provide safety for each other and to construct a space in which more complex growth and learning interactions could continue to occur. We will discuss this and much more in Chapter 2 and in subsequent chapters. We'll build our book around these observations of paraverbal interchange, first conceptualized in the parent–infant studies, the conclusions from which we then apply to our videotapes.

Now we'll consider why this mother–baby research hasn't informed psychotherapy more deeply. The parent–infant duo appears so obviously an analogue to the psychotherapy pair that we might predict much fertile crossover research, not much so far, however.

Many circumstances contribute to this curious disconnection between the two fields. First, in human relations–applied research, much time inevitably passes before laboratory findings ever impact practice. For example, one original thinker from the Stanford Graduate School of Education, whose name escapes us now, reflected that it took 50 years for a new idea, conceived and tested in the Stanford graduate program, no matter how helpful a concept, to become accepted in the average elementary school in Terra Haute, Indiana.

Psychodynamic therapy with all its historical quirks, to say nothing of the personal cults surrounding Freud and later luminaries, hardly represents the ideal proving ground to respond readily to new research information sent from the outside.

Also, in most cases, academics and clinicians usually reside in different professional camps with surprisingly little communication between them. When asked about the implications of her research for adult psychotherapy, Beatrice Beebe, a practicing psychoanalyst herself, noted that applying the mother–infant findings directly to psychotherapy represented a new and major challenge even for someone, like herself, well versed in both disciplines (mentioned during her address on Infant Research and Adult Treatment at the Harvard Medical School Conference, Boston, MA March 26, 2009).

Finally, clinicians and pure researchers lead different kinds of intellectual lives and hold different action values. They think and speak literally in different languages, although often about similar concepts. For example, a clinician may ask, "How do I use these paraverbal findings to understand this particular patient now?" The researcher might follow new nonverbal discoveries wherever they led, ignoring any immediate practical clinical application for specific clients. We can't overemphasize how these disparate stands, in general intellectual orientation, contribute to the difficulty inherent when one wing of the field attempts to transact with another.

However, we feel that we cannot allow these very real and long-standing obstacles to hinder us. That's why we began our project. We're faced with simply too much evidence that nonverbal happenings play a major role in the psychotherapy exchange. We want to explore these phenomena with our readers.

We'll start Chapter 2 by reviewing some of these extra-verbal data in detail. We need to investigate the significance of the paraverbal exchange as fully as possible, so that we can gain a further grasp of the therapeutic approaches that we already use. Our understanding remains incomplete as of now. Moreover, we don't just include dynamic treatment. Almost every psychotherapy involves the counselor sitting face to face with one or two clients in a helping situation. We want to know as much as possible about the less obvious nonverbal aspects of this exchange.

We'll see that we probably need to include detailed descriptions of the patient's appearance, gestures, voice tones, eye contact, and so on. We also require the same attention to the paraverbal presence of the therapist. What do his or her speech tone and prosody, body position, facial expressions, and other such expressions reveal?

As we'll clarify in Chapter 2, others have already made strong forays into this thicket of questions and research challenges, particularly the Boston Change Process Study Group (BCPSG, 2010) and Beebe and colleagues (2002, 2005). We'll document their findings and their arguments at length, as well as the contributions of others.

Investigation into the paraverbal interaction may represent a third evolutionary advance in psychotherapy. This potential propels the study of more nonverbal interaction and follows in the steps of the object relations and the relational therapy developmental progression.

The exploration of paraverbal phenomena seems already underway, as the findings from the mother–infant communication studies just now begin to push hard into the perimeter of our field. Establishing that nonverbal communication demonstrably takes places in therapy, and assessing its influence on the interchange constitutes the primary focus of our research narrative.

B. The Psychotherapy of the Nonpsychotic, Character-Disordered Client

The nonpsychotic character-disordered patient and his or her treatment represents another illustration of an emphasis on paraverbal communication entering the field, but again slowly and through the side door, in the same manner in which the mother–infant data now seem to seek a place at the table. We return to our principle that once we invite particular ideas, or particular clients, into the office, unintended, at first unrecognized, major consequences can follow.

What happened when we decided to include in our psychotherapy the spectrum of personality-disordered patients? We'll see that paraverbal exchange with these individuals becomes all important, and it's almost a necessity to add this perspective into our understanding of their treatment. Marvin, the angry dismissive man, from our introductory cases on page 1, probably demonstrates signs of quite serious personality disorder. For example, his anger feels so excessively inappropriate. If we ignore his nonverbal messages, we'll never understand Marvin in a helpful way.

Historical Perspective

After fully absorbing, now in 2016, the influence of Balint, Kernberg, Kohut, and Winnicott, it's hard to remember that the question of accepting into the therapy clients, with challenging character issues, provoked such heated debate in the 1960s, but it did.

In 1965, I (Jim) entered a psychodynamic graduate program in clinical psychology. My teachers made much of the oedipal versus pre-Oedipal distinction. The latter purportedly formed a poor alliance and a chronically ambivalent transference. They seemed prone to shallow or rageful relationships. Most distressing of all, they could rapidly regress into bouts of poor reality testing in the unstructured therapy situation. They sometimes seemed poorly regulated and do not have a cohesive self.

These clients might participate in successful treatment, maybe, but only if the practitioner introduced certain "unanalyzable parameters" into the therapy, such as extra support, controlled free association, restricted use of the couch, interpreting at slow pace and at minimal "depth." Clearly such people did not represent ideal treatment cases and certainly not the ideal candidates to become therapists in training.

Five to ten years later, however, in the 1970s, Kernberg (1975), Kohut (1971), Maltsberger and Buie (1974), and many others more routinely began to extend the application of dynamic therapy to clients who displayed these same nonpsychotic character issues (Wishnie 2005, p. 18). The fascinating story of how and why this era in our field unfolded, and continues to develop, represents too complicated a narrative to follow here in the detail that it deserves. We'll radically summarize.

The explorers in this new area of treatment reported one common conclusion: Clients with greater or lesser personality disorder put exquisite pressure on the therapist through their strenuous use of (1) *acting out* and (2) *projective identification*. In the former mode, the patients notoriously enacted their conflicts *behaviorally*, and *nonverbally*, rather than investigating them with more regulated verbal inquiry. They might cancel sessions precipitously, walk out of meetings, yell at the therapist, threaten self-destruction, the destruction of others, the destruction of the therapist, and so on.

In the second problem area, *projective identification* (Scharf and Scharf, 1991, pp. 55–59), the client projects his or her unacceptable feeling to the therapist, who then unconsciously carries it for them both. The client treats the therapist as if that affect actually arises in that therapist, as if she actually does display rage at, or uncaring indifference, toward the client, for example.

Buffeted by projective identification in this way, the therapist may begin to respond with her own counteraggression and mounting annoyance. The counselor can then become guilty, frustrated, perhaps angry, and feel that the patient has set out to hurt him or her or blame him or her, which in a way that the patient has. The therapist might then project back anger at, or fear of, the client.

If this process remains unacknowledged, the office can quickly transform into a Dutch oven on boil: a cauldron of anger, guilt, despair, revenge, and misunderstanding, all propelled by projections this way and that, thus the Maltsberger and Buie unforgettable title "Counter-Transference Hate in the Treatment of Suicidal Patients" (1974).

Both acting out and projection immediately usher in unmistakable para-verbal signs—raised voices, looks of sour disappointment from the patient, annoyed or guilty chagrin on the face of the therapist, bodily frustration on both sides of the room, and so on.

Maroda (1999, 2010), and Wishnie (2005), in particular, have offered help-ful guidelines about how we therapists can work to unravel our feelings in the midst of these stressful clinical showdowns and slowly help the client to understand himself or herself and to settle in with us. In Chapter 2, when we review the work of Tansey and Burke (1989), we'll explore in detail the role of counter-transference and projective identification as important therapeutic phenomena.

Inviting these character challenged patients into the practice turned out to be a fateful decision indeed because once we became more experienced in this work, many more clients seemed to have some form of borderline or narcissistic condition than we had ever guessed at the start.

Personality disorder clearly represents not a discrete state but occupies an ever-shifting place on a continuum of emotional functioning (Howard Wishnie, personal communication, Sept. 8, 2009 and J. G. Allen, 2013). In other words, it becomes clear that some hold these discrete severe diagnoses in full force, but many more display sub-diagnostic traits of these conditions, for example, a subtle, but important, chronic ambivalence over intimacy (Jennifer Dotson PsyD, personal communication, April 20, 2009).

The changes in technique demanded of the therapist, once these more intense clients entered the office, has led some practitioners to redefine the role of verbalizable insight in psychotherapy. Stern et al. (1998), Stark (1999), Maroda (1999), Schore (2003 a & b), Wishnie (2005, p. 31), Fonagy (2006, 2014), Wachtel (2008), and many of the rest of us have discovered that often, to improve from therapy, or even to continue in the work at all, the client must know that the therapist captures and *feels in herself* some crucial emotional experience of that client. Sometimes it's no longer about insight, if it ever were. The therapist must show paraverbally, behaviorally, her connection with the patient.

Failing this basic affective connection, the treatment with these more inaccessible people, may fall flat or drift along a meandering, confusing, sometimes boring path. The client complains of the same symptoms or interpersonal conflicts, and the therapist suggests some possible meanings or clarifications, which sound more and more hollow, even to her, no matter how sincerely she tries to engage with her client.

Glacial progress and ennui represent one important challenge here, but some of these treatments, lacking a crucial emotional connection, can become outright dangerous, to either client or therapist, and quickly. Now paraverbal signs abound in the office—screaming or angry, silent, disgusted patients, perspiring, confused, agitated therapists, and on and on. Consider my physical response to Marvin's provocations. I sat up rigidly in the chair, fixed him with my gaze, and asked a somewhat sarcastic comment but also productive question. "Why would you return to someone so inept?" We have to learn to work with these bodily reactions, in both of us, across the spectrum of patient acuity.

In Chapter 4, we'll encounter an almost always frustrating, and often frightening, Asian-American lady who used all her paraverbal force ostensibly to defeat Jim, her therapist, and to render impotent his attempts to offer any help. Both participants enacted an intricate series of extra-verbal responses and counter responses in this harrowing therapy, which we'll carefully review in that later chapter. At one point, this lady slashed her arm the night before our meeting and arrived to wave her wounds in my face, demonstrating to me my abysmal shortfall as a helper. In this one dramatic flourish, she communicated how I had failed her and in how much danger she remained.

Enactments—in capital E and lower case e:

These sometimes intense Enactments, with an uppercase E, can become the focus of the therapy. Clients on the personality disorder spectrum introduce many such confrontations into the office. They also react to the treatment in an often puzzling fashion. My chronically suicidal Asian patient, just mentioned above, repeatedly refused offers of a medication consult, DBT, or day hospital and also rejected any interpretation connecting her despair to the rest of her life, particularly to her relationship with her harsh abandoning grandfather.

She said she couldn't comprehend how any of these additional interventions or psychological observations might help her. I don't think that this is simply resistance. I think she really didn't see or feel any relevance to her situation. She did grudgingly admit, as the treatment progressed, that she felt more calm in her life, but she had no picture of how that greater peace had come about. These clients may denigrate the treatment, but they also keep coming and often improve. The therapist, however, is usually forced to fly blind using only her internal reactions as a guide, with no positive feedback whatever from the client.

I think she improved because my relaxed (sometimes), jousting with her sarcastic putdowns and my capacity to listen to her unrelenting despair, helped her, paraverbally, to "self-regulate" and to "soothe" herself in Beebe's words (2005).

I was also inadvertently offering coaching in "mentalization." What feelings did she have? What did they mean to her? How did they differ from mine and how did she perceive her life, or anyone else's, in an emotional way (see J. G. Allen, 2013)? Almost all of our work then fell "beyond interpretation," the title of John Gedo's 1974 book, one of the first efforts to explore extensively this paraverbal, preverbal world, that we're still pursuing 40 years later, perhaps with less progress than we had hoped.

My patient and I developed a teasing debate over the value of my suggestions, an interchange that we both enjoyed, mostly, and which probably represented a key element in the therapy. She could tell from my joking and grinning that I liked her, no matter how frustrating I found her and no matter how little she often liked me or herself. There was affection and connection, as well as consternation, from my side of the office.

Our interaction became a highly paraverbal one: smiling, grimacing, waving our hands to emphasize a point, raising our voices in a very animated way. As we'll later see, I think our therapy may also have represented a fumbling, non-insight-oriented, highly extra-verbal, bootstrap DBT strategy to help her gain increased self-management. If I could understand her and stay with her emotionally, her fury would not seem so frightening to her and she could gain some acceptance and control over it. My approach modestly succeeded in those goals, goals of which I remained consciously unaware until recently.

Lowercase "e" Enactments

It's a mistake, however, to overemphasize the significance of these major confrontations the like of which I've just described. For one thing, perhaps we can't put them out of our minds, but thank God, they happen infrequently. Moreover, I think that they may influence us to look in the less helpful direction for meaningful therapeutic nonverbal enactments, toward the distant most extreme stretch of our experience, rather than toward the proximal end, our day-to-day therapy exchanges.

Certainly these uppercase E Enactments force us into a paraverbal interaction and teach us just how important extra-verbal communication can loom in psychotherapy, a major contribution to our knowledge base. More importantly, they introduce the question that if the nonverbal connection feels so crucial within these highly charged confrontations, perhaps that paraverbal dimension also plays an important, although less obvious role, in the more quotidian exchanges that typify so many treatments. Most of our interchanges with clients are not deeply intense or upsetting, but many of them do include a some form of important paraverbal interchange. What if we followed those subtle communications more precisely?

A majority of enactments, in fact, come with a lowercase "e," that is, relational, often nonverbal exchanges, sometimes, at first below awareness to one or both of the participants. Nevertheless, for one of the first times in the literature, these extra-verbal engagements may bring great influence to the therapy, as we'll see in a minute.

Even a nontherapist can't miss potentially catastrophic confrontations, blatant suicidal threats, and the like. That observer could instantly spot the arrival of some momentous development, a knife-ripped arm, for example, although he might not know how to respond to it. But we offer, as the main thesis of our monograph, the necessity of not overlooking less obvious, smaller gauge paraverbal exchanges that regularly occur throughout our everyday treatments. What if much change in psychotherapy comes about partly through these hardly observable nonverbal interchanges?

Subtle facial expressions, hand movements, shifts in voice tone, or in rhythm, compose the stuff of psychotherapy each session and each week, not the occasional high-pitched, shouting face offs. The tapes and case vignettes, which we'll study, offer example after example of these mostly below-the-radar exchanges.

Beebe et al. (2002, 2005) and Stern et al. (2010) track these paraverbal communications and argue that they might mark the center of our understanding of the therapeutic relationship and of change in psychotherapy. We agree and will investigate how the Stern–Beebe approach helps us make sense of our observations about paraverbal interchange.

For instance, at the start of Chapter 5, we introduce a videotaped consultation interview, in which I (Jim) meet with a soft-spoken, wispy, 22–year-old young lady, at the time almost literally the age of my oldest daughter, of whom I'm very fond. The client, in turn, reports a close, supportive relationship with her 30-year-old brother.

I like my young patient right away and as her heartrending story unfolds, my respect for her grows. Also, I'm used to talking to women of her age because I chat with my daughter and her friends as much as they'll let me. As the tape runs, the observer cannot miss my interested, friendly, protective, avuncular tone, and relaxed body language with her. The scoring systems we use (see Chapter 3) capture this style in the therapist and likewise reflect that this young woman sits increasingly comfortably exchanging with me. Maybe I remind her of her nurturing older brother.

By the second half of the interview, she decidedly opens up, in both body posture and in the expressiveness of her voice, emphasizing her points with hand gestures and using a new sharp tone, with increasing emotional force. She speaks more powerfully, gets more involved, and lets us both see how upset she can get. She becomes more intimate and transparent in the content of her verbal communication as well.

I too speak with more intensity and authenticity. I point my hand, talk more loudly, raise my voice strongly at one point, lean toward her, and do not turn my gaze away. She inclines toward me. Our eyes lock. On one occasion, I finish an important sentence that she begins.

We synch through these lowercase "e" enactments. If we weren't studying our nonverbal communication, we might overlook many of these signs on the video. However, we see a trusting relationship that surprisingly quickly builds, verbally, but also behaviorally, between a 46-year-old male therapist and my 22-year-old female client, whom I've never met previously.

If we analyze the tape carefully, we cannot miss that this move to a greater depth between us, is mediated with words, obviously, but also with gesture, with body language, and with verbal tone. We cocreate a surprisingly authentic engagement, with one another, in a short time and work toward a productive culmination to the interview, "a moment of meeting" in Stern parlance (see Chapter 2). Analyzing this kind of developing interchange from the nonverbal perspective represents the focus to which we regularly return.

This, and other cases, suggest that we might track paraverbal joining to understand and to guide the interaction, not just in extraordinarily high-amplitude confrontations but in our daily therapies. We may need to turn away from too exclusively studying the words only, and look also at the subtle shifts in body position and verbal inflection through which the participants, mostly unconsciously, conduct their relationship.

THE THREE INTRODUCTORY CASES

If we return to our starting place, we can understand these three scenarios a little better now.

Case #1 Marvin and Ann—Marvin gives strong signs of personality disorder. He has few or maybe no friends, has retired early from his profession, seems to ignore his wife on purpose, and angrily picks fights with family members, strangers, and me.

Now I feel mad and insulted by Marvin. It's not just his words; it's his disgusted tone. I reviewed the case with myself and with others, and I decided that I needed to initiate a "real relationship" intervention with Marvin. When they came in the next time, I asked him his reaction to the last session, and he ignored my question; is that the way he feels he should do? Lie and say he's satisfied? I tell him I feel angry and abused. Does he want to repair our relationship?

He says no, and I ask him if he has similar interactions in his private life. Ann says that he does, and she can't stand it. I ask him if he can remember any relationship that worked smoothly. Ann volunteers that he and his demented grandfather did very well together. Marvin treated him with great respect and patience, and they genuinely enjoyed each other's company. I turn to Marvin and say "Marvin, everybody's grandpa." The room begins to calm down.

I conclude with "So Marvin feels saddled with a clown (his word), for a counselor. Ann is desperate, and I feel angry and ill-treated—(all the while I'm smiling at the absurdity of the situation)—so how about another session everybody?" We all chuckle and arrange another meeting. We agree that we'll schedule the appointments one at a time.

I have to take a paraverbal action here. My tone and facial expression tell Marvin he has hurt me but that I also want contact with him. He waves me off, but he listens a little more intently for the balance of the hour. He may return to his derisive self next time, but I'll interrupt him with "everybody's grandpa, Marvin, even me." I'm implying, but not stating, that he's capable of enjoying those who don't threaten or disappoint him. I'm also demonstrating that he has little to fear from me.

Case #2 Pat—The silent veterinarian—I approach Pat, "I'll sit with you as long as you need. I'm sorry you're suffering" (verbal and paraverbal offer of my continued presence, delivered in a gentle tone). Finally, in the seventh session, he confronts me, "How could I excuse him from his cowardly act of deserting his dog? What kind of person does that make me?" I smile and reach my hands toward him, "It was my honest answer that you had no choice. You can let yourself off the hook." He disagrees but begrudgingly begins to speak again.

In a soft voice, with slow prosody, I tell him I was worried about him, wrapped up in his angry silence, and that it seemed to me that he, at that time, hated himself. He grins back a little. A real relationship, beyond the words, a concerned mostly nonverbal connection at last has eased our impasse. Since I could wait out the troubling test of six silent sessions, he feels I care for him even if he sometimes can't understand why.

We go on to complete a productive therapy. He graduates, leaves town to continue his training, and sends two letters to me over the years. In the first, he says he's married to the woman whom he'd brought to our therapy for a few meetings during termination. In the next, he announces the birth of their son.

Case #3 Pamela and Fred—I suggest to this couple that her smile had tender feelings behind it, that I could see she really cares for Fred. Fred continues to feel frustrated by her tentative shyness. I offer Fred, "Never mind how much she talks, just watch for that smile—if you get it—you're both in good shape." He grins broadly but still wonders why she doesn't converse more. I answer, "Look at her face; she's interested in you." I smile broadly. The atmosphere in the room warms. This interaction represents almost entirely a paraverbal one. We discuss smiles and exchange those smiles back and forth between the three of us. Pamela and Fred leave, arms around each other. We'll certainly require future interventions, but we've experienced a new level of acceptance and affection for this couple. We don't know where this will go but we've made a beginning.

Paraverbal offers from the client seem to beget paraverbal responses from the counselor and to and fro. We've just started following our journey. We'll learn more about these nonverbal puzzles as we continue into Chapter 2 and particularly in Chapters 4 to 7, which center exclusively on the details of the nonverbal exchange between real clients and their therapists. If you emphasize relational therapy as a field, the study of nonverbal exchange soon comes into focus.

RESEARCH STRATEGY

Beyond simply asserting that nonverbal messaging represents key information in the therapy interchange, we clearly need a method of data analysis, a scoring system that will specify and differentiate these extra-verbal communications. This we introduce in Chapter 3.

In Chapter 2, we outline a model of the treatment relationship grasped at an instant in time, based on the findings of many previous students of psychotherapy, most of whom we've mentioned in passing, here in Chapter 1. In subsequent chapters, we then carry this matrix forward to organize the clinical material that we discover through each videotaped interview or case excerpt.

We'll study, at length, a total of four videos depicting the work of three experienced therapists. These investigations, and the study of a number of additional clinical vignettes, compose the subject matter of the book and begin in Chapter 4. Along the way, and particularly in our final chapter, we develop suggestions about potential alterations in technique that we can devise using a paraverbal focus.

As the reader works his or her way through the text, a list of questions will probably come to his or her mind: First, does this line of inquiry about nonverbal therapeutic interchange make intuitive sense? If so, how can I, the therapist, describe the shifts in my client's extra-verbal behavior and in my own? Does this series of unsaid exchanges trace a different, sometimes deeper, certainly more subtle, parallel intimacy developing between us, than any record of simply the actual spoken words? Should I call attention to my client's extra-verbal communications, when and to what end?

Should I directly comment on my own nonverbal messages, and should I alter these to influence the treatment in important ways? When and how might I do this? It's with this matrix of challenges and reflections that we want to engage our reader, as she considers, more thoroughly, the significance of the paraverbal world that may suffuse the psychotherapy in which she takes part.

In Chapter 1 so far, we've touched on the broad sweep of the evolutionary history of dynamic psychotherapy in the past 45 years. We're offering our beginning hypothesis that a next step may involve the more careful study of mutual paraverbal relating between client and therapist. We're trying to contribute to that movement forward.

THE ANATOMY OF EVOLUTIONS

We've also learned a little in general about how change tends to come about in our field. Evidently for paradigm development to occur, three sets of conditions need to take place roughly at the same time but in no particular order. (1) New types of patients clamor for admission into our clinics; earlier we observed what happened when those with personality disorder requested and received services (Wishnie, 2005; Allen, 2013). Now the newcomers represent the less-educated, possibly immigrant, possibly gay, Latino and African-American people, all of whom quite appropriately request services. They may require more paraverbal intervention since they're maybe less comfortable with the standard English language.

(2) We observe a shift in the cultural zeitgeist. In the 1960s, a new egalitarianism was afoot. In 2016, we see about us a societal change supporting personal availability, transparency and informality. The President of the United States appears regularly on television in his or her shirt sleeves. Clients may seek and expect a less formal more present therapist. (3) New theories of treatment arrive that support modifications in technique. For example, Attachment Theory (Allen, 2013; Fonagy and Allison, 2014), the New Neurobiology (Cozolino, 2014; Schore, 2014), and third physical interventions to treat psychological ills, that is, Sensorimotor Psychotherapy (Ogden and Fisher, 2015) and Therapeutic Yoga (Emerson, 2015), all have recently come upon the scene.

We're perhaps on the cusp of another paradigm shift in psychotherapy— this one reaching more toward the physiological, nonverbal foundations of behavior, for example, brain function, than previous schools of thought. Paraverbal relating fits within this wave. Physical action includes speaking loudly, leaning toward one another, all express, reflect, and beget shifts in brain activity, heart rate, and the like. Our research, like a good deal of contemporary work, focuses on the body as well as on the mind and sees these as a unity not a polarity.

In addition, the bodily presence of the yoga practitioner, the sensory motor counselor and, particularly of, the paraverbal therapist, takes a more central focus in the treatment room. What influence will this more active counselor bring to the therapy?

Amidst this welter of emerging approaches, though, our book turns on one basic question. What do you discover when you analyze a treatment session from an extra-verbal viewpoint? A new perspective may open. How will we find ways of incorporating this fresh knowledge into our extant treatment techniques?

In Chapter 2, we study the research data that constitute the scientific foundation for this exploration of paraverbal phenomena within the psychotherapy encounter.

Chapter Two

Brief Psychotherapy

A Model of Relationship Exchange, a Venn Diagram, a Research Review and Two Unconscious Worlds

To note our progress so far in Chapter 1, we first offered three illustrative cases posing different extra-verbal challenges. Then we traced each step in the gradual historical movement toward wider exploration of nonverbal communication in therapy. Finally, we explained the difficulties in studying this area but established the importance of continuing the work nonetheless.

Here in Chapter 2, we present the research foundation for our project. We introduce a general model of "relationship exchange," which we'll use to explore our videotape data. We summarize the previous findings germane to each dimension of that model, but we definitely emphasize the previous studies of paraverbal relating that represents our main topic.

BRIEF PSYCHOTHERAPY

First, let's address part one of our chapter title—"Brief Psychotherapy." Psychotherapy, in the majority, takes place in the short form. Budman and Gurman (1988) tell us that most treatment episodes last fewer than 20 sessions per calendar year. However, with certain striking exceptions (Gustafson 1984, 1995; McCullough 1997; Levenson 1995; Safran and Muran 2000), most technical writing purporting to teach psychodynamic and relational, theory and technique, derives from the study of long-term intensive treatment, often multiple meetings per week, stretching over several years. This disproportion in emphasis does not, of course, exist for arbitrary reasons. We have more data about extended cases, so they're easier to explore in comprehensive ways.

Many of the teachers providing these texts about longer-term therapy offer us fine work indeed (Greenson 1967; Mitchell 1988, 1993, 1997; Stark 1994, 1999; Wishnie, 2005; Maroda 1991, 1999, 2010), but this unbalanced distribution, within the available literature, poses a problem for the psychotherapy student at any level of experience. The publications, upon which he or she needs to base his or her understanding of her mission, describe longer-term work and match up jaggedly, at best, with her daily clinical activity, perforce usually shorter therapy.

To compound this difficulty in discovering appropriate learning materials, few authors present extensive verbatim therapy exchanges for study, a problem strongly underscored by the late Hans Strupp, a long-time psychotherapy scholar (Strupp, p. XI, forward, Levenson, 1995). The (student) "doesn't have enough case material in front of her to develop a deep understanding of the issues."

We've aimed our project to address these short falls in educational opportunity. We focus here sometimes on long-term treatment but mostly on brief work, often one-session consultations, and do a through careful examination of lengthy videotape excerpts and of extended case segments. The reader will have "enough material in front of her," if nothing else.

We study these data using a range of research instruments—all described in Chapter 3. (1) The authors lean most heavily on the Accessibility and Congruence scales (Donovan, Osborn and Rice, 2009), but we also include (2) the ATOS, Achievement of Therapeutic Objectives Scale (McCullough 1997 and McCullough et al 2003) and (3) the ATOS/Therapist (Osborn, 2009). In addition, we use the Control Mastery Scale (adapted from Sampson and Weiss, 1986) and a transference/counter-transference model suggested by Tansey and Burke (1989). We utilize all of these to track the verbal and extra-verbal exchange between the doctor and the client through a single session.

In our clinical Chapters 4–7, we offer a great deal of primary, word-for-word, gesture-for-gesture data, and we use objective rating scales to start our analysis of that information. We hope that this plan will feel helpful to working therapists, since the material we introduce so closely parallels the moment-by-moment exchanges that they experience with their own clients. Because we present a great deal of information about a few cases, the reader and the writer can proceed together, drawing on a common reservoir of shared clinical information. At the end of each chapter, we all should have a pretty full idea of what just happened between the participants on the tape or within the case illustrations.

A model of relationship

Let's continue to the second phrase in our chapter title, "The Dimensions of Relationship Exchange." John Norcross has offered us an indispensable book

Psychotherapy Relationships that Work (J. Norcross, Ed., 2002), describing from the viewpoints of many distinguished authors, relationship interchanges that help the patient toward constructive growth. More recently, Paul Wachtel (2008), in his turn, has given us a valuable historical summary and an in-depth understanding of the "relational" psychotherapy school, expanding on and adding to the ideas introduced in the Norcross volume, and by Mitchell (1988, 1993, 1997) and many others.

We aim to study the interactional therapy relationship as fully as possible. Therefore, we require a mutually accepted definition of "relationship." In a moment, we'll present a Venn diagram that captures the pathway along which we'll analyze each of our videotapes.

We all may not thoroughly agree upon a full definition of "relationship," and therefore, we may remain hazy about how we actually make exchanges within it and along which dimensions. When we imagine, write, or say "relationship," we assume that all of us refer to the same general concepts but possibly we don't. Most of us grasp several crucial variables contained within "relationship," but until now perhaps, we've never tried to integrate those into one model.

Consider the rough Venn diagram in Figure 2.1. Our friend Nick Covino, PsyD (personal communication, April 10, 2008) assures us that, if we're just alert enough, we can represent any important set of observations or ideas using a Venn diagram.

Dr. Covino seems correct. This Venn diagram captures something very important. It pictures "relationship" at a moment in time. In our book, we apply this schematic to our series of psychotherapy tapes, which illustrate the clinical work of three experienced practitioners. Our discussion centers on the paraverbal exchange, but we need, at least, to include these other sectors to assemble the complete mosaic.

OVERVIEW OF THE DIAGRAM

This picture certainly does not speak for itself. We require much more expli-cation, which we'll offer at some length. A few points stand out right away. The diagram is bidirectional describing the interaction between any two par-ticipants. "Relationship" feels suspended in air between the two, cocreated by them; if one or both suddenly withdrew, it could crash, although it might well remain alive in the conscious and/or unconscious memory of one or both.

Any pair of people can and do co-construct relationship: therapist–patient, parent–child, husband–wife, sibling–sibling, friend–friend, coworker–coworker. Relationship exists between the two and has a minute-by-minute, but also often a potentially long-lasting, independent existence. Analogue of the cocreated "analytic third" could enter the discussion here. The participants

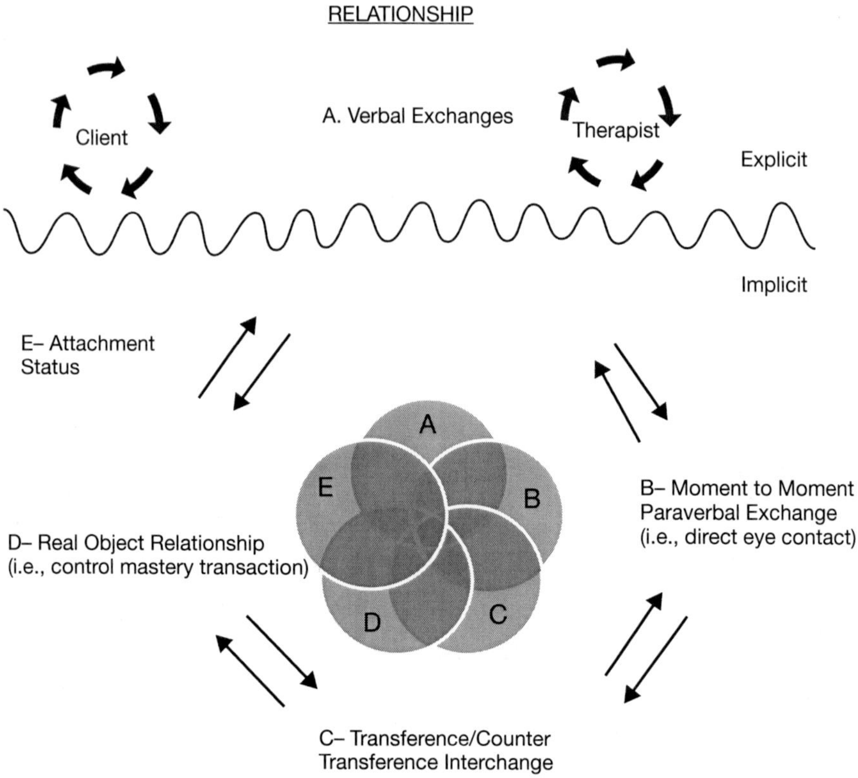

RELATIONSHIP

Figure 2.1 Relationship: A Venn Presentation

construct something new that stands between them but, like the gingerbread boy, it may, but not always, take on a life of its own.

Relationship has multiple components, each of which become more or less prominent at a given instant. We may have missed some crucial dimensions, which the reader can add for himself or herself, but relationship includes at least all of the circles within the diagram. We can leave none out. For the remainder of this chapter, we'll take up each of these five sectors in turn and briefly discuss the key contributions of different authors within each area. So Chapter 2 conveys a full description of this Venn Diagram and it also includes a brief summary of the important research germane to each section of the schematic. We cannot study paraverbal communication in a vacuum. It represents a key part of the whole puzzle, but it does not exist in isolation. The therapeutic partners exchange paraverbally but also about some specific topic, perhaps a verbally introduced idea, or transference feelings, and so on.

We'll explain each area as we traverse the diagram in the clockwise direction. The authors start with verbal communication in Section A, (B) the paraverbal mirroring, (C) the transference/counter-transference exchange, (D) the "real object relationship—control mastery" transaction and (E) attachment status, all take place usually, though not always, in few or no words. We'll spend the most emphasis on the theoretical and research literature from Region B, paraverbal interactions, since that's our central focus. Interestingly, only one domain here seems primarily verbal, Oval A, which we'll approach first.

Before we move much further into the matrix, we'll make a few additional observations about this picture as a whole. First, no one circle looms larger than another—all regions count, and all potentially, finally carry similar weight. Of course, one area might assume greater emphasis at a given moment. All the regions intercept with all the others, but they retain their own individual existence as well.

Therefore, we can at times, for instance, study paraverbal mirroring in pure case, not in intersection with other contiguous regions. The epicenter of the mosaic shows each oval overlapping with all the others, to depict "relationship" in its essence. It is this multipartite Venn diagram, which we'll use to explore the videotapes, we closely study in later chapters. By now it's evident that relationship does not represent one indivisible entity, rather several interlocking phenomena.

Clearly, the Venn illustration potentially introduces an enormous amount of information to the reader. Different authors have contributed multiple volumes highly relevant to one or another region in our sketch. We will carefully review a selected few of these books and papers in each area of the matrix, but, even then, we'll have to summarize dramatically.

WHY ADD THESE OTHER SECTORS?

Our narrative focuses primarily on paraverbal interaction. However, we must include these additional areas of "relationship" to give us as complete a naturalistic image of the whole exchange in therapy, as we can construct. Once again, the authors need to clarify that *nonverbal relating* sometimes feels central to these additional dimensions of psychotherapy: transference/ counter-transference and so on but sometimes less so. This leads us to our final point in this section. Dividing "relationship" into five sectors allows us an in-depth understanding of each but introduces artificiality as well. All the parts often interact.

Clearly, these regions do not usually progress separately. Therapists and patients, for example, often give voice to transference and counter transference feelings partly paraverbally and partly in words. We can't see the diagram as one linear plane; it's a multidimensional model and different parts illuminate at different times, sometimes in concert with others, sometimes not.

Region A—Verbal Exchange

Here, the majority of us feel most comfortable. We can, and have hundreds of times, carefully studied the verbal interchange between the client and the therapist. Perhaps we've read texts describing such interactions (Greenson, 1967; Balint, 1968, 1972; Wishnie, 2005; Wallin, 2007). Perhaps we've compiled a written case summary; perhaps we've made an audio tape of a session. All of us have prepared a verbal report of our own cases or listened to those from a student or from a colleague. We know a lot about how to search for the psychodynamic and the affective core of *the patient's*, but probably not of *the therapist's*, world. After all, we try to put the client's affective issues into words, many hours every day.

Here, in Region A, we can pretty adeptly operate as a Martha Stark (1999), psychodynamic, interpretative, Level 1 practitioner. We've become good at speaking well thought-out words to our clients, colleagues, and students and awaiting verbal responses to our offerings. Region A, verbal insight, feels so familiar to us and Greenson (1967), Malan (1979), Gustafson (1995), Stark (1999), and many others have written so well about this area that we do not need to retrace the sound steps of previous masters.

However, as we begin to circumnavigate the Venn diagram further, we feel a stronger and stronger awareness that the interchange between any therapist and any client encompasses much more than simply what they say to each other, much more than Region A alone, the verbal-insight circle. Of course, we know this. *How* we say the words (Wachtel, 2011) and *how* we look at each other or fail to look at each other carry crucial significance. Nevertheless, we find it helpful to state this point explicitly, and often, since we're prone to let it slip by unnoticed.

We don't wish to sound overly concrete here when we speak of the verbal region. We need to clarify our argument. The verbal interchange rarely stands alone. In other words, relatively few words are spoken by either participant without some affective or paraverbal elaboration. Nevertheless, the verbal cognitive pole might carry by far the greatest emphasis in any given exchange, as we'll see.

Now we'll try carefully to describe the next pieces of our puzzle as they come more fully into view. Once we take a few steps away from predominantly verbal content, we quickly enter regions drastically less thoroughly mapped. Returning to our sketch and moving slowly in a clockwise arc, we come upon Region B, which we discuss next.

Region B—The Moment-To-Moment Paraverbal Interaction

At this point, we delve into a literature perhaps unfamiliar to many of our readers. Here at last, we meet Beebe and Lachmann (2002), Beebe et al. (2005), Stern (1985), Stern et al. (1998, 2002, 2005, 2010), and Tronick (2007). Now we step toward the research foundation of our project.

Introduction to Region B

First, the explicit/implicit structure of the Venn schematic, a feature that builds on a similar direction taken by Beebe and Lachmann (2002, p. 35), requires further explanation. The double arrows show that communication can take place within or between all divisions of the relational diagram, but the wavy line implies that explicit exchange may not happen in any manifest or complete form and can become steadily or intermittently disrupted or may never take any conscious shape at all. The exception is verbal communication that remains explicit. After we leave Oval A though, much of the interchange between the different regions and between the two participants often takes place in limited or in no words.

Please notice that only region B bears the stated title of Paraverbal Exchange, but we'll find that many of the other ovals also carry a heavy load in that extra-verbal universe. For example, as suggested earlier, we'll see verbal exchange, Region A, often accompanied by paraverbal messages from Region B.

Region B, the mother–baby psychotherapy analogue

Let's move slowly into Region B, the paraverbal interactional moment. Since, after we leave area A, many readers are not conversant with the scholarly studies from these subsequent areas of the diagram, we will pay great attention to these data starting now. The Stern and Beebe and Lachmann findings feel so central to our paraverbal research focus that we'll review them in detail.

For example, drawing on their own studies and on the work of Stern (1985), Tronick (1989), Sander (1995), and Stern et al. (1998), and many others, Beatrice Beebe and Frank Lachmann (2002) have developed a dyadic systems model based on findings about mother–infant interaction, which we'll carefully summarize here. Next, Beebe, Lachmann, and Stern all apply their mother–baby model to the adult psychotherapy exchange; we'll follow their thinking there as well (Beebe and Lachmann, 2002, p. 27).

The mother–infant relationship mirrors adult psychotherapy?

Beebe's research review suggests that the paraverbal psychotherapy interchange *may* represent the adult analogue of the mother–baby "conversation." The latter must, perforce, unfold as an intimate relationship carried on in the paraverbal world; one of the participants can't talk, but we'll learn, he or she certainly can communicate. Beebe and Lachmann suggest: "Any theory of psychoanalysis (or psychotherapy—clarification ours) ultimately must address the nonverbal or implicit (procedural/emotional) as well as the verbal or explicit dimension of the interaction" (Beebe and Lachmann, 2002, p. 33).

This one sentence captures much of the rationale for the book. We use the mother–infant studies as the entry point to analyze the psychotherapy videos, so understanding this former research, is crucial to unravel our new data from the tapes.

Beebe and Lachmann establish the position that mother and infant, and therapist and client, interact verbally and nonverbally in order to cocreate a space between them in which the emotional exchange can serve the fundamental purpose of facilitating *self* and *mutual* regulation. Tronick (2007, p. 1) offers precisely the same point.

This position marks a breakthrough in the study of intimate communication, within psychotherapy or otherwise, and places Beebe and Lachmann's and Tronick's work in the forefront of the research effort exploring relational psychotherapy. (Once again, for an excellent review of the relational psychotherapy perspective, please turn to Wachtel, 2008.)

Psychotherapy: The centrality of self and mutual regulation

If we expand Tronick's and Beebe and Lachmann's positions just a little further, we realize that these explorations carry strong implications for the understanding of psychotherapeutic action. What if the internalization of this self-regulatory relationship represents a primary source of *change* in treatment, adding to the insight gained through mostly verbal exchange? Also, research findings, and intuitive conviction, tell us that the paraverbal quality of other intimate relationships: parent–child, teacher–student (Richard D. Mann—personal communication May 5, 1970), wife–husband (Dicks, 1967; Donovan, 2003) may also make a key contribution to the self-and mutually regulatory development of each member in those pairs.

However, our field usually stops just short of unambivalently believing the same facts about self—and—other regulation in the psychotherapy relationship, as we do about the mother–infant interchange, since the latter so clearly contributes to mutual self-management.

Maybe we can't view the therapy experience as fully analogous to the mother–infant one because it seems so difficult to differentiate the nonverbal exchange in psychotherapy from the verbal interchange, conceptually, or in any imaginable research design. Or maybe we don't quite grasp how to study the extra-verbal current in psychotherapy because it registers more subtly there, than in the parent–child relationship. The mother frequently actually holds the baby as she speaks to him, unmistakably soothing and regulating her infant.

The mother–infant coupling represents so obviously a nonverbal, as well as a verbal one, that it might seem fundamentally different from the psychotherapy connection, but maybe it's not. For example, concrete bodily touching obviously doesn't take place in psychotherapy, but it does in some forms of therapeutic yoga (Emerson, 2015) and behavioral medicine. Ogden and Fisher (2015) do not actually touch their patients but regularly suggest to their clients to experiment with changes in their posture and in their tone of voice, and so on. In other words, they ask the patients to shift their bodily position to gain more regulation and comfort.

So the mutual regulation in therapy is more ambiguous than that between parent and child. Moreover, it's so hard to relinquish the idea that what we think up to say to the client carries a great proportion of curative power, versus how we say it or how we don't say it. It seems so difficult to believe that, in psychotherapy, the extra-verbal universe would exert an influence similar in power to our verbal interventions, which we work so assiduously to construct. The rational, our carefully assembled, carefully stated thoughts, seem so superior to the irrational or to the nonverbal. What great weight could our spoken tone or facial expression really have in comparison to the cognitive thrust of our ideas?

However, as one example familiar to all of us, consider the 2008 Presidential election. Did the majority of us simply, reasonably, and philosophically, strongly believe in Barack Obama's platform of proposals, or did we also feel swept away by his astounding, courageous, personal story, and his charismatic physical presence and spoken delivery? We can't possibly separate these two sources of influence. How much did his verbally rendered or written positions swing us, or did the physical, extra-verbal presentation of the guy carry us away? Now, in 2016, the emotional power of his first campaign has passed. Many probably view President Obama in a more dispassionate and perhaps more critical way.

Stolorow, Brandschaft, and Atwood (1987), Mitchell (1988), Stark (1999), and Wachtel (2008) all advance this same general argument that the paraverbal sector can bear great weight in psychotherapy. They, however, do not take this stand as pointedly as Beebe and Lachmann, Tronick, or Stern, and they, unlike these latter groups, certainly do not cite reams of research evidence to solidify their position.

To clarify, Beebe and Lachmann offer us a two-part proposition: (1) the extra-verbal mother–baby interaction serves a self-regulating function for soothing, pacifying, holding, expressing love, interest, and relationship and (2) the adult psychotherapy relationship, to some major extent, also represents an extra-verbal world, parallel to the influence of the mother–baby universe.

Here, self and other regulation also unfolds, and here possibly the injuries from earlier parent–child relating, or mis-relating, can begin to receive redress in this new context. Following Beebe, the therapist offers to the adult patient many of the same holding and supporting experiences that the mother extends to the infant, clearly in a different form, but maybe not fundamentally so different. The therapist may smile at, nod at, lean toward, and speak gently to her patient as might an attentive mother.

Region B continued—The mother–infant studies

At this point, we'll interrupt our narrative for a few minutes to review a sample of the mother–infant research data to introduce, or to reintroduce, the reader to these discoveries, although to summarize this area in any comprehensive way would entail hundreds of pages of thorough analysis. We need to examine these findings in some depth, though, because the mother–baby research carries major significance for our ideas about nonverbal relating in psychotherapy.

In the following pages, we offer a few examples of the parent–infant communication findings. Beebe and Lachmann (2002), Beebe et al. (2005), Tronick (1989, 2007), and Stern (1985, 1998) cite multiple studies, many of them ingeniously strategized, which indicate that mothers and infants in interaction both exert their self-regulatory and mutually regulatory influence, which we noted just above. Tronick terms the process an MRM, which stands for mutual regulation model. The majority of the research in this area derives from the second-by-second analysis of mother–infant videotapes, which reveal striking phenomena. Rarely has anyone undertaken so painstaking a study of psychotherapy videotape, however.

Tronick, for instance, suggests that studies, which compare the relational style of depressed mothers with their infants, versus normal, depression-free mothers with theirs, lend us one window into the mother–baby mutual regulatory choreography. During face-to-face interaction with their babies, depressed mothers engage in positive social play less than 10% of the time and look away 20%. Normal mothers engage in social play 40% of the time and rarely look away (Tronick, 2007 p. 160).

Maybe not surprisingly, infants of depressed mothers have higher cortisol blood levels and heart rates (indicating exposure to stress) than controls, and have less-developed attachment status at one year and also later at 4 years of age (in Beebe and Lachmann, 2002, p. 75). The difference in the nonverbal relating styles of the two sets of mothers may account for the differences in the emotional regulation of their infants. For example, as just noted, babies of depressed mothers have less evolved attachment stance.

In Tronick's Still Face experiment (in which the mother, by design, for a minute or two, suddenly stops any facial expression in response to her baby), the infant's adaptive, or less adaptive, reactions to the situation predicts attachment status at one year. (We strongly encourage readers to view the Tronick YouTube video, the Still Face Experiment, 2007. Without words, this segment shows the powerful mutually regulatory, paraverbal relating between a mother and her one year old.)

Babies with depressed mothers react maladaptively to the anxiety of the Still Face Experiment. They become either frantic or apparently indifferent. Babies with depression-free mothers behave more flexibly in the situation and do not become overwhelmingly distressed (Cohn, Campbell and Ross, 1991). In another research, Tronick reports that 85% of the children, whose parents have panic disorder, showed marked behavioral inhibition, further evidence of an undermined mutual regulatory process (Tronick, 2007, p. 307).

Beebe and Lachmann (2002, p. 127) found that infants with problematic, insecure avoidant styles may reciprocally influence their parents. The feedback thus returns from child back to mother. Toddlers avoidant in attachment status manifested little responsivity, in any modality, to their mothers" vocal behavior, and the mothers then became more anxious, vigilant, and more determined to shift their gaze toward their toddler than did those of normal range toddlers.

In other words, we don't know where this interactional circle starts, but the babies certainly do not represent simply passive players in it. To summarize multiple studies, researchers have compared the interaction between depressed mothers and "good-enough" mothers and have shown that relational interchanges with the babies from these two different types of parents evolve in dramatically contrasting ways. Depressed mothers warmly interact with their babies much less than the comparison group, for instance. Predictably, the two groups of babies function at different levels of attachment as time goes on.

J. G. Allen (2013) reviews much of the research correlating the attachment states of infant and parent. He reports that the baby's adaptive behavior meeting a stranger, for example, differs greatly depending on the parent's attachment level. The more evolved the parent's attachment, the more relaxed and engaged the baby's behavior toward the newcomer. We have little extensive proof yet, but we can imagine that these differences in the tone of the mother–baby dyad have long-term consequences for the adjustment of the infant as she grows up.

To sum up to this point, Stern (1985), Beebe and Lachmann (2002), Tronick (2007), and Allen (2013) citing their own work and that of others, point to voluminous evidence that the "good-enough" mother relates to her baby in a way that provides mutual regulation for both and greater security, attachment, and personal stability for the baby, who in turn responds positively to the mother or to strangers.

When this primary bonding lacks vitality or regularity, the baby seems to react by becoming more anxious, less trusting, less related, and showing less attachment capacity. Touch, gaze, and bodily flexibility or rigidity, tone and rhythm of speech, all seem to carry relational value well beyond any actual words spoken (Jaffe, 2001).

We do not see a linear or black-and-white pattern unfolding, however. The interchange between mother and baby rarely plays in perfect coordination. Our authors report that "messy" misses in synchrony, which the pair quickly move to mend, seem to work better for developing mutual regulation than any perfect mirroring between the two (Tronick, 2007).

Jaffe et al. (2001), referred to in Beebe and Lachmann, (2002, p. 137), found that when mothers and their four-month-old infants coordinated speech rhythm at the mid-range, the babies were most likely to achieve secure attachment status at one year. Disorganized and insecure attachment at one year followed very high or very low speech rhythm coordination at four months.

Now turning back to the psychotherapy analogue for a moment, close, but far from perfect, rhythm coordination between therapist and client seems to predict positive treatment outcome in one preliminary research project (Beebe—personal communication, March 26, 2009). What if we could replicate this last conclusion over many studies? This would seem to suggest an important new dimension to the psychotherapy exchange.

Tronick (2007, p. 14) uses the MRM to introduce an extended discussion of momentary mismatch between mother and infant, and of their mutual efforts to redress those misalignments. When the two can reconstitute their rhythm, Tronick reports that they can move on to a higher order and more complex interpersonal challenges together.

We've come full circle now when we return to psychotherapy research because several important authors such as Loewald (1960), Kohut (1981), Blatt and Behrends (1987), and Saffran and Muran (2000), all of whom presumably had only a limited knowledge of mother–infant research, placed this same general dynamic, of rupture and repair, at the center of psycho-therapeutic change—a disruption occurs, vital learning takes place when the pair creatively react to the missed step and try new approaches to mend the mix-up.

In sum, all these studies imply that the paraverbal style of the mother, (for example, depressed versus not depressed) greatly impacts the behavior and the psychology of her baby. Would we then find the same type of interactional effect within the psychotherapy pair? Would the therapist's and the patient's nonverbal styles greatly influence each other? For example, the warmth and relatedness of the mother seem all important. Is that equally true in psycho-therapy? Would the therapist fill some analogue of the mother role here? If so, how should we build that understanding into our treatment technique?

In a moment, we will close this section by discussing the *noninterpretive* model of therapy interchange developed by Beebe (2002), Tronick (2007), and Stern et al. (1998, 2010) based on these many mother–infant investigations, but first let us discuss the concept of suicidality.

Predicting suicidality

We cannot go forward without exploring one rarely cited study, striking in its conclusions and in its implications, that seems to support the argument that an unconscious, nonverbal communication system, possibly parallel to the mother–infant bond, wraps around the counselor and the patient and might carry major significance in any treatment interaction.

Heller and Haynal (1997), in Switzerland, examined the psychiatric evaluation of suicidal patients using a unique strategy. The admitting psychiatrist interviewed 59 in-patients who had made a recent suicide attempt. The research team videotaped the faces of both the doctor and the client and scored that data using Ekman's Facial Activation Coding System (FACS, 1978). The researchers then asked the psychiatrist to predict which patients would reattempt suicide in the next year.

The doctor identified future reattempters at the 29% rate, no greater than chance. But the facial activation scores discriminated reattempters at the 81% level. It was, however, the *doctor's* facial activity scores, and *not* the *patient's*, which so powerfully singled out the reattempters. Toward those latter clients, the psychiatrist's face showed more expressiveness, more frowning, and she took more time directly looking at the clients; she spoke more as well. The authors conclude that the psychiatrist responded unconsciously to a felt fragility in her patient.

Beebe and Lachmann (2002, p. 41) commenting on this work suggested that the psychiatrist's greater activity represented both an unconscious means to regulate her own troubled state, as he interchanged with a very distressed patient, and her urgent attempt to communicate with these clients about their fears and to help them regulate themselves.

This research seems to demonstrate that at least under particular highly stressful conditions (here an in-patient interview following a suicide attempt), the unconscious paraverbal transaction between a doctor and a patient may reflect a universe at least as deep in meaning and power as the usual verbal communication so familiar to us, the psychotherapy students.

We know of no move, worldwide, to replicate this study or to construct any similar one. Perhaps the findings just seem too unlikely. But what if paraverbal data in psychotherapy often accounts for a major proportion of the mutual interpersonal influence that takes place, as it seems to in these Swiss interviews? Maybe across many quotidian situations, not necessarily evaluations of acutely disturbed patients, paraverbal factors might also carry significant influence on process and outcome. Beebe and colleagues have begun intensively studying the therapists" facial expressions, vocal tones, and postural change as they interact with their clients (Beebe and Lachmann, 2002, chapter 6).

Next, we move into a consideration of a new model of psychotherapy suggested by the mother–infant findings. We'll use this representation of the treatment interaction as we later try to make sense of our clinical materials in Chapters 4–7.

Region B continued—An alternative psychotherapy model

The Boston Change Process Study Group (BCPSG; Stern et al., 1998, 2002, 2005, 2010), Tronick (2007), and Beebe and Lachmann (2002) have all constructed similar alternative models of psychotherapy exchange based on their mother–infant interaction studies. These different researchers (Daniel Stern, Beatrice Beebe, Edward Tronick, Frank Lachmann, and others) have influenced each other heavily, and have worked and published together on different occasions, so we can propose an extra-verbal alternate therapy system, based on a fairly smooth integration of their various contributions. We'll see that this approach unfolds in three overlapping areas of interaction. To start, we'll lean mostly on the Beebe and Lachmann outline (2002).

The paraverbal psychotherapy model—Beebe and Lachmann

1) Ongoing Relations—a notion very akin to Stern et al.'s (1998) idea of "moving along." We'll quote Beebe and Lachmann's description of "ongoing relations" at length, since it captures so well the extra-verbal ebb and flow of the psychotherapy reality.

> The structure of the dialogue itself, *irrespective of its verbal content* (italics ours) is the object of study. Patient and analyst construct characteristic ways of asking each other questions, wondering aloud together, taking turns in dialogue, and knowing when to pause and for how long. In the process both are *constructing expectations and disconfirming fears* (italics ours), of being ignored, steam rolled, intruded on, misunderstood or criticized. These interactionally organized expectations and disconfirmations are represented and internalized *whether or not* they are verbalized (italics ours). This process constitutes the therapeutic action of on-going relations. (Beebe and Lachmann, 2002, p. 188)

We've just heard a keen description of the implicit give and take of every day psychotherapy.

2) Disruption and Repair: Here Beebe and Lachmann seem to incorporate Tronick's work into their model, summarized in Tronick, (2007). We'll summarize, too. The unfolding of the interactive relationship can suffer upset and discomfort from many directions, by an interpretation not readily accepted,

by a difference over the bill, by a transference or counter-transference conflict, by a communication misunderstanding, or through any lapse, or perceived lapse, on the part of either of the participants.

Almost invariably paraverbal as well as verbal signs accompany these breaks in the relationship: eye contact recedes, voices become raised or muffled. An angry, lifeless, bored, or disappointed silence may descend. Occasionally, the client precipitously leaves the office, perhaps never to reappear. Such breaks in the relationship require reconstruction and redress for therapy to continue in any meaningful fashion. A positive response to the disruption will represent a cocreated effort from both sides of the dyad, or the triad, in the case of a couples treatment.

As we mentioned earlier, several authors feel that this fence-mending represents the center of the curative process in long- or short-term psychotherapy (Loewald 1960, Kohut 1984; Blatt and Behrends, 1987; Safran and Muran, 2000; Wishnie, 2005; Safran et al., 2014). The thrust of the treatment must now depart from the disruptive, perhaps traumatic, experiences in the client's past.

The therapy needs to offer something different this time, something more open and more healing. Balint (1968) put it succinctly. The therapy must contain a "new ending to an old beginning" (Balint, 1968). Following Racker (1968) and Wachtel (2008), the therapy must alter the old "vicious circle" of relationship failure.

In this repair, the client can gain a new sense of value in herself, and in that way, a *new self* (Loewald, 1960; Tronick, 2007, p. 14). Both the mother–infant dyads and the psychotherapy pairs now attempt slight but important changes in direction. They check on the response from the other and inch their way toward greater harmony and warmth. The cooperative effort to mend often brings the two closer together.

3) Heightened Affective Engagements: They mark a shift to a deeper level of intimacy between the participants, perhaps signified by verbal exchange but definitely by paraverbal signs such as direct eye contact, leaning toward each other, mirroring body position, and perhaps sharing tears, from one or both (Beebe and Lachmann, 2002, p. 139–140).

Now moments: (Stern et al.'s contribution)

Stern, Tronick, and the BCPSG have studied these intense affective events carefully and have proposed a scenario as follows: At first, the psychotherapy relationship, or the mother–infant twosome, evolves in quite an ordinary way. Trial-and-error exchange helps each member of the pair toward achieving general goals, for example, mutual support and regulation. Stern et al. refer to this process as "moving along."

However, at unpredictable intervals something unique may happen. We'll discuss this shift at length; it appears to be one key to psychotherapy. At these points, "a present moment" becomes hot affectively, and full of portent for the therapeutic process. This event might or might not be an instance of disruption in the pair. The BCPSG calls these caesuras "now moments." When a "now moment" is grasped and responded to with an authentic, specific, personal action from each partner, it becomes a "moment of meeting" (Stern, et al., 1998, p. 909).

For Stern then, a "moment of meeting" represents one that lights up subjectively and affectively, thrusting both participants more fully into the present.

From Stern, et al.:
The known, familiar inter-subjective environment of the therapist patient relationship—has all of a sudden changed or risked alteration. The current state of the shared explicit relationship is called into the open. ... It does not have to threaten the therapeutic framework, but requires a response that is too specific and personal to be a known technical maneuver.

Now moments ... demand an intensified attention and some kind of choice of whether or not to remain in the established habitual framework. And if not, what to do? They force the therapist into some kind of "action" be it an interpretation or a response that is novel relative to the habitual framework, or a silence. In this sense "now moments" are like the ancient Greek concept of *Kairos*, a unique moment of opportunity that must be seized, because your fate will turn on whether you seize it and how.

The most intriguing now moments arise when the patient does something that's difficult to categorize, something that demands a different and new kind of response, with a personal signature, which shares the analyst's subjective state (affect, fantasy, real experience, etc.) with the patient. (The analyst becomes more paraverbally transparent, as a person, at these times—our clarification.) If this happens, they will enter an authentic "moment of meeting" (pp. 911–913).

These are the essential elements that go into creating a "moment of meeting." The therapist must use a specific aspect of his or her individuality that carries a personal signature. The two are meeting as persons relatively unhidden by their usual therapeutic roles, for the moment. Also the actions that make up the "moment of meeting" cannot be routine, habitual or technical; they must be novel and fashioned to meet the singularity of the moment. Of course, this implies a measure of empathy, an openness to affective and cognitive reappraisal, a signal affective attunement (note all the paraverbal words Stern has just used—"empathy," "openness," "attunement"), a viewpoint that reflects and ratifies that what is happening is occurring in the domain of the "shared implicit relationship," that is, a newly created dyadic state specific to the participants. (p. 913).

Stern et al. close their discussion of heightened communicative events and implicit relational knowing.

> ... most of the inter-subjective environment (belongs) to implicit relational knowing which gets built into the shared implicit relationship in the course of therapy. The process of change, thus, takes place in the shared implicit relationship. Finally we anticipate that this view of altering implicit relational knowing during "moments of meeting" will open up new and useful perspectives that consider therapeutic change. (Stern et al., 1998, p. 918)

The BCPSG in later papers introduces the concept of the "local level," "moment-to-moment" activity in the therapy (Stern et al., 2002). Such ideas imply that much of what transpires in a treatment does not enter reflective consciousness or explicit exchange. These small, "local" interactions appear "spontaneous," "creative," and "created" (Stern et al., 2002, p. 1054).

Stern et al. also suggest that finding a fit between client and therapist represents an inexact, trial and error, "sloppy" process (Stern et al., 2002, p. 1056). Ultimately, the two persons move toward inner coherence and new initiatives become possible. Change often comes in small not highly charged moments. Change enters, usually unnoticed, after tiny mutual shifts in implicit relational knowing. Chaos theory seems to predict that such change may well follow a "fuzzy," improvisational, redundant path (Stern et al., 2005). Recall, Tronick's, (2007) discussion on rupture and repair.

In sum, following the BCPSG, growth can often occur without explicit verbal reflection by either party, and in split second intervals, a radical assertion (2005, p. 697).

> Most of the affectively meaningful life experiences that are relevant in psychotherapy are represented in the domain of *nonconscious implicit knowledge* (italics ours). This also includes many manifestations of transference. Therefore much of what happens at the local level is psychodynamically meaningful though not necessarily repressed (remember this last sentence for later—our note) ... The fact that the dynamically repressed unconscious can also be an active influence at the local level is not our focus. We are simply calling attention to a different level of process. (2005, p. 698) ...
>
> (We'll expand on this idea of two unconscious worlds in a few pages.)
>
> We believe the level of therapeutic activity has its *own complex structure* and *organization* (emphasis ours). It is at this moment to moment level that implicit relational procedures are enacted and evolve. However, our focus on the local level is not intended to imply that the background and meta-theory of the psychoanalytic framework are not relevant as well. In fact, future work will need to focus on integrating the local level and the level of larger psychodynamic meanings and narratives. (Stern et al., 2005, p. 698)

The group continues to study material at the local level to tease out the alignment of verbal and extra-verbal intentionality.

> Whatever approach is taken, however, it is inescapable that every analyst is simultaneously interacting with the patient at the micro level (usually paraverbally—usually unconsciously—our note). And any approach will have implications at this level. It cannot be ignored in any view of treatment, whatever the orientation. It has changed our clinical sensibilities.
>
> Where do the novel elements come from in the analytic process that make it such a surprisingly specific term? One could say that sloppiness is to a two person psychology what free association is to a one person psychology. That each add the unexpected specific detail. These "now moments" create the surprise discoveries that push the dyad to its uniqueness. (Stern et al., 2005, p. 721)

"Now moments" and the concept of "implicit relational knowing" mark a dramatic departure from our usual understanding of psychotherapy and represent the distinct fulcrum in our argument about the centrality of extra-verbal relating in psychotherapy. Stern et al.'s view of the therapy relationship clearly reflects their earlier studies of the mother–baby interaction.

Stern's implicit relational world differs from an intrapsychic world because the former is largely unconscious but not repressed for dynamic reasons, guilt, and so on. However, the implicit relational space is not conflict free. Toddlers have distress over attachment to parents who inadequately comfort them, for example. In addition, implicit relational knowing usually remains mostly unconscious but the therapist does on occasion make interpretations explicitly focusing on it. Third, Stern et al. imply that the later intrapsychic world, particularly that of transference/counter-transference, may emerge from the original implicit relational space. However, they also seem to suggest that intrapsychic conflict often has a life separate from the earlier implicit world. They are not entirely clear on this point (Stern et al., 2010, pp. 154–155).

The core of the book

We've organized the analysis of our videos based on the Stern and Beebe models. These excerpts from the Stern group suggest four important observations illuminating the foundation of psychotherapy: (1) Therapy and the mother–infant implicit relational knowing process bear striking similarities. (2) These descriptions of the treatment interaction feel highly paraverbal— "attunement"—"analysts personal signature." (3) Tiny, brief, local-level interactions co-construct the implicit relational matrix. (4) Change in psychotherapy occurs mostly within the implicit relational knowing interchange.

Stern and colleagues studied hundreds of hours of videotape to gather their original parent–baby findings. We might observe parallel phenomena if we analyzed many hours of adult psychotherapy videotape using substantially the same methods. Stern et al.'s narrative feels insightful but still rather vague and confusing. To evaluate his findings, we probably need to use specific videotape or case examples of psychotherapy, maybe analyzed with an "objective" scoring system.

Stern, Tronick, and the BCPSG make clear the conviction that many of us have long considered. Spontaneous, very personal encounters occur in therapy which patient and therapist often remember for a lifetime and on which the power of the treatment seems to pivot. Change takes place because of a shift in implicit relational knowing within the pair (Stern et al., 1998, p. 918). These change moments usually happen at the local level in a flash and have sometimes verbal, but also inevitably paraverbal, thrust. These paragraphs above from the BCPSG seem to shadow our earlier thoughts in Chapter 1, about the consequentiality of moments of nonverbal communication in psychotherapy.

Some of these "moments of meeting" have achieved a historical immortality to us, the psychotherapy students: Balint encouraging his patient to somersault across his office and Winnicott reassuring Guntrip in their first meeting, "I don't have anything to say, but if I say nothing, I'm afraid you'll think I'm not here" (Guntrip, 1975)—Wachtel telling his client that he, Wachtel, also had overprotective parents and that as a child he had never learned to ride a bicycle. However, as an adult, he had asked his wife to teach him on a rental in Central Park (Wachtel, 2008).

Stern and Beebe and their colleagues have offered us a startling alternative view of the psychotherapy process, based on their understanding of paraverbal and often preconscious data. Most of us can contribute from our own practices, and personal therapies, moments of meeting that have befallen us and our clients, and that will probably stay with us forever.

Stern, Tronick, Beebe, and Lachmann all practice both as mother–infant researchers and psychoanalysts. They find themselves in the unique position to explore, with doubly expert eyes, a vast number of clinical and research findings illuminating the self-and mutual-regulatory functions embedded within paraverbal communication behavior.

Stern attempts to define implicit relational knowing more precisely. To him it does not simply mean preverbal or nonverbal.

... the implicit can be revealed through verbal as well as nonverbal interaction (our note—as we'll see) however the implicit aspects of meaning are not in the content of the words themselves. The implicit meaning exists, so to speak, between the lines, ... while with development, verbal exchanges increasingly become a part of interactions with others, the "rules" or syntax underlying interactions are noted through affect and intension cues from the beginning of life and are rarely raised to the level of conscious verbal description. Instead they remain a part of our implicit relational knowing. (Stern et al., 2010, p. 153)

After reviewing the Stern work we, and perhaps some of our readers by now, find ourselves left with little doubt that paraverbal data, that is, facial activation and expression, particularly smiling, and the power, pitch and prosody of speech, postural orientation, head and arm gesture, self and other touching, and so on may all beckon us toward an over-looked parallel universe to our studies of the verbal exchange within psychotherapy.

Additional points emerge from these last few paragraphs. The Stern-Beebe-Tronick group, from their mother–infant studies, has provided a map for us to understand paraverbal relating. Stern posits that change comes from the implicit relational knowing universe and happens gradually. Occasionally, we come upon a distinct breakthrough when the implicit knowing suddenly becomes explicit. The therapist and patients join in a personal and transparent event and make personal actions to address this new happening—the moment of meeting. But all along they relate affectively, unconsciously, or preconsciously and create small shifts in connection and mutual recognition that change their inner selves. The mother–baby analogue fits. The parent and infant slowly build wordless internal structures of connection upon which they can both count. This represents implicit relational knowing and is central to development.

Sometimes, client or counselor directly speaks out their implicit affective state, that is, "I suck, I suck" for example. In summary, many important moments in the relationship between the counselor and client seem to turn on the implicit relational foundation, and we can best enter that world by tracking the paraverbal exchange. Our study of the videotapes will uncover this pattern.

For instance, Heller and Haynal (1997) suggest strong evidence that the unconscious facial expression of the therapist helps to identify suicide reattempters at three times the accuracy of conscious professional judgment. This represents only one project; nevertheless, maybe it suggests we need to consider reassessing and augmenting our conventional explicit (verbal) understanding of the communication inside the therapy to include a definite implicit connection.

We, and the Stern, Beebe, Lachmann, Tronick camps, propose that the mother–infant communicative bond represents the analoge to the paraverbal exchange in adult psychotherapy. These research scientists mount a sophisticated convincing argument that two parallel spheres do unfold in a mirror-image fashion, but they remain well aware that they lack substantive proof to validate this position.

Although the co-construction of the intersubjective field is currently of great interest to psychoanalysis, detailed clinical material illustrating the nonverbal and implicit dimension of this process remains rare. (Beebe et al., 2005, p. 89)

We have plenty of mother–infant research data and reports at our finger-tips, but we lack available comparative video tape data and rating systems for the adult psychotherapy exchange, for a host of reasons, research funding and confidentiality concerns among them. The latter represents a minor issue in videotaping mothers and babies as research subjects, but psychotherapy patients require far more privacy. Also, as we've mentioned, we simply do not know how to describe and to organize extra-verbal information very well as yet.

The present authors, however, now do have videotape materials, extensive case reports, and systematic methods of analysis at their disposal. Exploring the correspondence between the verbal and the paraverbal information on these tapes and comparing these findings to the mother–infant research model is the major goal of our study and comprises much of the focus of the remaining chapters. Responding to Beebe's suggestion, we want to supply some of the "detailed clinical materials" illustrating the nonverbal dimension of this process.

Stern et al. do not represent the first to describe these important moments of meeting between an open counselor and an open client (for example, see also Greenberg et al., 1993).

We're left, however, with a major question to which we'll return shortly. If "implicit relational knowing" represents so important a dimension of the psychotherapy exchange, why can't we spontaneously recall many more "moments of meeting" from our experience as therapists or clients? Some immediately come to mind, we can search for additional ones, but the final number in our memory seems to remain fairly small. Why? More in a few minutes.

Region B concluded—Unconscious World I and Unconscious World II: Two Unconscious Worlds

As we follow the track of the Stern et al. 1998, 2010, Beebe and Lachmann, 2002, and Lyons-Ruth, 1998, 2005 writings, we slowly realize that they offer us a complex argument that indirectly seems to propose an unconscious divided into two separate regions at its base.

Unconscious World I

We refer to this universe as "first" because it appears earlier developmentally. Stern's (1985) "core self" and "inter-subjective self" and Beebe and

Lachmann's preverbal self leads us toward an unconscious based on implicit relational knowledge. All of us have "forgotten" the paraverbal "going on being" experiences that make up our entire early interpersonal world prior to age 2, when we acquire some speech and shortly after that certain kinds of autobiographical memory (Siegel, 1999).

These early preverbal experiences, however don't go anywhere. They remain stored in the brain and continue to grow in the nonverbal unconscious, presumably largely in the right frontal cortex (Siegel, 1999, 2012; Schore, 2003 a & b, 2014).

When we encounter a new person who makes us smile or laugh or with whom we rapidly feel physical and emotional comfort, to whom we relate in some automatic natural way, we quickly sense, "I feel like I've known him all my life." It's true we have because this stranger has stimulated a "Representation of Interactions Generalized," RIG (Stern, 1985, p. 97). The new acquaintance fits into an old relationship pattern that started to become internalized before words.

The vast majority of brain events, like this one of sudden warm recognition, never become fully conscious. Consider Pally.

> The fact that so much in the brain occurs unconsciously and without words suggests that emotional nonverbal exchange may play at least as much importance in analytic treatment as does verbal exchange (Pally, 2000, p. 99). Some 80% of brain events probably never reach consciousness (Pally, 2000). Analysts and patients may influence one another's bodily sensations, imagery, thoughts, behaviors and even words, through non-consciously processed nonverbal cues of emotion such as autonomic changes, (flushing, dry mouth) and behaviors (facial expression, posture, gesture). These nonverbal cues are evident in the *analyst* (emphasis ours) as well as in the patient. Since the brain is organized so that individuals impact each other so much at the nonverbal level, this work suggests that *how* the analyst communicates may be as important to the therapy interaction as *what* the analyst says. (See Wachtel, 2008, once again, our suggestion.) Additionally, *how* the analyst behaves and feels may be as much an indicator of what is going on unconsciously *in the patient* as anything that is consciously known by the individual. (Pally in Beebe et al., 2005, p. 199; Also see our Chapter 7.)

Stern (1985) in the brilliant insight upon which he and his coworkers originally based their theory of implicit relational knowing, pointed out that the preverbal selves, that is, "core self" and "intersubjective self," do not just disappear when the verbal self emerges but continue to expand and to exert influence, throughout the life cycle, as an active, extra-verbal self, usually playing a motif in the background, often obscured by the spoken dialogue of the "verbal self."

This paraverbal self probably contributes a strong part to any psychotherapy, even if it evades our usual focus (Stern, 1985, chap 11). We'll see repeated evidence of it as we watch the videos. Pally captures the imprint of this unconscious implicit relational universe. She also answers our question from just above. We can't remember many "now moments" because they fleetingly register in just barely the conscious or just barely the unconscious world. From now on, we'll refer to the Pally and Stern–Beebe space as Unconscious World I. Our paraverbal relating apparently comes mostly from this Unconscious World I, the nonverbal language originally connected with early intimacy and associated with the right side of the brain.

Unconscious World II

Freud brought Unconscious World II to our awareness in 1900 with the publication of *The Interpretation of Dreams*. The content in that unconscious, however, represented the fears, longings, excitements, we have suppressed for psychodynamic reasons: that is, guilt, shame, anger. This second unconscious world, Freud's unconscious, seems all about memories and feelings kept repressed by conflict.

In Unconscious World I, normal childhood amnesia, in the inarticulate right side hemisphere, originally keeps these memories out of awareness. Some similar force renders implicit relational knowing experiences mostly unconscious as we grow older. Dynamic issues do not act to repress this material; it can usually emerge, implicitly or explicitly, like any other non-conflicted memory.

This division between the implicit relational Unconscious World I, and the dynamic, psychic conflict dominated Unconscious World II, makes intuitive sense and seems consistent with the research data (Infants quickly enter the implicit relational universe of Unconscious World I. They can distinguish their mother's face and voice, from those of others, within hours of birth, and they have a developed social grasp and interactional capacity by age 60 days.) (Stern, 1985).

Psychodynamic conflict represents a real phenomenon, but it probably appears much later than Freud suggested. Babies and toddlers in the laboratory do not seem conflicted over their eating or bowel issues, and so on and are usually remarkably open and attuned with their holding/attachment figures, just a few weeks after birth (Stern, 1985).

Beebe and Lachmann (2002), Beebe et al. (2005), Tronick (2007), and Stern et al. (1985, 1998) have all suggested changes in dynamic theory that carry significance for our understanding of psychotherapy. As we noted, they argue that much crucial learning in therapy arises within this sphere

of implicit relational knowing and not through the interpretation of unconscious dynamic conflict. This implies that change processes in therapy often
emerge from Unconscious World I from which extra-verbal communication
originally comes as well. In the balance of our book, we'll study these two
unconscious worlds from multiple angles, relying in part, on our small array
of structured research instruments (see Chapter 3).

Since it seems likely that dynamic conflict arrives after we enter the
epoch of speech, our tentative working hypothesis implies that the paraverbal behaviors we can observe in psychotherapy exchanges relate mostly to
Unconscious World I, the originally wordless but now ongoing right brain
space. The language of implicit relational knowing stretches back to the
human infant and the mother. We see direct evidence of this reappearing in
later intimate interactions particularly in the psychotherapy relationship.

We also suggest that much, although not all, of the *dynamic* unconscious information emerges from the post-verbal time period and lingers
in the left or verbal side of the brain—within Unconscious World II, in
other words. However, Stern et al. (2010, p. 155) further in their book,
hypothesize that intrapsychic conflict may represent the later product of
earlier defensive conflict within the dyadic, implicit, relational space. In
other words, apparently dynamic conflict can be an outgrowth of original
difficulties from the implicit relational world. Stern et al. do not develop
this idea further.

Also, an important exception to these distinctions between Unconscious
World I and Unconscious World II enters the argument when we consider
preverbal trauma. Schore (2003 a & b, 2014) and many others have suggested
that such early trauma resides in the right side of the brain, but it clearly does
not represent implicit relational knowing. It's a separate, wordless, recollec-
tion that can reemerge without words, often in visual images, at unpredictable
times, and can lead to inexplicable extreme dysregulation. Ogden and Fisher
(2015) and Emerson (2015) approach the treatment of these traumatic resi-
dues through physical movement since they originally had little to do with
words. In sum, there's more on the right side of the brain than implicit relational knowing, and the contents of right side and left side brain can certainly
intermingle.

We must take the notion of these two unconscious worlds as a very provi-
sional model, about which we need to learn much more. Nevertheless, to our
surprise, we now begin to realize that Pally, and Beebe and Lachmann, and
to a lesser extent Stern, have posed an important redefinition of what we had
thought of as the unconscious.

It appears that, unbeknownst to us, we therapists may have been dealing with phenomena from two unconscious locations and not one. As we'll
soon see, this hypothesis offers us considerable potential value as a tool for

understanding the differing dimensions of mental and emotional functioning that we observe in our treatments and on our videotapes.

The differentiation of the two universes represents no perfect dichotomy and can quickly break down. Messages from the two wells of the unconscious easily become entwined. For example, an implicit relational knowing nonverbal incident that seems too unexpected, or too intimate, can provoke anxiety or guilt, that is, the patient suddenly hugs the therapist at the close of the session.

However, the central point remains that if we look at issues as just dynamic or as just "moments of meeting" or "local actions," we'll miss the other half of the crucial meaning. The authors continue to track and label the differing messages from these two regions of the unconscious as our narrative progresses.

Additional Unconscious Worlds

At the risk of confusing ourselves and our readers even more, additional Unconscious Worlds have recently become identified. Ogden and Fisher (2015) explore Unconscious World III, the sensory motor unconscious sphere. Their position extends Stern et al.'s and our own, although they work with mostly Unconscious World II conflicted affect. In particular, in the case of the traumatized patient, the authors find that the unconscious memories seek expression motorically, for example, as a downward glance, a frozen smile, stooped shoulders. The author's treatment method focuses on a "predominance of nonverbal body based implicit processes over verbal explicit processes" Ogden and Fisher (p. 25). They mutually explore these physical movements for signs of underlying affect, much the way Beebe might use matching speech processes and soothing voice tones to connect with the patient right brain to right brain (p. 47).

Ogden and Fisher introduce a fascinating behavioral medicine dimension to their therapy. They teach the client to become more aware of their postural communications, but they also coach the patient with homework assignments to realign their spine and their chin, for instance. In other words, they use direct physical interventions as well as Unconscious World I implicit relational intervention strategies. A change in body position translates into a change in mind; a physiological action represents a strategy to modify feelings. We'll return to their work later in the book, since it poses an interesting parallel to our own.

In Unconscious World IV, Hassin, Uleman, and Bargh propose "The New Unconscious" (2005). They, and multiple contributors, describe a very active *cognitive* unconscious world that we have only recently begun to understand. "The new unconscious is much more concerned with affect, motivation, and even control and metacognition than was the old unconscious. Goals, motives and self-regulation are prominent without the conflict and drama of the psychoanalytic unconscious" (2005, p. 6).

The editors and their colleagues introduce a plethora of methods to study these new unconscious cognitive processes from "neuroscience and social lab experiments to naturalistic observation and field experiences" (p. 6). In other words, human beings have a readily observable cognitive unconscious to anticipate and understand the expectations that the person confronts in his, minute-by-minute, real-world negotiations.

For example, scientists have found experimentally that subjects have multiple sub-selves that can, for instance, measure just how familiar a new person seems compared to their unconscious image of a significant other, and "people can perform complex, flexible, goal oriented behavior unconsciously" (p. 7). They can work to change a rigid personal attitude, such as a racial prejudice, for example. We previously had thought that this activity came under the control of conscious mastery, but apparently often unconscious forces are usually at work here as well, according to this present research. We emphasize that this new "unconscious" is non-dynamic and relatively non-relational, so that as fascinating as the findings seem, the Hassin et al. work pertains mostly to advanced cognitive psychology and probably is not highly relevant to our own investigation.

Odd as it may appear, we've now encountered probably four Unconscious Worlds that function often separately from one another but all of which have great significance for human interaction and behavior. Other students will probably discover still more unconscious places, as they continue their own research. Myself and my coauthors had no idea that we'd encounter two distinct Unconscious Worlds as we started to study the videotapes, and now we're up to four. We're as surprised as the reader.

Region C: Transference/counter-transference exchange

With this hasty introduction to Unconscious World I and Unconscious World II, (and a very hasty mention of Unconscious Worlds III and IV), we're again ready to move, clockwise in our diagram, to an area as deeply psychodynamic as any but still one where paraverbal transactions also centrally take place. Recall from Chapter 1, Jacobs" (1991) description of Ms. C, who while lying on the couch wordlessly, turned her back to him, as if to shun him, expressing her angry feelings nonverbally.

We include this section in the diagram to explore that Unconscious World II (psychodynamic conflict) holds a strong place in "relationship" as well. Evidence of transference/counter-transference in Unconscious World II, readily appears on our tapes. We will also indicate how transference matters relate to Unconscious World I issues.

Region C: A brief introduction to transference issues

Early on, Freud (1912) offered his colleagues the image of the dispassionate surgeon as a model for the ideal analytic stance. In theory, the transference feelings of the patients would then project onto a "blank screen" for doctor and patient to study and work through. At nearly every cost, Freud tried to avoid any impression that the analyst might suggest meanings to, or hypnotize, the patient, as so often took place in the contemporary psychotherapeutic universe of that era. Freud fought all his career to prove psychoanalysis a fact-buttressed, objective scientific discipline akin to the other medical specialties (Wachtel, 2008; Gay, 1988).

Today's current obsession with evidence-based therapy brings us to déjà vu all over again. Some find themselves desperately trying to prove psychotherapy a science conforming to empirical laws, that is, this particular procedure really does remove this particular symptom. Why do we care so much about a narrow definition of treatment and of efficacy? Patients get better within our contextual, nonmedical treatment. That's the important point (Wampold, 2001; Norcross, 2002; Wachtel, 2008, 2010).

Over the next 80 years after Freud, well-meaning analysts, attempting to follow his dictum tried to keep their persons and their feelings out of the treatment. With the advantage of historical hindsight, we can now see that, in the process of adhering to the supposed blank screen guideline, the therapist often committed mistake after mistake. He sometimes made the patient and his "transference" responsible for every feeling exchanged between the two participants, including ones based on the fact that one member of that dyad spoke so infrequently to the other and seemed so distant and sometimes so uncaring.

We now know that we need to appreciate, fully, how the therapist's person, feelings, and behavior influence the patient on both nonverbal and verbal planes. A blank-screen therapist represents an impossibility; the valence from the therapist remains inescapable. We have to understand that influence, and bring it constructively into the treatment, not try to banish it (Maroda, 1991, 1999, 2010; Wishnie, 2005).

Ironically, Freud himself apparently spoke a great deal in the therapy sessions, revealed facts about his personal life to clients, sometimes accepted research funding from them and, on occasion, lent them small sums of money (Gay, 1988).

Region C continued

A Model of the Transference/Counter-Transference Transaction: Tansey & Burke

Many such as Reik (1948), Racker (1968), Winnicott (1965), Searles (1965), Greenson (1967), and more recently Jacobs (1991), Maroda (1991,

1999), Stark (1999), Wishnie (2005), and Wachtel (2008) have offered us invaluable insights, which begin to unravel the crucial, but so complicated, role of transference/counter-transference interaction in psychotherapy. Space does not permit any summary of their specific contributions with which many readers have familiarity in any case.

However, Tansey and Burke (1989), have, more completely than anyone else, carefully explicated how the strands of projective identification, transference, counter-transference, and empathic response interweave into one comprehensive model. We'll lean heavily on the Tansey and Burke matrix and introduce it, in detail, as we explore this third area of our Venn diagram, transference/counter-transference issues.

We must include the area of dynamic transference and counter-transference to give a complete picture of the interactive relationship. The Tansey and Burke data also include multiple examples of paraverbal messaging, as we'll soon see. In short, these authors clarify that it's impossible to study psychotherapy interaction without including an explication of transference and counter-transference communication.

To begin, the Tansey and Burke system links projective identification, countertransference and empathy along one integrated pathway: *transference → projective identification → counter-transference → empathic response. (We've added transference at the beginning of the Tansey and Burke sequence to make it more complete.)*

Terms

Let's start by defining these terms in order. Transference refers to all the affects, memories, and associations the *client* feels toward the person of the therapist, conscious or not, realistically justified or not, clearly transferred from earlier relationship figures or not. This is the "total" definition of transference versus more restricted ones, a distinction enunciated by Tansey and Burke (1989).

Counter-transference, in turn, refers to all the affects, associations, and memories that the *therapist* feels toward her client, objectively accurate or not, originating in her early life experiences or not, including both her distorted, "neurotic" reactions toward her client and her more realistic ones.

Given what we now know about implicit relational knowing, we can quickly see that a restricted specified view of transference or counter-transference represents an epistemologic impossibility. Brain events to the tune of 80% remain unconscious, so we could never confidently and completely relate any action back to any particular early relationship. Many other associations could be attached to the particular transference reaction, which might only come to light later, if at all.

Further definition of terms

Projective identification describes a largely unconscious process in which one person, usually, but not always, the client, transmits some part of his mental/ emotional life into the therapist. The counselor unconsciously identifies with the projected material, modifies it, and projects it back toward the client. This process is now complete. Both the therapist and the client identify with the projected material and little by little the client forms a new self, a new object that has become real, at least for a time, between them. Finally, mutual projective identification occurs because, even as he projects, that client receives projections back from the therapist. The unconscious transaction continues in a circular manner (all of the above adapted from Scharff and Scharff, 1991, p. 55–59).

Several conclusions follow from this sequence. Projective identification represents a powerful, mostly unconscious, form of communication and influence. It will carry particular force in any intimate pair: parent–child, therapist–client, husband–wife. Introjective identifications, new creations, some lasting, some not, can come to life. People really do create new objects and change each other, sometimes permanently, sometimes not, during projective identification. Projection often occurs wrapped in paraverbal messaging, an anxious stare by the client, for instance.

The painstaking exploration of this projection trail represents the important content of the Tansey and Burke monograph (1989). Empathy, the final step allows the therapist a deeper, more multileveled understanding of his client, and of his client's message and renders him better equipped to communicate back to that person with helpful content and feeling.

We can now more thoroughly review Tansey and Burke's model: (1) transference—the client reacts affectively to the therapist's person with, an accurate, or less than accurate, response → (2) projective identification—the client then projects important, but as yet still unconscious, self and object images and conflicts into that therapist. → (3) counter-transference—the therapist reacts to the projection and seeks to understand and validate his response to it. → (4) introjective identification—the therapist takes in the projection and reworks it into a trial identification (Jacobs [1991], for example, captures, with remarkable specificity and poignancy, the inner world of the therapist as he gropes to understand these feelings projected and provoked by his client.) → (5) empathy—the therapist returns to the client a verbalized response, often paired with a paraverbal communication (a smile, a sigh, a look of sympathy), "Yes, it has been (that way) for you" (from Stern et al., 1998, p. 914).

This response captures the client's dilemma and strengthens him to use the new emotional and cognitive grasp the two partners now have on the conflict.

The empathy brings the patient and the therapist closer as a dyad and nurtures the alliance between them.

As we continue to explore this picture, additional tentative ideas emerge, which carry important implications for our study of psychotherapy interchange. *First*, the Tansey and Burke framework strongly suggests a continued active presence of projective identification, which underlies the psychotherapy enterprise, exerting greater or lesser influence at any point but always potentially present. Forces from this usually unconscious process occasionally break out into the conscious minds of the participants and become available for direct discussion, but usually these remain in the background.

As of now, no researcher has marshalled empirical evidence to support the existence of the omnipresent exchange of projective identifications, but many writers have persuasively argued for the importance of this dynamic. They suggest that the core object and self images that lie within the projective identification sequence, so skillfully captured by Tansey and Burke, almost certainly exert significant power on the unfolding of the treatment (See Racker, 1968; Jacobs, 1991; Stark, 1999; Maroda, 1991, 1999; Wishnie, 2005).

Unconscious World II as reflected
in the transference/countertransference interaction

If we step back and reexamine Tansey and Burke's sequence as a whole pathway, we can grasp that they too have mapped an unconscious world for us—but a very different one from Stern's or Beebe's.

The conflicted, psychodynamic shards of the repressed seem gathered within the Tansey and Burke's model. For example, they offer an important case illustration in which a therapist feels subtly rejected by his client and struggles with this countertransference feeling toward his trying, childlike, only somewhat verbal, young Asian woman patient (Tansey and Burke, 1989, pp. 171–186).

We can see the dynamic unconscious universe of conflict, anger, fear, frustration, wish, and hope played out in the transference and counter-transference with this client and with others that Tansey and Burke introduce. According to their model, the therapist (and the client to some degree as well), mostly unconsciously, strive to grasp the projections involved and to modify them, to contain them and ultimately to transform them into empathic responses to the other and to the self.

Clearly this represents a crucial process inside dynamic therapy but a contrasting one, unfolding side by side, with the more naturally occurring, unspoken "implicit relational knowing" model offered to us by Stern, Beebe, and their colleagues.

Table 2.1 Unconscious World I and Unconscious World II

Unconscious World I (Implicit Relational Knowing—Stern 1985, 2010; Beebe et al., 2002)	Unconscious World II (The Dynamic Unconscious— Tansey and Burke, 1989)
• Centers initially on preverbal material which later translates into paraverbal communication • Right side brain related • Implicit relational mode of communication • Local level micro-process • In therapy, little direct verbal focus on these issues • Usually a place of benign extra-verbal unconscious feeling, not actively repressed • Moments of meeting: paraverbal selves of client and therapist collide in a deeply personal way	• Centers on repressed dynamic issues, that is, guilt, anger, disgust, etc. • left side brain-related, verbal expression common • transference and countertransference matters abound • projective identification—often mode of communication • wide use of empathy pathway (Tansey & Burke, 1989) • In therapy, verbal interpretations/observations, likely

If we reflect on the case of the young Asian lady mentioned just above, and on Tansey and Burke's contribution, we can more fully realize that they've given us largely a model of Unconscious World II, the dynamic unconscious subterranean space. We can sketch a chart beginning to summarize some of the differences between the two universes.

In this chapter, we've tried to talk about both unconscious worlds, a little, and to give a rendition of the part both play in "relationship." Paraverbal communication, since it probably originates in the early wordless stages of life, retains a deep connection with Unconscious World I, implicit relational knowing. But Unconscious World I does not own the extra-verbal exchange. Plenty of such interchange goes on there, but also in Unconscious World II— remember Ms. C literally turning her back to Jacobs, paraverbally acting out a hostile transference, through her different postures on the analytic couch.

Implications of Tansey and Burke's work for our research

Three topic areas, which Tansey and Burke highlight, hold particular relevance for our project.

First, the authors reintroduce us to the dynamic unconscious. Their model seems all about conflicted affect. Their client projects often unacceptable or distressing feelings onto the therapist who then must face his or her own memories, and ambivalently held self and object images, to respond constructively.

The Stern-Beebe "implicitly relational knowing," usually gentle unconscious and the Tansey and Burke projected, affectively hotter, conflicted
unconscious, represent two often, but not always, separate entities, it appears
(see p. 53). We've stumbled over a sometimes split unconscious—(1)
Unconscious World I organized around an initial wordless core self and
inter-subjective self and (2) Unconscious World II constructed mostly around
post-verbal, repressed, dynamic affect. In later chapters, we'll continue to
explore these two universes, sometimes as two different realms, but ones that
cross over and interact at important times. Much paraverbal communication
can take place in both.

For example, Tansey and Burke's contribution feels very relevant for
our objective to carefully analyze ten-minute video segments of specific
psychotherapy interchanges in terms of extra-verbal communication. In the
psychodynamic unconscious world into which Tansey and Burke usher us,
barely conscious projections, trial identifications, and empathic counter-
projections represent the principal players in forming the transference/
counter-transference matrix underlying the interchange. These often make
themselves known subtly and paraverbally—recall Jacobs and Ms. C.

We'll use the Tansey and Burke model, almost exclusively, when we study
the specific details of transference and counter-transference, Unconscious
World II themes appear in our tape selections. We'll see a complex process
that emerges from the Tansey and Burke matrix. Little by little as the projections become modified and returned to the client, a new object, an optimistic
client, for instance, may gradually come into being.

Region D—The real object relationship: Control Mastery Theory

Now, we'll move to the next subsection of the Venn diagram—a place further
removed from the moment-to-moment therapeutic interaction but one where
momentum also usually becomes enacted paraverbally. Introducing the control mastery theory allows us to examine the broader relationship offers that
client and therapist exchange. Here, as well, extra-verbal data loom large
because, as we'll see, little is usually actually said in the treatment about these
relationship exchanges, however major a role they may play.

In its turn, the Control Mastery perspective will help us to understand
more completely the action on our videos. The real relationship seems to
emerge out of Unconscious World I mostly. Previous authors describing this
"real relationship," that is, Greenson (1967), carefully distinguish it from
Unconscious World II dynamic conflict and study it as a separate phenomenon. These earlier writers, however, did not have the advantage of the neuropsychological, or the implicit relational, perspective and so they could not

pursue the real relationship as far as can we. For example, Stern's "moment of meeting" represents an obvious real relationship phenomenon taking place between the two participants.

Control Mastery study began with the work of Alexander and French (1946) who explored the curative action of the emotional experience between the client and the therapist. We'll return to their work in a few minutes. Almost 20 years later, the important contributions of British (originally Hungarian) psychoanalyst Michael Balint (1968, 1972) took up this path. Balint pursued a lifelong examination of the negotiation of focal relationship offers, versus interpretations, between clients and therapists, students and teachers, and general practitioners and their medical patients (Donovan, 1989). For instance, find below Balint and his client exchange in real relationship terms. Balint makes no interpretations but supports his client through the treatment with his genuine listening and encouragement.

Vignette #1—The Stationary Manufacturer

Consider the celebrated case of the paranoid business executive, the Stationary Manufacturer (Balint et al., 1972), a man briefly introduced in Chapter 1. This client tortured his wife with a ceaseless inquisition into her sexual relationship with her former fiancée—whom she knew, and left, before she ever met the patient.

In a deft treatment Balint does not interpret to the Stationary Manufacturer the patient's possible fears of weakness and castration or his possible homosexual wishes to identify with the wife's former lover. Rather Balint lets the client lean on him psychologically and use him as a "sounding board," the client's phrase, supporting the patient to wrestle out loud, over and over, with his excruciating dilemma. He loves his wife, but her possible sexual behavior, earlier in her life, pushes him toward disorganizing, jealous mistrust and destabilizing anxiety and fury.

After 27 meetings, carefully spaced intermittently over two years, this businessman, almost miraculously, begins to regain his former composure. All this in 1972, before the widespread arrival of SSRIs, for which, given his ceaseless ruminations and bitter interrogations of his wife, this dangerously symptomatic patient, would have become a strong candidate. Balint over the next few years remained episodically in touch with the client, by post. He apparently retained his positive equilibrium.

In this landmark case, Balint clearly uses a specific relationship offer, the "sounding board," instead of any particular interpretations (or medications). In his outline of the session by session work, Balint includes a heading "therapeutic interventions thought of but not given." He consciously avoids the explicit verbal, Level 1, intervention and consistently turns to the authentic relationship offer—an unusual stance for any psychoanalyst, at any time, but particularly then in the late 1960s.

Balint's relationship offer included a supportive, man-to-man, acknowledgement that his patient had won. His wife was his and not the former suitor's. He did not need to question his masculinity or her fidelity. In another harbinger of modern technique, Balint included the wife in some of the sessions to reassure her of her husband's stability and to gauge the seriousness of the marital stress. However, he wanted to let the patient see that he, Balint, would not humiliate him by competing with him for his wife's regard. Many aspects of Balint's self, not just his interpretive skills, seem present in his treatment, thus the "real relationship."

We so intensely wish that we had videotapes of this therapy and could discover the paraverbal, relational trail, which no doubt, took place within it, given the remarkable outcome with such a pressured patient. In other words, this probably represented, in part, an implicitly relational knowing case, but we can never be sure without the video data. It certainly represents a Level 2 object relations intervention; Balint becomes the missing supportive object.

Later Gustafson (1981) and Weiss and Sampson (1986) built upon Balint's work and began to teach us about what they then termed "control mastery theory." Within the Sampson and Weiss system, the client enters therapy burdened by a negative "hypothesis," a "pathogenic belief" about herself to which she tightly clings, in her unconscious, but which she desperately wishes to discard. Effective therapy moves in one direction only, disproving the negative hypothesis.

Our Stationery Manufacturer needed to prove his masculinity and to assure himself that the wife's former boyfriend had not bested him. (His own father was apparently a sadistically competitive man.) This conviction that the other man would emerge the victor, represented our patient's pathogenic belief. Balint helped him disprove it.

Following Sampson and Weiss, the "negative hypotheses" or "pathogenic beliefs" or "chronic and enduring pains" (James Mann, 1981) often revolve around survivor or separation guilt. Consider these hypothetical examples: "My father felt himself a failure at work, if I'm successful in business, he'll feel totally defeated, beaten out even by his own son" (survivor guilt), or "If I leave my weak mother and let others love and care for me, that desertion will kill her" (separation guilt).

The real relationship with the therapist potentially introduces the antidote to the pathogenic belief because it can disconfirm the hypothesis. The earlier book by Alexander and French (1946), introducing "the corrective emotional experience," gives us further clues about how the therapeutic interchange supports the patient to question, and eventually to modify, his self-hating assumptions, work which often takes place unconsciously and without words.

For instance, Alexander's patient, the Glass Manufacturer's Son, felt controlled and dismissed by his wealthy powerful father. The young client, in turn, provoked the father and Alexander with outrageously rebellious behavior to escape what he felt his inevitable subjugation at the hands of these twin tyrants, the father and Alexander, the doctor.

But Franz Alexander grasped the test right away and didn't strike for the bait. He treated the young man with patience and forbearance, no matter how recalcitrant and annoying his youthful companion became. The patient sat in Alexander's chair, jeered back at his interventions, and so on. Alexander *held* his client with a real, respectful, accepting relationship and "disconfirmed" the hypothesis that he represented a bothersome disappointment as a patient and as a son.

The client ultimately began a constructive alliance with Alexander, curtailed his acting out, started to like both himself and his therapist better and began to work on issues with his internal father. He experienced a "corrective emotional experience" in the office with Alexander.

As Gustafson (1981) explains, in a control mastery engagement, the patient feels reassured that, within the relationship, he can lift (or *control*) a central defense, for Alexander's young man, his fantastic rebelliousness. The client has satisfied himself that the therapist really differs from the troubling parent. This step, in turn, supports the client then, to *master* his hidden fear, that he's a worthless nuisance, only someone for his father to dominate and to disregard.

Note that the therapist and patient rarely refer directly to the pathogenic belief. Control mastery theory is all about paraverbal interchange. The disconfirmation of the negative hypothesis often becomes enacted through nonverbal means in the relationship transaction. Through Unconscious World I, the therapist communicates his regard and support toward the client, which thaws the defense. Balint will not, above all, crush his patient, in a masculine competitive match. In Chapter 6, Jim follows this same strategy with a rigid vigilant man within a couple's therapy consultation. He learned this approach from reading Balint. Balint extended the Stationary Manufacturer virtually no verbalized clarifications whatever but provided him the invaluable genuine "sounding board."

In control mastery theory, the unconscious worlds sometimes intertwine. The Manufacturer's son acts out his rage and transferential anger, so this content is from Unconscious World II. We don't know whether Alexander interpreted any of the client's hostility, but we do know that he calmly accepted and patiently valued his patient in an Unconscious World I real relationship offer. We can almost see Alexander, unruffled, parrying the client's endless provocations. Here, Unconscious World I and Unconscious World II each play major roles in this therapy.

The reader may have realized, a while back, that control mastery theory decidedly represents an object relations Level 2 approach. The therapist, Alexander, for instance, offers his recalcitrant patient a real and positive object who accepts him and his dilemma. Then the client can more fully embrace himself and rid himself of the conviction that he's simply an irritant and a bother to adults—a real object relationship transaction underlies the control mastery experience much of which is negotiated without words in Unconscious World I terms. The therapist passes the test. He never moves to brush aside his client.

The Sampson and Weiss idea represents a new, creative way of thinking about psychotherapy and has two strong additional advantages for us. First, Sampson and Weiss (1986) and their colleagues have amassed empirical data, from studying multiple audio tapes, which over and over illustrate how a test appears in the psychotherapy. Can the therapist help dispel the negative hypothesis? The treatment takes a positive turn, when the therapist passes that test, or a negative one, when he doesn't. We have modified some of the Sampson and Weiss (1986) instruments to score our own data on the control mastery dimension. We'll describe these adapted scales in Chapter 3.

Second, the Sampson and Weiss approach aptly fits the paraverbal, implicit relational framework. The two systems hold much in common. Sampson and Weiss argue that clients do not willfully resist relinquishing their "negative hypothesis." They want to rid themselves of these harmful convictions and hope that the therapist can help them do so—hopes that rest initially on the unconscious level. Can Balint support the client to dispel his terrible sexual vulnerability?

The testing of the therapist, and his reaction to that test often are enacted largely paraverbally—within Unconscious World I in other words, through smiles, steady gaze, reassuring hand movements, respectful voice tone, and so on. We'll discover that the extra-verbal defeating of the pathogenic belief appears surprisingly frequently in the tapes and cases that we'll encounter as well.

A "moment of meeting" in the implicit relationship framework, in which the client and therapist step out of role and become fully human to each other, often corresponds closely to an experience of *disconfirming the pathogenic belief* in the Sampson and Weiss matrix. Alexander's Glass Manufacturer's Son, all of a sudden, realizes that his therapist does authentically value him as a person and actually likes him. Alexander does not see him as an annoying bother. Only a real response from the therapist will allow him to pass the test.

Region E—The Mind and the brain: Their relationship to Attachment Theory

Before we close Chapter 2, we need to complicate our mosaic one more time. Readers may already have realized that in this discussion, our patients and our therapists may represent embodied speakers, but also their minds reside within an embodied brain. Subtleties of brain function directly influence our paraverbal relating. Amen, 1998; Siegel, 1999, 2012; and Schore 2003 a & b, 2014 have pioneered the investigation of the role of neuropsychological process in relationship exchange.

Siegel (1999) illustrates the point that two people in close communication mirror and affect each other's feeling states but also their bodily sensitivities and their brain functioning. Consider:

a thirty year old woman sits quietly in a chair in her therapist's office. She looks puzzled as her therapist repeats his question: "How was your visit with your mother last weekend?" She bites her lip, looks away and gazes down towards the floor, saying nothing. She reaches up and covers her eyes with her arm. Her breathing becomes more rapid and shallow. She taps her foot nervously on the floor. Silence. The therapist's heart begins to accelerate. He finds himself looking down at the floor and notices his own foot tapping. The therapist's own state of mind is revealed in nonverbal signals: facial expression, eye gaze, bodily motion, tone of voice and the timing of verbal signals (whether fast, slow, in response to other comments, or the like). His voice is low in volume and he slowly says, "Oh ... it was a hard weekend." [Notice the therapist appears to match his voice prosody and pitch to his patient's - suggestion ours] His head feels as if it's about to burst. [Clearly the patient's projections highly influence the therapist's state of mind—recall Pally—the free associations within the counselor's mind offer the best clue to the client's most pressing concern at the time.] "Horrible" the woman suddenly exclaims. The pressure in the therapist's head dissipates with a sense of relief. The muscles in his own face begin to relax from their drawn, tightened state as hers also relax. The patient's body becomes less tense. "Horrible ...," she moans, now with tears in her eyes.

As this therapist and patient illustrate, engaging in direct communication is more than just understanding or even perceiving the signals—both verbal and nonverbal—sent between two people. For "full" emotional communication, one person needs to allow his *state of mind* (emphasis ours) to be influenced by that of the other in highly extra-verbal ways. In this example, the therapist's sensitivity to the patient's array of signals allows his own mental state to become aligned with that of his patient. (Siegel, 1999, p. 69)

We've quoted this passage at length because it illustrates two important, but easily overlooked phenomena, both of which speak to our core hypotheses about paraverbal communication within psychotherapy. First, the patient's actual mind, as in her brain workings, affects that of the therapist directly and vice versa. One dimension of psychotherapy represents an interchange of mind, a neuropsychological interaction, between the two participants.

Second, this Siegel vignette pictures a common adult patient/therapist interchange, the report on a troubling visit home. Patient and therapist mentally and emotionally share the former's reaction to the latest encounter with mother. But here Siegel spells out for us, in detail, the *therapist's* paraverbal attunement and reaction to each of his patient's affective and neuropsychological messages and bodily communications, as well as to her verbal ones.

She bites her lip. She taps her foot more and more quickly and glances down. He taps his foot, and he glances down matching her posture and her actions. His head feels as if it's about to burst. Finally, she says "Horrible," and the pressure in his head releases.

Nothing remarkable here, a so ordinary therapeutic interaction, except few have described, as precisely, the wordless mirroring between the two players, the mutual regulation at all levels between the therapist and the client. Every therapy unfolds in double exposure, one camera on patient, one on therapist, as they choreograph engagement and soothing at multiple levels, including brain function. Here Siegel pictures for us the neuropsychological substrate of the Beebe and Lachmann description of "Ongoing Relations."

Freedman et al. (1983), furthermore, tell us that graduate student therapists engage in more unconscious self-touching when treating patients they perceive as "difficult" versus those not so designated. The patient impinges on therapist's brain, who returns nonverbal signals back to the patient. He fidgets with his hands. The client in turn reacts to the therapist's neuropsychological response and probably sends a counter message back to the counselor once again. Here we see paraverbal relating and brain functioning comingle.

Attachment theory and the brain

Siegel's illustration also introduces another important possibility. Read from one perspective, it appears that the two participants are working to further develop the young woman's attachment status through their neuropsychological interactions. She may function at the ambivalent level at this time—note the conflicted relationship with the mother but by reflecting and supporting her mental state, the therapist is leading her to home base and becoming her mentalizing partner. The Siegel case further suggests that attachment and brain function closely interact—(more below).

We know from our prior review of Beebe et al.'s writing that the attachment status of the mother and toddler match at one year and four years. This implies that the baby must absorb his mother's "attitude with respect to Attachment" in micro level interactions through the first four years. In very brief, "local level" exchanges the parent explores, mirrors and joins with the infant's mind as he passes into toddlerhood and beyond. The process takes place in a "herky jerky" pattern but gradually leads to increasing emotional development, probably for both participants.

This suggests that attachment engagement looks surprisingly like implicit interactional knowing in Level 3 relational psychotherapy, and also very much like "teaching mentalization." Gradually psychologically, and neuro-psychologically, Seigel's therapist will support this woman toward more differentiated attachment.

Allen's description of mentalizing, "plain old psychotherapy" captures the interactional process too, exploring the feeling states of each other in the verbal and paraverbal spheres, and in a transparent, nonjudgmental fashion.

> The heart and soul of this treatment approach is maintaining a mentalizing stance, which for therapists, entails being curious, inquisitive and open minded about what's going in the patient's mind and relationships, including the relationship with the therapist. Therefore therapists also must remain curious about their own thoughts, feelings and motivations in the relationship. Therapists who maintain this stance may thus inspire their patients to join in this stance: as in development, mentalizing begets mentalizing. Therapists and patients will lose this mentalizing stance for the same reasons—feeling disgusting, or frightened or angry or ashamed and, more generally, feeling defensive and thus being closed off or in a self-justifying mode rather than being inquisitive and open-minded. (J. G. Allen, 2013, p. 194)

Allen, as Wallin (2007) has observed before him, outlines the likely interaction between therapist attachment level and that of the patient. He points out that insecure ambivalent clients will likely hold too tightly to the therapist and then push away. Avoidant people, if they seek treatment at all, keep their distance; it takes a long time for them to move closer. Unfortunately, patients disorganized in attachment usually cannot develop deeper relating with the therapist. Any treatment is likely to fail with these people.

On the other hand, securely attached clients readily involve themselves with the therapist—particularly if that therapist offers a secure attachment base, and the two can readily set up a mentalizing exchange in which they are open to the minds and feelings of each other (J. G. Allen, 2013, pp. 174–186; Diamond et al. 2003; Slade, 2008, also see Seigel 2009, chap 3, p. 74).

Attachment status usually seems communicated in Unconscious World I terms through implicit relational knowing. In the Heller and Haynal study (1997), the presumably securely attached therapist became unconsciously distressed by her inability to connect with the isolated patient, who secretly retained the decision to die but would not discuss it. The doctor then worked even harder but failed to reach these avoiding or disorganized patients.

All these efforts registered paraverbally for the therapist, she over-talked, frowned, and so on. In sum, the clients" difficulties in attachment level presumably prevented them from the potentially lifesaving therapy connection that they required, no matter how industrious the doctor.

Balint's Stationary Manufacturer demonstrated a highly ambivalent and desperate attachment to his wife. Balint's calm secure attachment gradually settled down his agitated client. This represents the most economic explanation of the positive outcome in this challenging therapy.

From the start, Winnicott engaged with Guntrip in a similar way—offering gentle verbal and paraverbal attachment messages. "I have nothing much to say as yet but if I don't say something you'll be afraid that I'm not here." In this brief, but telling exchange, Winnicott embodies the definition of a Securely Attached therapist representing home base. This brings us to the tentative conclusion that we can apply our final lens to our case excerpts and videotape segments by observing the attachment status of both the client and therapist in each vignette and by examining ways in which the client's level of attachment gradually and subtly may increase through the interaction.

If we return to the remarkable Tronick's Still Face video (2007), we see that the engagement between the paraverbally related mother and baby almost inevitably will increase, little by little, that baby's level of attachment. She's so attuned to him for most of the interchange. We can say the same for the, adult-to-adult, mentalizing stance in psychotherapy, much of which we'll find out takes place through paraverbal interaction. It's pitched to augment attachment for the client.

The right and the left side of the brain

As we watch our tapes, we'll observe the interchange of attachment levels between patient and therapist. We will study these and report on them. But in a closely related series of observations, it's likely that we'll notice that the two participants interchange, in part, through their right side brain functioning. These communications will usually become mediated paraverbally.

Schore (2003 a & b, 2014) establishes that preverbal relationship experiences particularly traumatic ones, but positive interactions as well, possibly register first in the *right orbital frontal hemisphere* of the brain, and do so with specific emphasis during a neuropsychological growth spurt in the first two years of life. These findings introduce multiple implications of major significance to the study of psychotherapy, in general, and also for the purposes of our discussion now, we'll concentrate on only one.

Verbal capacities develop in the left orbital frontal hemispheres and apparently do so one to two years later than visual nonverbal imagery, which registers in the right side. This suggests that many of the most important phenomenon with which we deal in psychotherapy, primarily with words, started as preverbal and extra-verbal, without words, experiences.

Gedo (1979), Lyons Ruth (1998, 2005), Stern et al. (1985, 1998, 2002, 2005, 2010), Schore (2003 a & b), and Allen (2013) have taken on this confounding issue in a series of important discussions. For example, perhaps the issues central to the mostly verbal medium of psychotherapy may have had little to do with words in their original form. By age 2, the average child has a vocabulary of only 70 words. Children remain quite limited verbally for several more years, but during those years they certainly have many formative experiences. What happens to those? They don't disappear. Often they are expressed through attachment relationships and often through paraverbal communication, emerging mostly from the right side of the frontal region.

We now find ourselves with a central conundrum in our field, one which we've encountered before in Chapter 1 and here again in Chapter 2. How do you describe the ineffable in words? To some extent, it begins to seem as if when we struggle to undertake psychotherapy, we're trying to complete an important, complex, business transaction, but always in a foreign currency, one with which we're mostly unfamiliar. How to use words to grasp nonverbal convictions?

Our discussion here leads us to hypothesize that we can gather information about the experiential memory locked in the right hemisphere, from the *paraverbal behavior of the client* and *from our own* extra-verbal interactions with that client. What paraverbal associations do they engender in us?

A client's rapid speech, a forced smile that does not include crinkling at the corners of the eye, a recurrent downward glance, speaking in a whisper that is too low for the listener to hear completely, all will readily communicate a great many clues about that client's basic relationship and attachment assumptions and about the feelings he or she now experiences with us, the counselors. We need to track this information carefully, but it's data hard to capture clinically in words, since neither participant may have conscious left side access to much of it.

We know that the quality of the alliance more strongly influences therapy outcome than any other factor (Gustafson, 1995; Wampold, 2001; Norcross, 2002; Wachtel, 2011). Maybe alliance comes down to which pair exchanges Duchênne smiles, who trusts, who feels chemistry, who "clicks," (from Balint, 1972), who "fits," (BCPSG, 2002, 2010; Wampold, 2002), which client and therapist join in "implicit relational knowing" on the right side of the brain (Stern et al., 1998, 2005, 2010; Schore, 2014). Who can engage in mentalizing together (Allen, 2013; Wachtel, 2011, p. 124)? The alliance seems probably largely mediated extra-verbally in which the brain function of the two participants synchronizes (Seigel, 1999).

"Chemistry" appears about *how* we say it, and see it, much more than about *what words* either client or therapist actually speaks. The right hemisphere involves experiential material. How we find an entrance to it, falls directly at the center of the therapy we undertake and seems closely related to extra-verbal expression.

Many crucial treatment happenings may emerge first from the right side of the brain: attitudes with respect to attachment, relationship expectations, possibly traumatic fears, or shameful memory visualizations, but also positive experiences, such as the projection of optimism received from the face of a friendly, relaxed therapist.

This means that, to some extent, as therapy students we've looked in the past partly in the wrong place. We've tried to account for right-side paraverbal experience with left-side verbal constructions. If we grasp this paradox, it might point us down the path toward explaining important insights in our field that before we have never quite fully articulated. They seem to slip through our fingers at the last moment, confounding our progress in more completely exploring psychotherapy.

For example, EMDR (Shapiro, 1995) and DBT (Linehan, 1993) apparently treat many of the same conditions: physical and relationship traumas and the spectrum of personality disorders, respectively, for which we used to pre-scribe long-term psychodynamic therapy almost exclusively. However, when efficacious, these new procedures seem to act more quickly than our earlier conventional techniques.

These two strategies, EMDR and DBT, with mindfulness training as a third candidate, and sensory motor therapy (Ogden and Fisher, 2015) as a fourth, clearly employ some kind of paraverbal methods that remain difficult to define precisely at this time. To us, EMDR appears a hypnotic technique and DBT a meditative one. Furthermore, long-term therapeutic yoga successfully treats seriously traumatized patients (Emerson, 2015)—which comes first the mind or the body?—this now appears a meaningless dichotomy.

Following Schore's reasoning, it seems likely that these four methods, EMDR, DBT, yoga, sensory motor interventions, focus largely on the life transpiring in the right prefrontal lobes of the brain. This important hypoth-esis represents a question open to direct neuropsychological investigation (Amen, 1998; Siegel, 1999). We can now map brain events, with PET scans, for example, and we could apply this methodology to what happens during therapy interventions like EMDR, DBT, or yoga, or even "plain old psycho-therapy." To our knowledge, little such work, with this focus, has started.

Over the past 50 years, a series of brilliant scholars have addressed various sections of the jigsaw puzzle we're assembling here: Fairbairn (1952), Balint (1968), Racker (1968), Winnicott (1971), Gustafson (1981), Mitchell (1988), Stern et al., (1985, 1998, 2005, 2010), Stark (1999), Beebe and Lachmann

(2002), Wishnie (2005), Wachtel (2008), Fonagy (2008), Allen (2013). All sought to understand the moment when the mind and body of the two participants profoundly connected and moved forward in mutual recognition.

We suggest that these original thinkers, without knowing it, strayed from the left into the right frontal hemispheres. They started with the verbal methods, but they went beyond words to touch on right side, Unconscious World I experience. Maybe they began on the left side and migrated to the right side but then became somewhat confused because they didn't realize that they and their client had a brain bi-laterally divided and, to some extent, an unconscious bi-laterally divided.

For example, Balint's (1968) Basic Fault, poignantly describes a relationship emptiness, a bottomless abyss, an overwhelming attachment disorder. With our 2016 eyes, we can see the Basic Fault as mostly a right hemisphere issue, the result of profound, immutable, preverbal trauma. It also sounds like highly Avoidant or Disorganized Attachment.

Balint began his 1968 book by telling us that experienced and inexperienced practitioners fare equally poorly with the Basic Fault subgroup. Now we can see why. The difficulty of these clients lies beyond words because it began before words. It represents a serious disorder in attachment, not an insight missed, and one not reparable, in the slightest by any Level 1 therapy.

When Winnicott tells us, "There's no such thing as a baby," his sentence makes no verbal-rational sense whatever. It projects no left-side, level-1, verbal understanding, but we never forget it because, in his poetry, he has captured the right hemispheric experience. The baby cannot exist without the mother holding him or her in every psychological and physical way. The woman cannot become a mother without a baby to hold, but it's difficult to describe this striking, double, extra-verbal image more vividly in words than to say, "There's no such thing as a baby."

Once you realize that you're functioning within the right side of the brain, nonrational, often paraverbal phenomena become much more understandable and suddenly fit into the mosaic of our position of two unconscious worlds, functioning simultaneously. It's very important to realize in which of those worlds you presently stand, as you try to make sense of what is happening between you and your client.

THE THREE EVOLUTIONARY STEPS UP TO THE PRESENT

Let's go back to the beginning. Psychotherapy's first shift in paradigm took us out of the verbal insight sphere to the object relationship world and to the self-psychology universe. The second development brought us into relational therapy and into the attachment world, mediated often through the transactions of the brain's right side. Now a third evolutionary shift may lead us to investigate the adult therapy exchange, beyond the words, by directly studying paraverbal communication and sensory motor reactions. We're circling back closer and closer to the right side of the brain when we do this.

This broad area of inquiry represents a major challenge in therapy research for the early twenty-first century. Advances in neuropsychology (Amen, 1998; Siegel, 1999, 2012; Schore, 2003 a & b, 2014; Ogden and Fisher, 2015) have given us a clear idea of a productive focus and of possible investigatory techniques that our predecessors could ever have dreamed of. What is the language and the logic of the right hemisphere? How do we enter this world and function experientially and therapeutically within it? In the balance of our monograph, we'll suggest some possible means of learning to do so.

THE MAP OF THE BOOK

After we introduce the specifics of our research instruments in Chapter 3, in Chapter 4, at long last, we'll meet actual clients and therapists in interaction. We'll study videotapes and case excerpts contributed by three experienced therapists illustrating different treatment approaches. Our counselors, Kristin Osborn, Jim Donovan, and Paul Wachtel also differ in age and obviously in gender.

Our first two chapters have offered the preamble to these encounters, setting out the regions we'll track on each tape and in each case presentation, and as well some of the relevant research attached to each of these regions.

We started out to study paraverbal relating, but we realized that we can't explain that specific area without including the rest of the landscape—verbal exchange, transference/counter-transference development, control mastery theory, levels of attachment. Perforce we include all these dimensions in the model that we'll use to study the clinical data as we continue.

No one dimension represents the most central or the most important, but like fingers of a hand, each acts independently, although coordinated with the others, to help the therapy participants to do their work of relating. Nevertheless, we'll regularly return to emphasize the paraverbal lens in the analysis of all the clinical data. That's maybe what's new here.

As we examine all five regions—verbal, paraverbal, transference/counter-transference, control mastery, and attachment issues—perhaps we can make discoveries amplifying a little bit the Balint, Winnicott, Mitchell, and Wachtel contributions. We offer this report to emphasize that maybe too much evidence has accumulated, from too many quarters, for us to dismiss the study of paraverbal information as a part of a third evolutionary step in psychotherapy research and practice.

Our book describes constructing a model and putting it to heuristic test. If it really helps us toward an explanatory, at least somewhat empirically buttressed, X-ray picture of a therapeutic exchange, a verbal and particularly an extra-verbal one, at one local moment in time, then we've made our contribution.

Using our Venn diagram to organize the material, we'll report on what happens on the tapes, and in the cases, particularly at the paraverbal level. This fresh knowledge may stimulate readers to experiment with their own clinical approach. After closing the book, they'll have to decide if they now wish to practice, playing in a slightly different key.

Next, in Chapter 3, we turn to a discussion of our methodology, and of the research instruments, that we'll use to investigate this kaleidoscope of clinical data that awaits us.

Chapter Three

Our Research

The Strategy and the Instruments

WHICH TAPES TO STUDY?

Most Thursday mornings for four years, we three authors met to frame our project and to screen and score videotapes.

We studied 12 full tapes, illustrating the work of eight therapists. Kristin and Jim had libraries of their own videos. Since we understood our work best, we concentrated on these first. Ultimately, we decided to include two from Jim's collection and one from Kristin's in the study. These we felt illustrated strong examples of paraverbal relating between the therapist and the client. Mine dated from the 1980s when our department often taped sessions. Regrettably we no longer have that capacity.

Kristin knew Paul Wachtel slightly, and I not at all, but upon viewing his work, almost immediately we realized he formed a strong extra-verbal connection with his client, which fit our model well. We sought Paul's and the American Psychological Association's permission to include his tape in our study. Including Dr. Wachtel's, these four videos seemed to illustrate valuable examples of a spectrum of paraverbal connectivity between the client and the therapist. They obviously do not represent a random sample.

CAN WE MEASURE PARAVERBAL INTERACTION?

Ten-minute segments of videotaped psychotherapy encounters and extended case dialogues make up our source material. We use an array of approaches to study these primary data. As practicing clinicians, we first analyzed the tapes and the additional clinical material qualitatively. What paraverbal actions by both participants seem to reflect, or to direct, the thrust of the interview? We then added quantitative instruments to the design. Some of these measures enjoy widespread use in psychotherapy research. Others we crafted ourselves because no method existed to examine the data from the particular angles we required.

For the first class of instruments, a record of reliability, validity, and research application exist, which we'll review shortly. For the new methods, however, which we constructed specifically for this study, we'll explicate these in detail but, obviously, can cite far less psychometric evaluation to report on them.

The primary question that we try to answer here in Chapter 3 focuses on whether we now have or can foreseeably develop research scales that will reflect, in meaningful and replicable ways, the paraverbal exchange we see on psychotherapy tapes or in case excerpts?

Our quantitative strategy takes four directions. We use (1) the ATOS (McCullough et al., 2003 a & b), (2) the ATOS Therapist (Osborn, 2009), (3) the Accessibility and Congruence Scales (Donovan, Osborn, Rice, 2009), and (4) the Control Mastery Scale, adapted from Weiss and Sampson, (1986). For the ATOS, we can report on a good deal of directly related prior research findings, for the Control Mastery Scale less, so for the ATOS therapist and for the Accessibility and Congruence measures, none at all.

In the remaining sections of this chapter, we describe each of these four instruments and review the quantitative findings we can derive from each, as well as their validity and reliability, when available.

We start with the ATOS because it's the most widely used presently and its properties have been the most thoroughly studied.

The ATOS

We scored segments from all the research tapes on the ATOS (Achievement of Therapeutic Objectives Scale) and on the ATOS/Therapist (an instrument of Kristin Osborn's invention, which measures the extent to which the therapist supports the patient to reach the ATOS objectives—see below.)

First the ATOS proper—Leigh McCullough et al. developed this measure, beginning in 1995. Over the past 15 years, it has enjoyed consistent use at the Harvard Medical School in Boston, at the Norwegian University of Science and Technology, NTNU in Trondheim, Norway and at the Psychiatric Clinic—AFFORI, Universita Statale, in Milan, Italy. The ATOS, therefore, as much as any psychotherapy research instrument, can boast of truly cross-cultural findings from these three distinctly different countries and ethnicities.

In this preamble to our discussion of research measures, we should first establish certain basic facts about psychotherapy efficacy. Psychotherapy does work. Clients in treatment consistently improve more than controls (Wampold, 2001; Lambert and Ogles, 2004). The *relationship* appears a key mediating variable in the psychotherapy process (Norcross, 2002) and seems to account for some 22% of outcome variance (Bohart and Tallman, 1999; Lambert and Ogles, 2004). Well and good, but we next need to ascertain what specific aspects of the therapist–patient interaction contribute to that finding.

McCullough et al. (2003 a & b) joined this debate by pointing out that we know what the therapist said, but we do not know what, or how much, the patient *took in* and used. Here arrives the ATOS. This scale measures the response of the client to the therapist's interventions. McCullough and colleagues have studied thousands of hours of videotape assessing changes in client behavior in reaction to active therapist contributions.

McCullough derived her seven therapeutic objectives (see below) by studying client self-reports of helpful treatment events and by observing patient behavioral change on tape. Unfortunately, Dr. McCullough prematurely died in June 2012. Over her lifetime, Leigh probably had watched more hours of psychotherapy videotape than any other person. At the time of her death, she supervised the research of 100 graduate students at the NTNU in Trondheim.

McCullough's focus on "adaptive affect" stands at the center of her theory of therapy and of her research. By "adaptive affect" she meant that the client could acknowledge and deeply feel authentic reactions to her emotional life, that is, reacting with profound sadness to the loss of a beloved parent, becoming truly angry at an abusive spouse. McCullough builds her theory around the hypothesis that conflicted emotion leads to self-thwarting thoughts and behavior and to neurotic symptomology, in other words, to the opposite of mentalizing. Adaptive affect leads the client toward self-actualization.

The ATOS scale turns on the proposition that change happens in psychotherapy when the client, through her interaction with the therapist, gradually becomes more and more comfortable with an adaptive affect. In other words, she becomes "desensitized" to her fear of "negative" important feelings, that is, anger or shame, thus the title of McCullough's treatment manual *Treating Affect Phobia* (McCullough et al., 2003). Notice that McCullough has just melded dynamic and behavioral theories of change. Exposure decreases fear of the stimulus.

The authors derived the **A**chievement of **T**herapeutic **O**bjectives **S**cale (ATOS) by studying multiple tapes of short-term dynamic therapy, but further research indicated that these goals, which we'll spell out in a moment, overlapped with the treatment goals from other orientations, such as cognitive behavioral therapy (CBT). Apparently, the ATOS applies to techniques beyond short-term psychodynamic psychotherapy alone.

The seven treatment objectives, which comprise the ATOS Scales include:

1) Awareness/Insight (defense recognition). How clearly can a client see and feel his maladaptive pattern or defensive behavior?

2) Motivation for Change (relinquishing defenses)—how much does the client wish to give up his maladaptive and self-defeating behavior?
3) Affective Arousal or Affective Experiencing—measures the patient's degree of emotional arousal within that particular adaptive affect during the session, whether consciously experienced and verbally expressed by the patient and/or based on visible behavioral or physiologic signs, that is, crying over a significant loss.
4) New Learning (affect expression)—how much has the client learned to express new adaptive thoughts and feelings, in face-to-face encounters outside the session or, if relevant, with the therapist within the hour?
5) Inhibition—Reflects how much inhibitory feeling, such as anxiety, guilt, shame, or pain interfere with adaptive affective experiencing.
6) Constructive change in sense of self.
7) Constructive change in realistic sense of important others.

An ATOS researcher scores ten-minute segments of videotape at a time, so a 50-minute interview would generate a sequence of 5 sets of scores.

Of these scales or factors, Arousal and Inhibition, dimensions 3 and 5 respectively, correlate most strongly with improved treatment outcome, in the following way. Exposure to adaptive affect (scale 3) and the reduction of inhibitory feeling about that affect (scale 5), empirically, most surely predict positive results in short-term dynamic therapy, and curiously, in cognitive treatment as well (Bhatia et al, 2009). Therefore, a composite factor, "desensitization," derived by subtracting the amount of inhibitory feeling from the level of active "arousal" of adaptive affect best foreshadows outcome in short-term dynamic and short-term CBT therapy. The "exposure" mechanism, in other words, apparently plays a central role in therapeutic change. More exposure to the adaptive affect paired with less inhibition leads to positive growth. The increased capacity for realistic assertion, without self-destructive guilt, for example, represents "desensitization." By the end of treatment, improved clients in short-term dynamic therapy, or in cognitive/behavioral therapy, appeared more desensitized to conflicted feelings when compared to clients not improved (see Bhatia et al., 2009).

Reliability of the ATOS

ATOS authors (McCullough et al., 2003a, Bhatia et al., 2009) report on several investigations of correlative reliability for the ATOS (see below). McCullough et al. (2003), have refined and adjusted the ATOS over the past 14 years and have developed a web-based training module to teach the ATOS scoring system to new raters (McCullough et al., 2003b).

Groups of psychotherapy graduate students received at least 15 hours of training on the ATOS scale. Using calculations from the interclass correlation measure, ICC, McCullough et al. found that the majority of these judges, in groups of three, achieved ICC correlations at moderate, .60 or better, or at substantial, or at 80 or better levels.

Validity of the ATOS

In Montreal, Bhatia et al. (2009) correlated changes in the ATOS scales with shifts in the SCL 90-R (D. Rogalis, 1994), and the Inventory of Interpersonal Problems, IIP (Lazarus, 1994) and the Rosenberg Self-esteem Scale (RSS, 1965) in an attempt to establish the discriminate and predictability validity of the ATOS. Desensitization on the ATOS (scales 3 & 5) implies an increase in affective experiencing and a decrease in inhibition feeling. As the scores on scales 3 and 5 went up, so too did the self-esteem measures on the Rosenberg and so too did the measures of symptom control on the SCL 90-R and the IIP. In other words, all these instruments moved in tandem and in predicted directions.

In sum, McCullough and her associates began developing the ATOS in 1995, 20 years ago, and have continuously refined it, tested it, and retested it, applying it in cross-cultural settings. They've published several papers on the reliability and validity of the ATOS and now have assembled a coterie of graduate students in Trondheim, Norway working extensively with the scale within a variety of research designs.

The ATOS today represents one of the most sophisticated measures of psychotherapy process and outcome available. Because McCullough et al. have framed a large number of present and future studies using the ATOS, we will hear much more about this instrument in the literature as time goes on.

The paraverbal ATOS dimension

ATOS scores reflect both the client's verbal statements *and* observed body language: tones of voice, visceral reactions, that is, smiling, crying, speaking very loudly or very softly, gesturing, and so on. Without these accompanying paraverbal signs, the client, on any of the seven scales, cannot receive an ATOS score above a 40, for a verbal contribution only.

It follows from this introduction, that ATOS therapists proceed with a virtually exclusive affective focus—what is the conflicted affect and how can we draw the client closer to it in an adaptive fashion? When we study Kristin Osborn's tape in Chapter 4, we'll see an unconventional treatment in which Kristin ceaselessly pursues her client's sadness and loneliness and, along the way, models adaptive affective functioning by openly expressing deep feelings of her own. The complete ATOS Scale appears in Appendix A.

ATOS/Therapist

Investigators have developed several scales in the past to evaluate the therapist's behavior, for example, the **T**herapist **I**ntervention **R**ating **S**ystem, TIRS,
(Gaston et al., 1994), but recent literature reviews do not reveal great attention paid to the therapist's responses or to one predominant instrument used to
measure that behavior. Wallin (2007) has investigated therapists" attachment
styles as they engage with specific client-attachment orientations, but he does
not do so in any quantified way.

We decided that if the ATOS measures the patient's reaction to the therapist's intervention, then we could devise an ATOS/Therapist scale to reflect
how much the therapist supported the client to achieve those ATOS objectives. We needed a way of tracking, in ATOS terms, exactly how the therapist did contribute to the session. In other words, regardless of the patient's
response, did the therapist do her job? Led by Kristin Osborn, we arrived at
the ATOS Therapist Scale (Osborn, 2009) which, in overview, unfolds like
this:

1) Insight—How much does the therapist provide insight into the client's
   maladaptive patterns?
2) Motivation—How strongly does the therapist try to increase the patient's
   motivation to give up the self-defeating defenses?
3) Arousal—How consistently does the therapist help the patient to expose
   and to experience the affects over which he has become phobic?
4) New Learning—How strongly does the therapist inquire about, or point
   out, new learning to the client?
5) Inhibition—How much does the therapist help the client to regulate his
   inhibition?
6 and 7) To what extent does the therapist support the patient in realistically
   improving her self-image, in accepting her strengths and vulnerabilities
   and, also in changing her view of others and in treating those others, where
   appropriate, with more acceptance, compassion, and trust.

Our group has begun to study the reliability and validity of the ATOS
Therapist but have no findings to report as yet. The complete ATOS Therapist
Scale appears in Appendix B.

A change in plans

The basic format and goals of the ATOS fit our project since we took a quali-
tative and quantitative orientation to our data and analyzed it in ten-minute

segments. Extensively working with the ATOS taught us how to score the verbal and paraverbal behavior of both the client and the therapist.

We do report on the ATOS and ATOS Therapist scores in some places in the text, but to our surprise, as we continued our work, we realized that we pursued paraverbal findings almost exclusively, and the ATOS did not. We concluded that we needed to customize instruments of our own to pursue those extra-verbal data more deeply. The ATOS remains a valuable measure of process and outcome—how much adaptive affect does the client portray at the end of a segment or of a full session? We can correlate ATOS outcomes with our paraverbal scores at certain places.

The Accessibility Scale and the Congruence Scale

At this point, we realized that we had no procedure to measure directly the paraverbal behavior of the patient, and of the therapist, on the videotape, or within case material excerpts. For the most part, neither did anybody else.

Previous research

A few experimental social psychologists have ventured into this area of nonverbal communication. However, the lack of research attention here is perhaps striking because as early as 1872, Charles Darwin published *Underlying the Expression of Emotion in Man and Animals*. He felt that extra-verbal emotional communication, particularly in facial expression, carried great evolutionary significance, not only for mankind but for the whole mammalian province.

Since that time, researchers in paraverbal behavior have focused on one discrete area of the human body or another as a communicative medium. The most well-known and important of these is Ekman, P. and Friesen, W. V, (1978, 2001, 2003). He studies human facial expressions only. He has discovered that consistently across cultures, genders, and ages, humans express the seven basic emotions in virtually exactly the same way. He found that anger, fear, sadness, disgust, contempt, surprise, and joy were mirrored by specific, similar, facial expressions in each society around the world.

Ekman has carefully tracked the involuntary movement of the facial muscles, which distinguishes each of these expressions of affective shift. The Facial Activation Coding System, (1978) captures all of these basic, nonverbal, facial signs. For our purposes, it turned out that the Duchênne, authentic smile of joy and warmth took a central place in our analysis of the tapes (Hertenstein, 2013).

Birdwhistell (1970) contributed early work analyzing nonverbal messaging conducted through nearly every part of the body other than the face, that is, linguistically, kinetically, and so on. Norbert Freedman and colleagues studied physical movements, particularly with the hands, in psychiatric patients and in their therapists. They found that some gestures by patients treated the therapists in an object-focused way and some hand movements expressed a noncommunicative self-focus (Freedman and Hoffman, 1967; also in Siegman and Pope, 1972).

Freedman et al. (1973) also studied therapists" behavior in working with "difficult" and "not-so-difficult" clients, again studying mainly the behavior of the hands that accompanied their speech. With the "difficult" often psychotic patients, the therapist movements were arrhythmic and disconnected from the exchange. The therapist with these trying clients also showed more soothing self-touch than with the less stressful patients. With the "NSD" client, the therapist tended to demonstrate object-focused, bridging, physical movements toward the patient.

Freedman and Grand (1984) suggested that the hand dysrhythmic gestures of either patient or therapist performed the function of shielding them from the distressing affect, and screening out disturbing, unwanted information.

Goldbeck T, Tolkmitt, and Scherer (1988, pp. 124–137) studied speech sound and found that acoustical parameters readily identified the major dimension of the speaker's affective communication both in intensity and in specificity. The sound of the voice definitely reflects the affect communicated. Stiles (1992) constructed an extensive and reliable taxonomy of verbal response modes: Disclosure, Confirmation, Acknowledgment, and so on.

Evidence of paraverbal communication

These groups of social and clinical psychologists have made important contributions to our debate concerning paraverbal communication in psychotherapy in a number of ways. First, they provide strong confirmation of extra-verbal communication in treatment, that bodily movement and speech characteristics accompany important affective shifts in the messages between the therapeutic pair.

Second, Freedman and associates, studied the nonverbal communication of the therapist, as well as that of the patient. As an exception, Ogden and Fisher (2015) describe the messages sent using the patient's entire posture—particularly the spine, not just one body area, that is, the hands.

Greenberg et al. (1993) described the bidirectional process between the client and the therapist but with no quantifying measures. Freedman, mentioned above, took that bidirectional perspective also. Likewise, we assume a focus on both the client and the therapist in our research.

We concluded that no model existed that filled our needs sufficiently to track the nonverbal communication between the therapist and the patient. The work of early researchers focused too narrowly on one behavior alone, such as facial movement. We needed to mount our own multidimensional scales.

Many therapy scholars would agree that the paraverbal dimension carries at least some weight in the interaction, but then what? Departing from the Birdwhistell, Freedman, and Ekman studies, we constructed the Accessibility Scale and the Congruence Scale in an attempt to pursue paraverbal communication in much greater detail and including multiple dimensions.

Expressiveness: The Accessibility Scale

We mapped our own seven-point scale to capture a wide range of possible nonverbal behavior in the therapy session. We included (1) facial expressions, that is, smiles, frowns, grimaces; (2) tones of voice, that is, gentle, loud, angry; (3) rhythm of speech, fast, labored, halting; (4) eye contact versus looking away; (5) other body language: self-touch, tracking hand and leg movements, as well as the physical posture taken in the chair by either participant.

After several iterations of reworking these data, we realized that nonverbal communication really translates into a message about how <u>open</u> or how *closed emotionally* the speaker appears to his or her companion, so finally we named our first instrument the *Accessibility Scale*.

We constructed a seven-point Likert measure. A low score of 1 or 2 represents a closed, rigid, inaccessible stance—lack of facial expression, no smiling, slow low tone in speech, protective huddled body posture. We designated the midpoint on this instrument at (4), the marker for normal, social, accessible contact, distinguished by appropriate facial movement, opening of arms, occasional smiles or light laughter, some range of affect in speech and verbal communication.

Scale points 5, 6, and 7 on the Accessibility measure correspond to an unusually open style of relating, ascending from quite open scale point 5, to extremely open and active at scale point 7, where we find frequent smiling, unmistakable communication of affect: sadness, anger, warmth, laughter, tears, tenderness, variations in speech intonation and rhythm, open bodily posture, that is, leaning toward the listener, very direct eye contact. In couples" therapy, when the pair look directly at each other, or gently touch each other, or mirror body language, this refers to scale points 5, 6, or 7.

We hypothesize that productive therapy probably includes a majority of exchanges in the 5, 6, and 7 accessibility area. The effective therapist, frequently, though not always, needs to feel very accessible and the constructive client at least somewhat accessible, according to this scoring matrix that we've just outlined. In the later chapters, we'll make discoveries about whether we, in fact, do find these paraverbal patterns, which we've just predicted, in productive sessions.

We've included the complete Accessibility Scale in Appendix C.

As we worked with the accessibility measures, assessing a series of patient–therapist videotapes, we quickly uncovered a problem. The speaker might express a great deal of affect and thus seem very accessible, but this feeling might not appear congruent with the present subject matter or with his or her clear underlying affect. For example, he might laugh, when sad, or smile, while also crying. True affect and expression here do not match.

The Congruence/incongruence Scales

Our task, therefore, did not end with our assessment of accessibility. We needed to estimate how congruent that expression with the speaker's discernible emotional state. We devised another seven-point Likert measure, the Congruence/Incongruence Scale. Scores of 1 or 2 here correspond to paraverbal behaviors that contradict the verbal or affective message. The client, for instance, laughs when apparently sad, smiles when angry, and closes up in body language when describing an intimate feeling.

A rating at Level 4, again, corresponds to usual human congruence—facial expression, voice, and tone that do, for the most part, match the evident affective state—body language reflecting affective content of words, head down if sad, smiling when feeling positive, and so on. However, we learn little extra from the congruent paraverbal picture at Level 4. The speaker's body expresses consistency with his or her emotional message, but his or her nonverbal elaboration only mirrors and does not add to that message.

At points 5, 6, and 7, all systems seem strongly congruent. For example, positive verbal tone, bright eyes, a broad smile, and arms open, all match positive affect in the spoken content. They enhance the expression of that affect. Or, in the case of more troubled feelings—when angry: a loud rageful tone, punching palm, much eye contact; when sad: teary, holding self with arms, and so on likewise represent high congruence. These paraverbal presentations, that we've just noted, fall well beyond the average social congruence and strongly augment the verbal message, so consequently we score them at the 5, 6, or 7 levels.

Earlier, Rogers (1951) and Greenberg et al. (1993) have called attention to the importance of the therapist's perceived congruence by the client. We, and other groups of researchers, have begun reliability and validity studies with our measures. We found that after working 3 hours together with several videos, our small coterie of three, could rate Accessibility and Congruence at roughly above the .60 level of reliability. The small size of the sample prevented more sophisticated statistical analysis. The complete Congruence/Incongruence Scale appears in Appendix D.

The Control Mastery Scale

For our final instrument, we adapted the previous work by Weiss and Sampson (1986, appendices 10 and 11, p. 372) to develop a Control Mastery Scale, parts A and B. As we reviewed in Chapter 2, the Weiss and Sampson framework identifies a central *Pathogenic Belief,* that is, "if I, the daughter, express myself in a sexy and attractive way, I will crush my mother who seems so dowdy and plain"—this conviction reflects separation guilt. The client comes to therapy with the hope that the interaction with the therapist will *disconfirm* her pathogenic belief. In this example, the relationship with the therapist will help the client find it acceptable to feel sensual and alluring and not to fear her internalized mother's dismay.

Part A of the Control Mastery Scale asks the judges to reach consensus on the *specific pathogenic belief,* within the treatment episode, that the patient longs to shed. In Part B, the judges rate the extent to which the therapist passes the test and helps the client to disconfirm this pathogenic belief.

The Weiss and Sampson seven-point scale ranges from (1) a clear-cut example of the therapist failing the test and accidently *confirming* the pathogenic belief, to scale point 7 in which the client responds to a definitive example of the therapist *passing* the test and helping the client begin to rid herself of the burdensome pathogenic belief. Working on various videos with the Weiss and Sampson scale, the three of us could reach an acceptable .60 reliability in rating after 2 hours of training.

Weiss and Sampson (1986) have amassed considerable empirical data supporting their Control Mastery paradigm (Weiss and Sampson, 1986a; Weiss, 1993; Silberschatz and Curtis, 1986). Within these findings, the authors report reliability and validity studies, which begin to establish the centrality of the Control Mastery test in psychotherapy. This deceptively simple Control Mastery Scale, which we've incorporated with a few minor changes from Weiss and Sampson, appears in full in Appendix E. There we offer a case example scored with the scale.

All these instruments set us on course to deepen our understanding of psychotherapy. We suspect for example, that high ATOS scores, high Therapist ATOS scores, high Accessibility and Congruence measures for both participants, and a high Control Mastery score, all will inevitably correlate with successful cases.

The exceptions to this pattern could feel almost as interesting. What is the significance to a low Accessibility and Congruence rating for the client but high measures for the therapist on these dimensions? What is the meaning to high Accessibility but a low Congruence score for the patient or for the therapist in a given session? How much do the Accessibility and Congruence ratings correlate with ATOS scores or with the outcome of a given session?

In the balance of the book, we report on what we discover when we apply these instruments to videotape and case study material. We lean more and more, as we noted, on the Accessibility/Congruence measures since they fit our objectives most closely—specifically how can we measure the role that paraverbal interaction seems to play in the psychotherapy exchange?

Now we'll move to Chapter 4. There we meet our first patients in the study. We'll begin to see how helpful this armamentarium of scales proves to carefully track the verbal and the paraverbal exchange in specific psychotherapy sessions across a spectrum of clients and across a variety of therapists.

Provisionally we've answered our question from the beginning of this chapter. We do now have instruments to measure paraverbal interchange. We don't have many, but we do have promising scales to pilot test. The remainder of the book will give us a stronger idea of the helpfulness and the limitations of those scales.

Chapter Four

Intense Paraverbal Enactments

Four Vignettes

Now we meet our patients.

In some therapeutic moments, the client and therapist strongly, unmistakably, directly confront one another—an engagement almost invariably initiated by affective expression from the patient. The treatment suddenly becomes unmistakably all about extra-verbal interplay. We start our narrative, here, to show paraverbal relating in its most vivid, most recognizable state. These represent the unmistakable moment of meeting in Stern parlance.

Now, we'll unravel several powerful meetings, some on tape, some not, to understand how these events characteristically unfold and, more importantly, to begin to grasp the extra-verbal meanings that they carry for the treatment. Finally, we'll start to see that we might apply this paraverbal experience across many psychotherapy exchanges, not just these highly charged ones.

SUICIDAL THREATS ON A DAILY BASIS: THE UNDERGROUND WOMAN—VIGNETTE #2—JIM DONOVAN

Some 14 years ago, I began a weekly treatment in an out-patient general hospital setting, with a chronically suicidal, Asian-American lady, a therapy that ultimately lasted 2 ½ years. Our treatment together represents a clear example of the therapy with the nonpsychotic, personality-challenged patient whom we've mentioned several times in Chapters 1 and 2. Enactments with these clients start with a welter of paraverbal defenses.

Our lady's life apparently hung in the balance, meeting by meeting, as I struggled to connect with her. With the stakes so high, I would have cheerfully altered almost any parameter of the treatment, if it held the slight-est promise to turn the tide. Similar cases appear in texts describing the use of counter transference with highly disturbed and highly disturbing patients (Maltzberger and Biue, 1974, Stone, 1990, 2006; Maroda, 1991, 1999; Wishnie, 2005). We introduce this therapy now, in detail, because in vivid fashion, her story and mine illustrate the important therapeutic activity often played out along extra-verbal dimensions, almost in pure state.

My moment of truth came at the hands of this young woman, intelligent and professionally educated, but probably burdened by a severe personality. She presented with nearly constant suicidality and an almost unbearably provocative anger, painful to herself, and all the more so, to whatever opponent she chose at the moment.

Particulars of her behavior rendered the treatment excruciating. First, this woman unfailing brought lethality with her, a brinksmanship that she used in highly destructive ways. At every meeting, she taunted me with her wish to die. My efforts to sway her in more constructive directions felt pathetically weak, especially to me, even as they left my lips. Each meeting centered on suicide, would she or wouldn't she kill herself this week? I can now see that she projected her desperation into me, so I could share it, and she could observe how I dealt with it—projective identification par excellence.

On several occasions, she forced me into psychotherapeutic high-wire acts. She would call to report an overdose, but often she would then refuse to give her location. Sometimes with the police on one phone, me on another, she on a third line, she would force me to guess her whereabouts through a series of clues, before the apparently quite deadly pills took their course.

I had no knowledge of the true facts. Had she really taken the tablets this time? Before our therapy began, she had made genuine attempts to die, but did this represent another bona fide crisis? She initiated a game of cat and mouse with me, pressuring me with what she had done or might momentarily do. We knew who was the cat and who was the mouse.

On a session-by-session, minute-by-minute, basis she enlisted all her considerable intelligence and sophistication to parry my suggestions and to brush aside my attempts to link her anger, and utter despair, to her traumatic relationship with her grandfather, who led the family. Of Asian ancestry, he appeared a remote frigid man, who took note of his one grandchild, and of his two children, only when they had a dangerous medical condition and perhaps not even then.

Against my will, I felt shoved into the grandfather box, required to earn my way out by demonstrating extraordinary concern and 24-hour care, which always seemed to fall just short anyway. Clearly, at least in retrospect, I had to deal with a transference/counter-transference weekly battle in which this lady tried to turn the tables of her childhood and make me the child begging her to listen and to live, while she played the frosty, indifferent, pitiless grandfather. Viewed in this way, her behavior feels more understandable and more meaningful. She was not traumatizing me for no reason.

I'll describe this woman's physical habitus and self-presentation and then turn to the moment of acute crisis in the therapy. Our lady was tall, exceptionally thin, in part due to poor nutrition, with long arms and legs. She gestured dramatically with those arms and those hands. She usually wore overly revealing clothing, which flopped open at regular intervals, but I was far too on edge to feel titillated. She spoke rapidly, articulately and nearly incessantly, mixing in various literary illusions and references to foreign languages and cultures.

I found her huge dark eyes unforgettable. She glared directly at me; those eyes burned with apparent hate and derision. I sensed she was trying desperately to get the hate outside of herself and into me. I felt she leered at me and mocked my earnest attempts to understand, with her stiff, painted grin. Her fast, self-centered speech often drowned me out and made it even more obvious that she had evidently little interest in my meager contributions. She exploded in wrath regularly, but she never cried at any session.

Her intense hopelessness, and near constant suicidal pre-occupation, made me wonder how she could possibly survive the rest of the week not spent in the office with me. She clearly enjoyed taunting me so much during our meetings that our one hour together did bring her some satisfaction and maybe some genuine support.

From the medical side, she had in the past, of course, consulted numerous psychiatrists and defeated them all. She did take a major tranquilizer. She found antidepressant medications not helpful and psychopharmacologists, in any case, trembled at the idea of prescribing them to her, given her dangerous behavior. Still, she had managed to accumulate a cache of pills from previous consultations, with which she continually threatened to overdose.

Although professionally qualified, she had no job and lived alone in a below ground apartment. There she drank wine in alcoholic bursts, over consecutive days and nights, and slept little. She was usually awake all night reading or studying Asian cultural writings. Her marginal, nocturnal, basement existence reminded me of Dostoevsky's Underground Man (1884) who existed in a similar self-imposed squalor in a dank cellar.

However, she never missed an appointment with me and often arrived early. By her report she had nothing better to do. She usually managed to cause a stir in the waiting room with her loud, sarcastic, provocative commentary. She regularly called me to task for any lateness or apparent absent mindedness on my part.

She sent a verbal and paraverbal message, then, of disdain for me and despair for herself. Her faithful attendance at the therapy, that she so pointedly devalued, of course, offered a different paraverbal message. She got something from our meetings, but she could almost never admit it or maybe realize it. She did experience attachment to me, then, no matter how unconscious and ambivalent. This represents a key factor, easy to overlook in the dramatics of the therapy, but onto which I, and any therapist in a similar plight, needed to grasp.

Consciously I felt utterly stuck with this patient. I could not make her stop her provocative teasing or get her to consider, seriously, the meaning of her suicidality or of her other outrageous behavior. Over the first year, I felt we could boast of few gains, but her lethality made it impossible to discharge her as an unresponsive case or refer her to an unsuspecting colleague.

She refused additional medications, scoffed at the possibility of adjunctive group therapy or of a trial of the then new treatment, DBT. Her suicidal behavior had already resulted in multiple hospital admissions before our therapy began, but none of the inpatient therapeutic programs seemed to offer any lasting help, at least by her report.

I'm sure my introduction, thus far, succinctly communicates that I felt well qualified to write the sequel to Maltsberger and Buie's "Counter-Transference Hate in the Treatment of Suicidal Patients" (1974).

The reader can grasp by now, that to some degree, I had lost control of the therapy. This inmate seemed on the verge of running this asylum. I should have sought expert consultation, which I didn't, although I did discuss this lady informally with several colleagues. I mostly just doggedly persevered.

The therapy luckily righted itself thanks, providentially, to a last ditch standoff between us, which felt more like a street fight than any psychotherapy technique.

After 1.5 years of once weekly treatment, we could point to only two accomplishments. The patient had not killed herself, and she had not returned to the hospital, but she still worked only very part time, and had few relationships other than massively ambivalent interactions with a series of inappropriate boyfriends. She spent a majority of her life regressed, underground, sitting in her apartment, depressed, usually drinking heavily, rarely sleeping. She experienced little peace or self-soothing.

Then one unforgettable afternoon, I ushered her into my office, which to her glee she frequently (correctly) observed as poorly decorated. She sat down, grinned insincerely at me, one more time, and announced that the night before, she had again slashed her arm. Pulling up her sleeve, she revealed blood dried along jagged gashes, ripped crosswise across her left inner arm, stretching from elbow to wrist. She had closed these cuts by haphazardly applying strips of scotch tape across them.

For some reason, this last touch put me over the edge. The sad, futile, careless, meaningless quality of the act of scotch-taping her arm, pushed whatever few of my buttons remained unpushed. I felt horrified, a little nauseated at the sight, and furiously angry.

For a moment, I forgot that she suffered more than I in this therapy, and I nearly blew my top.

One final time, she had taunted me with her extreme destructive behavior. She waved her grotesquely slashed arm in my direction, as if to prove to me my helplessness and incompetence once more. She had tortured me with her numerous crisis calls, but now she had brought her self-mutilation into my office as if to wipe it in my face—some paraverbal message.

I asked her if she had consulted a physician about her wounds, keenly aware that, for one more time in my career, I, no doctor, had not the slightest notion of the severity of those cuts. Through her frosted grin, she dismissed my suggestion, tossing back at me that she'd cut herself so often that she knew how to treat the injuries herself.

I found her response shockingly unrealistic, self-hating and hating toward me. Now after a serious suicidal gesture, perhaps an actual attempt to die, she wouldn't even take on the task of pursuing medical assistance, herself, but left it to me to browbeat her into self-care.

I couldn't stand the helplessness toward which this last act shoved me. I felt completely out of options, except to share my frustration and to force her to take back responsibility. From between grinding teeth, I told her that I felt sad and angry at her devaluing of her own well-being and of my efforts to provide her meaningful treatment. Further, I added that if she didn't go downstairs to the hospital ER with me directly after our appointment to consult medical personnel, I could no longer work with her.

I told her that I would not participate in a joke therapy, and she needed to stop playing Russian roulette with herself and with me. She had to choose to live or to die herself, and not to continually throw herself into harm's way for me to snatch her to safety.

This intense counter-transference communication, close to a counter-transference growl, apparently snapped home my seriousness and commitment to her in a manner that even she could not distort or dismiss. She now *knew* that *I felt* her utter despair but also that I could care about her even when, especially when, she couldn't love herself, or even stand herself. I had just literally, transparently, yelled at her. My loud voice, angry tone, direct stare, and chiseled face, conveyed far more than could any words alone. At this minute, this had become nearly an entirely paraverbal therapy.

She had gotten to me at most every session, but today I'd gotten to her. At that moment, she had control of her affective state, possibly more than I had of mine. I did not think her in need of psychiatric hospitalization, but after the appointment, she complied with my walking her to the emergency room for medical evaluation of her arm. Had she bolted, we both knew that I really would have ended the treatment.

This confrontation marked a turning point for us—a "moment of meeting" in Stern's terminology (see Chapter 2). The therapy changed and never returned to its earlier form. We both became more present as our real selves and for the first time began to work a little bit more as a team. She knew that I meant business now; our treatment had come to a crisis point. If she did not take the therapy, and her responsibility in it, seriously, I would resign.

The sometimes sadistic game of chance: the emergency calls, the near suicides, almost miraculously stopped. Our treatment came to an acute stand-off only once more, a few months later.

During that second episode, she assured me that she would kill herself on her birthday as she had attempted in the past. Her birthday was in January, and January approached. She threatened that this time she would go to her family's cemetery plot, overdose, and join her dead relatives, lying on their graves.

I confronted her once more with her difficulty tolerating and directing her anger adaptively, and with her need to act it out. She felt compelled to show everyone how they had failed her, her icy grandfather, in particular, for whom I usually stood as a proxy. We scheduled a meeting on her birthday, but she adamantly refused to cancel her self-destructive plan.

When she arrived apparently unmoved, I had prepared my own strategy, and kicked the emergency switch under my desk. The EMTs and security guards appeared on cue. I produced the Pink paper I had earlier completed. The staff rolled her out of my office on a gurney headed to the hospital, she spewing anger and sarcasm back at me, as they wheeled her down the hall—an unforgettable paraverbal goodbye.

She stayed as an inpatient only a few days and emerged for our next appointment, spiteful and belittling, but alive and a little more serious. I think she would have killed herself on that birthday, even though she really didn't want to. She seemed to feel determined to call my bluff one last time, maybe to reassure herself that I would really safeguard her, the way her grandparents hadn't.

Gradually she forgave me for intruding on her plot; she tested me no longer. She did not threaten suicide again for the remaining year of our two and a half year treatment together. I never had to resort to hospitalization with her again. She settled down and, surprisingly, suspended most of her provocativeness. We could joke for the first time without her needing to turn the laughter in a cruel direction. She did not express much more agreement with my attempts at interpretation, but she did listen a bit longer before she waved me off.

She began to work full time as a technical researcher. Her personal relationships became less chaotic. During a hospital stay previous to our therapy, she had, for example, made a death pact with another female inpatient, but there were no repeats of this level of behavioral chaos. Her relations with men did not seem much more intimate or supportive however.

One year after the enactment of the hospital commitment, my administration transferred me to a different site, inaccessible to the patient since she had no car. This set in motion the unusual scenario of the therapist, driving down the highway, leaving the patient, rather than the other way around.

We worked through a long termination during which we agreed that she had moved to a softer place psychologically and that she had begun to gain real satisfaction from her professional work, at which she showed great proficiency. She seemed sad, but not bereft, to see me go. She did not bitterly protest or stage a dangerous separation scene.

Some two years later, I heard from her that she had engaged a private practice therapist who accepted her insurance. She had already contacted this woman before our ending. Her relatively stable functioning apparently continued. She worked full time at her job, but she apparently had no steady close relationships with men or women.

Reviewing this case now, I'm struck with how self-destructive she could become and how deprecatory of psychotherapy she acted but that she had returned to therapy recurrently over several years. She formed long-term alliances with at least three counselors whom she allowed to help her. I represented the second of the three. All appearances to the contrary, she had an internal guidance system that allowed her to survive and to improve within therapy despite her constant disparagement of it. Devalue them she might, but she did gain from our meetings.

This story holds much in common with similar encounters with patients burdened by nonpsychotic personality disorder, described so well by Maltzberger and Biue, (1974), Stone (1990, 2006), Maroda (1991, 1999), Stark (1999), and Wishnie (2005). The uncooperative dangerously ill client, somewhat like a stubborn and mischievous child, puts the therapist under unbearable pressure to prove his caring and his deep understanding, and to express this concern with very strong affect and distinct paraverbal behavior—no modulated emotions permitted on the part of the therapist. I literally led her to the ER almost as I would a youngster.

However, following the showdown, a change takes place in the client. She now seems to trust the counselor at a new level and begins to work more consciously and maturely, dropping the threats to kill herself or upend the therapy. Most of us, who have put in career service as therapists, can tell some version of this story. A harrowing treatment comes to a dangerous impasse, but the crisis successfully negotiated, the sessions turn toward a deeper and more constructive level. Here we see the action of "disruption and repair" from Chapter 2, but writ large.

Any description of my case, or of a similar one, leaving out the paraverbal details would feel meaningless. This lady and her therapy appeared often about the slashed arm, the smoldering eyes, the red-faced exasperated therapist. The treatment of nonpsychotic character issues illustrates in its most dramatic form the necessity of including extensive extra-verbal information in our grasp of every case.

The words, in retrospect seemed so useless. I remember her taunting smile, burning eyes, the flippant waving of her hand. I responded in kind paraverbally—raised my voice, broke in, and refused to let her interrupt me. Much of this treatment took place in my body, as well as in hers, trying to hold my fear and choke back my frustration and anger. Sometimes, the client's communication to the therapist brings a contagion of assertiveness and even rudeness. She talked over me, but I pushed back and demanded that she let me speak too.

The paraverbal intensity of our meetings, sometimes genuinely unpleasant, at least for me, marked a path to our real selves. She was desperate and needed to know that I really was there for her. She kept upping the ante until I literally went over the top. Then she seemed satisfied and a new relative calm took over our treatment.

In a very important, implicitly related way, the extra-verbal confrontation made us feel closer, just as Stern would predict. At the moment of meeting the therapist steps, or in this case, leaps out of role and engages his personal self, his own signature into the therapy. He takes an action. He's transparently present. The two participants sit there, open, and face to face. Our selves touched in a new way this set off an affective event that led her to experience her life differently. She could really die and somebody else took that personally and seriously. In Unconscious World I, she realized that her life was truly important to me and to herself. She took a different direction.

This enactment, the moment when I demanded that she come with me to the ER, turned this therapy around. Without it, at the very least, the treatment would have remained mired in passive/aggressive acting out, mostly on her part, some on mine. At the worst, she would have ultimately made further suicide attempts, probably not actively wishing to die.

Two lessons to start

Reaching back to Chapter 3 and the "Accessibility"/"Congruence" axis, we see that this woman paradoxically behaved in an ostensibly expressive way, particularly around her feelings of anger and despair, but her participation lacked congruence. She had many needs for assurance and soothing, which she covered over with her annoyed scoffs. Paraverbal behavior remains ever important, but we cannot allow ourselves to lose the way and follow only the affective intensity without wondering about its true underlying content. If we do, we will miss its meaning.

In Accessibility, she scored in the range of 6 but in Congruence in the range of 2. The entire spectrum of affects "I'm afraid"—"I'm alone"—"care for me" undeniably seem present but did not register at all in her spoken or paraverbal presentation, a crucial discrepancy that we need to investigate. Certainly her ATOS Arousal numbers at 60 were very high but led to little self-soothing or New Learning, or New Views of Self or Others.

Our first lesson is that this case illustrates in bold type that the paraverbal interchange is the message, sometimes much more than the verbal exchange. She felt despair and made me feel it too. The second lesson suggests that strong *and* congruent affect are an even more significant marker of the genuine path of the interchange.

Alternative paths

This unfolded, in many ways, as a poorly organized treatment, even though the eventual outcome evolved into a solid one. The reader might well have many questions about my approach. I did. At this point, I lacked a crucial understanding of two specific phenomena, which repeatedly return through our book.

What is the first paraverbal gambit that the client offers? From the start, our lady challenged me to save her from herself. Before the crisis of the sliced arm, I did not feel that she listened to me. Her implicit paraverbal offer seemed, "rescue me but with no participation from me." I should have focused more clearly on this paraverbal paradox. It represented the pivot on which the treatment ultimately rested.

Second, what important part of her self had our patient "cast aside" (Wachtel, 2011)? This is another primary therapeutic question. As I review the case, I felt her afraid to ask someone to love her, since she was so convinced of the answer and presented herself in as unlovable a fashion as possible. At first, I felt pulled into this struggle but working alone. She had to love herself too. Only later would my paraverbal investigation identify these two related fulcrum issues, but more clarity sooner on my part, concerning these matters, would have lent the treatment a clearer goal.

In the first year, I struggled but failed to maintain regulation over the therapy. I was on the defensive trying to anticipate and parry her suicidal maneuvers. I allowed her and her case to interrupt me when I was with other clients and also at home once or twice. I fell into the position in which it became my responsibility to keep her alive, not hers—a dangerous place. At the very least, I should have sought more experienced consultation.

The consultant would likely have advised me to set limits more quickly and more firmly, a sensible strategy, given the mostly unconscious feelings I had of frustration and rage toward the patient. She finally pushed me to my breaking point, but paradoxically in a way, I could not have confronted her much sooner. The event that redirected this treatment would have had to come in a paraverbal, very personal form. A staged confrontation requiring her to join a day hospital group, for example, wouldn't have gotten us very far.

A second difficulty was that, to some degree I misunderstood the focus. I thought this represented a Level 1 → Level 2 insight-oriented, object relations treatment. I offered a series of interpretations about her early relationships, particularly those with her grandfather, in the hope that "understanding" could turn the tide. I'm not sure she comprehended anything important that I offered her in a verbalizable form throughout the therapy. Somewhat, unbeknownst to me, we pursued a paraverbal, Level 3 relational treatment.

So what did transpire here?

She screamed out her hatred, despair, and disdain, but the important transactions came when I could smile, reframe a little bit, and chip away at her black and white thinking. I made a counter-offer of paraverbal acceptance in other words. In this way, I pursued a poor man's DBT therapy to help her calm and regulate herself. At the time, 15 years ago, I had no knowledge of the DBT rationale.

I was also extending in Allen's (2013) words "plain old therapy," helping her to mentalize, that is appreciate her true feelings and some of mine and put them into perspective. She grew up in a home where evidently little mentalization took place. This represented new territory for her. She was used to bottling up affect and then finally acting it out in angry and destructive ways, although not directly confronting those with whom she had the issue.

However, in responding to my relatively calm, unflustered, usually warm, facial expressions and tones of voice, she picked up some capacity for self-regulation. I often felt inhibited by her biting criticism. Before our confrontation, I estimate that I probably functioned at about a Level 4 in Accessibility and in Congruence but during our "now moment," I reached Level 7 on both measures. Afterwards when I could fairly reliably work with her at the 6 position in both Accessibility and Congruence, I felt liberated. She now knew my position. Her Congruent functioning, after our showdown, reached and stayed at 5. Without the words, we both implicitly knew where we stood.

Attachment levels

In fact, I was also offering her an attachment-oriented holding therapy. She never missed a treatment hour, but we battled in the therapy for most of each session in the first two years. This describes the essence of her underlying highly ambivalent attachment. I let her act out her disappointment and fear as if she were a recalcitrant child who would not stop crying and screaming. Finally, she emerged from her tantrum and moved closer to me, verbally and paraverbally, indicating a resolution of some of the ambivalent attachment.

This represents clearly a more Unconscious World I therapy, than an Unconscious World II therapy, even though I didn't understand it at the time. Interpretation helped not one whit. The treatment evolved around tones of voice, smiles, grimaces, angry silences, sometimes a grateful grin.

Transference/Counter-transference issues and the Control Mastery test

We can also see here the Tansey and Burke sequence played out. She projected more and more calumny into me, and I modified it and returned it back to her in measured terms. Gradually she became a more composed person with more balance in her affective reaction.

In terms of control mastery, she tested me over and over, ostensibly about whether I would save her life in the contrived situations that she arranged, but actually the test focused on, would I guard her psychological and physical welfare, however provocatively she behaved. When she brought in her slashed arm, I did pass the test at a 6/7 level. Angry as I was, I became unmistakably personally upset, and I took moves to set limits for her safety. She then seemed able to listen to me a little more and settle down in the sessions with less tumult.

She became more self-regulated in her negative expressiveness. Her Congruence score rose from a 2 to a 5 level. We communicated more genuinely and didn't need to spar nearly as much. My calmer tone of speech, my gaze, and my more relaxed bodily movements probably reassured her.

An important meaning we can take from the Underground Lady's therapy is that it was, of course, conducted in words, but at its core it unfolded in the nonverbal relationship offers and counter-offers. Had I understood this way of working at the time, I would have felt less anxiety over this woman, and I could have offered her more real charity and soothing.

I authentically respected her for her ability to survive and to carry on despite her unbearable rage at herself and at her primary objects. Also, she displayed real talent and altruism in her work. She needed the catharsis of screaming out her rage at me. I had to remain in touch with her but not get so frightened about her next move. I had to realize that we were engaged in a paraverbal therapy, and not the slightest in an insight oriented one.

Now we turn to another very intense therapeutic coupling but one with an entirely different tone and meaning.

VIGNETTE #3—THE "I SUCK" MOMENT OF MEETING

I (Jim) had treated a 45-year-old white single man, weekly, for approximately 18 months. In a moment you'll understand why I came to refer to him as The Self-hating Architect. A small, shy, artistic child, he regularly recalled his miserable adolescence during which his large, loud, distant, preoccupied father and his hulking peers seemed to ignore or to mock his delicate appearance and "feminine" interests. His age mates sometimes taunted and threatened him about his lack of athletic skill and his aesthetic leanings. (I'm happy to report that he now earns $125 per hour marketing some of those "feminine" design skills.)

In one unforgettable session, my client continued to describe his unhappy self-blaming childhood and teen years. He suddenly burst out in misery, "I suck. I suck." He repeated this phrase several times, two or three meetings in a row, at each point in tones of more and more self-disgust, eyes downcast, tears flowing. Finally, his voice took on a timbre of utter self-loathing, and he began to yell out, nonstop, his self-hatred. "I suck. I suck."

I broke in, probably because I felt his "I suck" conviction represented his "pathogenic belief" (Sampson and Weiss, 1986, see chapter 2) at the center of his neurosis, but also, honestly, because I felt neither of us, particularly myself, could stand to hear, and feel him, lacerate himself any longer. So utterly painful to witness, it promised no constructive purpose. He would only feel worse about himself.

Much to my amazement, I found myself matching his intensity, volume, and prosody, using his own heart-rending words, I yelled back at him, "You don't suck. You don't suck." He looked up at me in disbelief, and he yelled it again, then I yelled back my disagreement, and away we went.

The therapy, already enjoying a strong alliance, took a still deeper turn at that moment. When I stepped out of my professional role and shouted my objection to his conviction, making obvious my personal and professional wish that he could stop castigating himself, over a self-denigrating, mistaken conviction about self, we came to trust and to like each other in a new deep way.

Together we refer back to this interchange as the "I suck" session. We "flag" the session (see Stern et al., 1998) when I just couldn't accept his self-hatred anymore, and I screamed back my protest. This exchange now symbolizes our bond to both of us, a "moment of meeting," a confrontation of our minds and hearts, which seems to have helped him also to reject his malignant self-assessment.

Pretty clearly, it's not what I said. It's how I said it. I intervened mostly paraverbally—red faced, yelling and waving my hands, and I wouldn't stop. I did not plan this intervention and felt a little shocked as I blurted it out. Since that time, five years ago, my patient has made a new marriage, started a private consultation practice and become a doting and imaginative father to his young daughter.

We both agree that none of these outcomes seemed likely when our therapy started. I give him the credit for grabbing his happiness. He tries to hand it back to me. In any case, now it's obvious that it's not just I, but he too, who believes he doesn't "suck." His new conviction has come to permeate all of his personal and professional life.

This dramatic confrontation represents a rather odd but unforgettable interaction, one that I'll remember for the rest of my life. The paraverbal intensity that he brought into the hour sparked off mine, as I felt his excruciating self-disgust. His screams penetrated to my middle. I became unwilling to listen further and shouted my protest back at him. At first, he couldn't accept my retort, and he yelled back at me.

This paraverbal edge moved us both into a very personal and transparent place. I stepped way out of professional role and expressed my complete disagreement with his self-assessment. We both stood utterly present "in self" in Richard Schwartz's terminology (2004). He deeply felt that I accepted him, and I deeply felt that he accepted me. This was our "moment of meeting," and we never would have got there without the introductory paraverbal exchange.

As with the Underground Lady, this "moment of meeting" helped us cross a river to take a new direction. He had an affective experience, which started an inner process that he could use to begin to build a positive view of self. We now meet every 2 to 3 weeks. Since that time we've had no issue about whether we understood each other, cared for each other, and whether we both felt committed to help him escape his destructive past. This treatment has many Unconscious World I paraverbal aspects: We hold direct gaze, smile, nod, lean toward each other, fully join in the project from both sides, express appreciation both ways, laugh together, let tears come to our eyes. We both feel free.

The therapy has continued in the same implicit relational knowing key. He assumes I will understand him. He lists his topics for the hour and knows that I'll support him grappling with these. I feel comfortable offering my assessments and also my genuine support and feedback about the efforts he's making in his family and in his artwork. We're in sync and if we weren't, in a given hour, either of us would feel unconflicted about pointing out that we had veered off course. Without the Stern/Beebe Unconscious World I, implicit relational knowing motif as a backdrop, we the students couldn't understand this therapy.

The notions of Accessibility and Congruence have direct application to the "I suck" moment as well. At this dramatic time, the patient and therapist would both receive Level 7 ratings on each measure. The Architect's tears and shouts mark obvious evidence of his affective openness. The heartbreaking tone of his repetitive "I suck" indicated that he was entirely congruent with his emotional expression at that time. These words come from deep within. My response, as well, represents an open feelingful one, as I shout back at him showing my authentic reaction to the situation and to my client. We need to grasp both accessibility *and* congruence when evaluating a paraverbal situation. In this case, both the architect and I rated high on either scale, indicating that these moments represented an authentic coming together.

At our regular meetings now, we each hover around the 6 levels on both measures but readily able to move to 7 at required moments. The ATOS and ATOS Therapist numbers on all relevant scales would reach or exceed 60. This suggests that when Accessibility and Congruence consistently move to Level 6 for both participants, the ATOS will indicate constructive outcome as well.

The Underground Lady did not display congruence in much of her affective expression, however intensely she communicated her feelings. When you're lucky enough to encounter congruence in both client and counselor, you can attempt a very straight-to-the-heart connection. This is what happened between the Architect and myself. The paraverbal relating made this engagement possible. Any description of this therapy leaving out those extra-verbal qualities would fall flat on the page. The implicit relating, sometimes carried on verbally and sometimes paraverbally, does not represent an intervention based on insight. Rather an internal affective change has taken place within the Architect, which registers on his face, in his voice, and in his bodily posture. This represents implicit relational knowing between us and within himself.

ALTERNATIVES

It does seem strange, however, to yell back at the patient and perhaps to rob him of some of his experience. The reader might suggest that the therapist support the client by gently communicating that he understands how upsetting these feelings and memories feel to him and how debilitating they have proved in his life. Does he feel what kept them active all this time? Does he need to retain them in this form? In other words, quite rightly, I could have helped the Architect explore more of this aspect of his self-image and gain perspective on it, rather than to jump right into his grief and self-hatred, strongly registering my disagreement. Frankly, I felt carried away by the spontaneity of the experience and had no plan of what to do next. I personally left my role.

The later progress of the therapy

We both shared these moments of openness; we knew how much it meant to both of us; beyond words. My client, perhaps a year after our "moment of meeting," left me a long, spontaneous voice mail stating how grateful he felt for the treatment and how he had never dreamed that he could experience these feelings within himself, let alone discuss them with anybody else. Almost in tears, he related how meaningful he found this therapy relationship. His phone message represented his response to the "I suck" session and to the general tenor of our treatment.

The client and I have not repeated this dramatic interaction in the subsequent years. As Stern suggests, there are times when a particular personal response feels utterly called for by both participants, but those moments feel rather rare. I certainly continue to have strong supportive feelings toward the Architect, and I'm probably more likely to offer him direct, personal feedback than I might with another patient. It feels natural to do so with him. As noted, we've each functioned at Level 6 in Accessibility and Congruence pretty consistently. This treatment has enjoyed an unusually open, secure "fit."

I meet him every 2 to 3 weeks, sometimes for an extended session, or a phone session. He continues to make strong gains, to grow into himself. He's now in his early 50s, and he becomes steadily more self-actualized. We repeatedly realize how his isolated childhood experiences and his odd, lonely, family interactions, in which his two wealthy, unengaged parents, maintained great distance from their confused children, had affected him. These experiences held the Architect back a great deal in his 20s and 30s.

Control Mastery

This previously self-hating man never proved so angry and potentially destructive as the Underground Woman. He related in a modest, kind, realistically grateful fashion, but their treatments show a surprising similarity along one important dimension. The Architect came to a crisis point where he needed me to respond to him with absolutely clear unqualified support, a holding that he virtually never received from either parent or from his first wife. Once I passed that test and proved myself different from the parent, he defeated the negative hypothesis that he "sucked," and he, surprisingly smoothly, moved into greater ease and agency in his work life and in his parenting.

Evidently, this face off with the therapist and the constructive aftermath represented a required experience for his therapy. The Control Mastery interaction reflects a 7/7 score. Recall Paul Wachtel's idea that this man had a "cast off" sense of himself as worthwhile and grown-up. The therapy supported him to accept or reaccept these parts of himself. The "I suck" moment represented a decisive step in that cocreated direction. He could feel no doubt that I deeply valued him in those moments. Gradually, cumulatively he internalized that feeling as we moved along in the treatment. Apparently, the "corrective emotional experience" with me yelling back at him started him on the path to self-acceptance that he required.

Further dimensions of this treatment

The dynamic Unconscious World II matters here revolved around inadequacy and shame. However, we dealt with those mostly through Unconscious World I methods, implicit relational exchange, trading smiles of appreciation and understanding, physically leaning in toward each other. I occasionally share a memory from my own earlier life.

Attachment level

In terms of attachment matters, we can see that from this man's voice tone
and transparent relating, as well as his intimate phone message, he experiences me as home base, a solid person to whom he can return with continued
issues and reflections.

Interestingly, his two older sisters, who understandably have developmental issues of their own, offered him strong support in his childhood. He could
depend on his two sisters for protection and understanding. All three siblings
rebelled, in very different ways, against their parents apparently rigid, arbitrary, unempathic attempts to structure their family in a similar way to the
families in which they had very unhappily grown up. The siblings formed a
gang of three, and the Architect stumbled through his latency and adolescent
years watched over by those older sibs.

Despite his lonely childhood, our patient has many aspects of secure
attachment within his character, which facilitates his using me as a constant
object. He, for example, has seemed to raise a very securely attached daughter. We guess that this attitude toward attachment originally came mainly in
interaction with those older sisters. In another serendipitous outcome of the
therapy, he's now the emotional leader of his original family, of his neighbor-
hood and of his business.

Transference/counter-transference

Initially, the Architect may have felt that I would judge him a failure as his
parents had. My shouting out "You don't suck" put those fears to rest. He was
able to project his sense of inadequacy into me, which I then could modify and
project back into him. Little by little, we cocreated a more confident, realistic,
self-loving person. He has stopped certain self-destructive patterns, for example,
a habit of eating large amounts of high sugar foods. We barely focused on this
behavior, but he reported these positive results spontaneously. He engages his
wife and daughter with extraordinary empathy. He doesn't hate himself any more.

This treatment vignette teaches us once again to reflect early and often, on
the paraverbal exchange and to add into the dialogue our own extra-verbal
participation when it feels helpful to do so (see Chapter 7).

Now we meet a different therapist, Kristin Osborn and her client, the
Starving Musician.

VIGNETTE #4—THE STARVING MUSICIAN

In this case excerpt, we'll study direct videotape data for the first time. Here,
Kristin interviews a 48-year-old Middle Eastern man, the Starving Musician.
We'll learn the origin of this nickname in a minute. Kristin is 38 at the time

of this meeting. These excerpts are from Session #8, so this depicts a brief therapy well underway.

The Starving Musician: his appearance and background

This gentleman initially appears a somewhat somber individual with glasses and trim curly hair. However, he has a soulful, often smiling face. In many ways he seems to feel all alone in the world. He left his native country at age 17 and came to the United States to pursue his education. He has not returned since, for political reasons. After he left, he never saw his parents again; both died subsequent to his departure.

A youngest son, he grew up with two older brothers, one who has died and the other he rarely sees due to his wives reluctance to visit and his inability to stand up for what is important to him. He reports a very close, supportive, early relationship with his mother who clearly deeply loved and admired him. The Starving Musician returned those feelings for her—she represented home base for this securely attached man. The interaction with his father was somewhat more ambivalent. The father, seemed a serious hard-working person, who did good works outside the family, but the patient reports his father felt less warm within it. The parents" marriage appeared solid. The client had a middle-class upbringing, though the family moved frequently.

In the United States, the Starving Musician has earned considerable professional success. He has multiple academic degrees and holds a sales and marketing job in the mechanical engineering sector.

Excerpts from the treatment

In an earlier section of the taped record, hour 7, the patient describes many symptoms of anxiety: heartburn, irritability, difficulty concentrating, fear of the unknown, preoccupation. He appears identified with his mother in these respects. "She taught me to internalize my feelings instead of asserting myself." The Starving Musician married some 15 years ago, and here his troubles seemingly began. His wife, originally from his same country, evidently finds it difficult to express affection and approval to her husband or to anyone else (maybe somewhat like his father?). She seems to experience him as not "kind" and attentive toward her but more solicitous to his children, to his friends, relatives, and workmates.

The two argue, in circles, over whether he is a "nice guy," or not, and if so, toward her or not. From his side, he reports that he does have many friends, but they return his warmth, and his wife doesn't. Our patient tells us that he finds his passion in music, playing and singing, native pieces, (which no doubt, reminded him of home and of his mother). Predictably his wife can't stand his music, discourages his playing because she finds it "lower class." He rarely plays anymore, his musical instruments remain packed in his basement from his last move, years ago.

The Starving Musician comes to therapy because he's "longing for love" (his words), and he's caught in a quandary over whether to leave his wife, or to try again to go to couples counseling with her, a course that she presently refuses to take. He also might decide to forgo marital treatment and just stay in this discouraging relationship, which he finds cold and unsupportive. He loves his two teenagers and doesn't want to leave them. He longs to play music again, and he's hungry for love and affection, thus Kristin offers to call him, the sobriquet, "Starving Musician."

Now we pick up the last ten minutes of hour 8 of the interview in which the client reaches levels of real sadness and feels deserted by, and held back by, his wife and her disapproval. He breaks into tears, we join them at at minute 50.

Kristin: You take the term "Starving Musician" to a whole other level. Musicians are known as being very poor, because they can't make money. In your case, you are able to make money, but your not playing music and your not in a relationship where you are giving and receiving love.

Minute 51 SM: Yes, that is true. What you said is very true. I'm very sad now, I'm very sad.

Kristin: See if you can stay with your sadness.

SM: That feeling has been inside me. That I'm capable of giving tenfold what I have given, and it's being suffocated, and I consider that really a suffocation. (direct gaze, outward movement of right hand) It's like somebody on a team knows, if he gets out there (slow serious prosody), he can score ten thousand points (Kristin cocks her head to the right, and nods up and down), but the coach just has him sit on the bench.

Kristin: Ahh! (nods head, eyes wide open)

Kristin: What is it like to be the kid who's on the bench, who's wanting to play? (Kristin cocks her head to the right, and uses slow prosody and low serious tone)

SM: It's really sad. You already can see yourself out there doing this (speaks very strongly and quietly, gestures with hand to the left). The reality is there so vivid. You know how, and it's so frustrating having somebody put a stop, put a gate! Can't and that someone, I don't" know who that is. Maybe myself or my wife. (slow tone, sad eyes). That's how I see it. A lot of time I thought about this, but not at this level, and it's funny you mentioned music. (Starving Musician is consciously aware of different, slightly dissociated parts of his self, now he's realizing who he really is. See Wachtel, [2008, 2011] I think that's probably where my intimate love is (gestures to heart with both hands), and when you touch bases on that, it's just feelings get a little bit more real—(real affects now). The definition of offering love and all that is too vague, too much, too different (slow prosody, quiet heartfelt tone).

Kristin: Uh hmm (head cocked to the right—this represents a "tell" for Kristin. When she cocks her head to the right, she's evidently intensely tuned in.)

Minute 55 SM: It could be mentally. It could be sexual. It could be this, but music is simple, love of the music. (slow prosody, strong direct tone, nods, powerful gaze toward Kristin) It's always been there. It will always be there and making it come out and releasing that (makes two releasing gestures with both hands) feeling through your instrument, through your voice, through your act. (gestures vigorously with right hand). If you suppress it, that's very black and white. (hand, palm down, to signify suppression) That's why I got sad, when you said that. (slow prosody, sad tone) Because that was very much a direct point! (His feelings are intense. Kristin riveted in gaze, nods slowly and gently toward him. She's zeroed in too.)

Kristin: What would your mom say to you, if she could be here? (soft tone, slow prosody)

SM: Oh, right away she would want me to play! No question! (powerful tone, an affirmation of his true self)

Minute 56 Kristin: How would she see you with your sadness? Would she hug you? (She slowly gently nods up and down—another "tell.")

SM: Oh yeah!

Kristin: What would she say?

SM: I can't talk right now. I just … (Silence, looks away, shakes head. Patient breaks into tears—His deepest crying seems connected to memory of his mother—his self-object.) (Kristin holds him with her direct gaze.)

Kristin: (Pause) Just sit with the feeling. Try not to push it away. (very gentle quiet supportive tone, slow prosody, she looks directly at him, head cocked to the right.)

SM: She wouldn't need to say anything, (waves hand—direct gaze) just her look, (a paraverbal sign from his mother) just her admiration, just brings the best out of you. That's what I missed about (her). (slow weighty prosody) Sometimes they don't need to talk to you. (tears, looks down at glasses—Kristin wipes away her own tears.)

Minute 57: They're there. You know they truly loved you. (very tearful now, very congruent) They give you that. It stands that you can do anything. (pauses thoughtfully—He has a strong implicit relationship with his mother.)But I haven't got that from, you know from work, yes, but it's all superficial. But feelings? I can't think of anybody.

Minute 58 Some of it you get from kids, but kids are kids. (slight tears) (Kristin cocks head to the left, nods. He nods.) Thinking about the music, I think from day one that we got married; this was an issue actually. That "you know musicians are really not the status that they should be." (paraphrasing wife—shrugs both hands) You're a professional engineer or this and that, the culture, you know? So it was suppressed. It was suppressed right from day one in that. It's doomed. It was doomed probably right from the get-go. (His music, represents his true self, which his wife apparently disdainfully rejects. His music, his marriage and his need for intimacy now all seem doomed, sad faraway look—silence)

Kristin: (wipes away a tear—a "moment of meeting")

SM: (wipes his tears with tissue—both riveted on each other in silent engagement) Sometimes, you're lucky, you're thinking that you're lucky, that somebody would understand who you are and bring the best out of you. (slow prosody—very serious facial expression of realization—the words he earlier applied to his mother)

SM: Sometimes you're unlucky that you end up in a relationship. Yeah there's good and bad but a couple of true principles that's part of you that if they're never understood, never appreciated, it could be suppressed. Guys like me probably just take it in and hold on, hold on, hold on. (major insight) This will get better. Things will change. Before you know it ten, twelve, eighteen years have passed. (Gestures back and forth with his right hand as if to mark the years—both nodding at each other and mirroring with comprehending expressions) And I think that's what's the core differences (between him and his wife). It's what I can think. (They lock each other with their gaze, both look sad; Kristin cocks head to her right) (A poignant description of a marriage gone wrong or one that never started.)

Kristin: So I'm going to hold in the back of my mind when we meet that you have a real longing for someone to be in your life, who is going to be loving toward you, and who's going to be able to accept your love. (Here Kristin takes a personal action. She's gentle, accepting, she has an authentic tone, a direct gaze, her head is cocked to the right, she makes circular hand gestures toward him. She's making a unique personal offer.)

SM: I'm hoping that's the first definition of a good partner (smiles ironically), and I have tried to be that partner. Maybe I never found the right way to express it or maybe the right person. (maybe the latter) (SM gestures outwardly with his right hand, as if to reach toward another person.)

Kristin: You're a musician and you're starving for love, you need be able to give and receive love. (implicit relational knowing)

SM: Yes! My definition of love, not the world's (gestures over his head to indicate the world). (slow prosody, serious authentic tone) (It seems as if Kristin has become his encouraging mother, self-object. They clearly have an ever deeper connection throughout this excerpt—it's one long moment of meeting.)

Scoring profiles

This is the final ten-minute segment of the tape. We also scored the two preceding sections and we found that the ATOS ratings sequentially increased over the three excerpts. By the end of this session, the patient had very high scores of 70 on Awareness, Motivation, Affective Arousal, and New Learning. Subtracting inhibition from affective arousal led to a score of 40, which predicts strong success in psychotherapy (Bhatia et al., 2009). Similarly, Kristin had markedly high ATOS Therapist ratings of 85 or 90 on Promoting Insight, Motivation, and Arousal.

On the paraverbal ratings for this segment, the Starving Musician had an Accessibility score of 6.8/7 ("This is where my intimate love is"—"Can't talk, not say anything."—patient begins to cry. Patient's verbal tone has a genuine inflection. He gestures vigorously with his hands to emphasize his feelings.—"I thought about this but not to this level.")

The Starving Musician's voice intonation, body language, and words all match. It's clear he transparently means what he says here, and we're drawn to his authenticity. ("She [my mother] would want me to play."—much feeling and tears "Releasing that feeling through music." —the patient begins to cry harder—heartfelt expression of his core sense of self.) In this segment, his congruence score reaches 6.8/7. When the patient's Accessibility and Congruence numbers are very high, constructive ATOS outcome ratings accompany them.

Similarly, Kristin's Accessibility and Congruence scores are both 6.7/7. She's responsive, encouraging, gentle, and affective; twice tears come to her eyes as she's speaking with her client. She deeply means what she says.

Postscript

We have had the privilege of participating vicariously in an intimate, interview in which a 48-year-old man, more and more deeply encounters, first his anger, and then his grief over his lifeless marriage. He almost literally starves to play his music and to give and receive love. We probably all wonder what direction he chose subsequent to the therapy. Did he find a way to approach his wife with more shared intimacy? Did he continue to starve and to suffocate himself or did he leave the relationship?

In fact, his life took all of these directions. After this session, the Starving Musician went home and unpacked his musical instruments and started playing music again, deriving great satisfaction from sharing his love of music with his children. He met with Kristin four more times for a total of 7 double sessions or 14 therapy hours. Then he tried to get closer to his wife in an effort to save the relationship and to convince her to seek couples therapy one more time. The pair attended several such meetings, but probably no surprise, this arrangement soon broke down. The Starving Musician left his wife and set out to find love on his own.

The Starving Musician: an overview of his treatment

This is a strongly Unconscious World I paraverbal therapy. Kristin and her patient, the Starving Musician, clearly share moments of meeting. He cries over his loneliness and his cold marriage; Kristin shares tears with him. He feels that she's personally supportive and in tune with his inner state. At this moment, Kristin becomes the giving Level 2 object and probably stands in for his supportive mother. As she cries with him, she takes an action. She's fully personally involved and a Level 3 therapist. The unmistakable extra-verbal accompaniment: the locked gazes, Kristin's head cocked to the right, the simultaneous tears, the matching, slow, weighted, thoughtful prosody. Kristin's strong encouragement to find the love he needs, all speak of an evident, paraverbal, implicit relational connection.

As with our previous examples, the client in an important way leads the therapist to the moment of meeting. The Starving Musician begins to cry remembering his encouraging mother, obviously comparing her to his discouraging wife. Kristin now draws closer to him. The therapist follows the client's lead into the implicit relational enactment. We didn't study the first 7 hours of the treatment, but here in the 8th session, the central paraverbal pivot turns on his authentically looking for love and finding support and understanding from Kristin. This inner experience touches off a process in which he can embrace his identity as a loving, expressive man. The implicit relational connection with Kristin allows him to start in a new direction, internally and externally.

We can see on the tape, the patient and therapist taking mirror image body positions, and we note Kristin's head cocking, a sign of her intense involvement. These journeys are not frequent occurrences in therapy, but they are crucial. We can't imagine the treatment of the Starving Musician without this poignant implicit meeting of the hearts, at the close. Likewise, the Architect led me toward him, when he started shouting "I suck, I suck" in clear painful distress and moved me into our "moment of meeting."

Transference/counter-transference development, control mastery testing, and attachment level exchanges

The Starving Musician has a positive maternal transference to Kristin who returns motherly feelings within her counter-transference to him. The Tansey and Burke progression of projection and counter-projection supports the creation of a new more transparent, self-loving, and self-confident musician who emerges from the treatment, no longer beaten down by emotional starvation and rejection. Apparently, he later goes out on his own to look for love; the love he needs so badly.

The Starving Musician came to the therapy with the negative hypothesis that his love feelings for his music and for his children and friends were possibly "low class" and excessive. After interchanging with Kristin, he embraces these feelings. He emerges with a rejection of his negative hypothesis at a 7/7 level. His attachment for his music and for his friends convinces him that at his core he's a loving man, whatever his wife's view. In Paul Wachtel's language (see Chapter 5), he reconnects with a formerly cast-off part of himself. As his pathogenic belief about himself recedes, we can see him come alive in the therapy. He embraces that he's a deeply related person. He regains the self-belief that he had lost.

With regard to attachment, it seems that the relationship with his mother has left the Starving Musician with secure attachment and an ability to use home base. Kristin now represents that home base, and he can depart with some assurance that he'll find the love that he needs. He undertakes a mentalizing exploration when he delves into his feelings about his wife, his music and his wish for more intimacy. He states, "I'm going into this at a deeper level now" (in case we had any doubt.)

Alternative directions

The reader might have other constructive ideas about how Kristin could have picked up the thread of this meeting. Kristin is an affect-focused dynamic therapist (Osborn et al, 2014) who relentlessly pursues more and more intense feeling, here specifically her client's loneliness and need for love. However, she might have offered her patient more perspective and maybe suggested that the relationship with his always loyal mother formed an ideal template, so he's reluctant to give up hope in any relationship with a woman. Or in a supportive noncritical fashion she might have asked, "How is it that you've stayed so long in this cold relationship?" "What are the barriers to leaving?" In other words, there are additional ways to approach this therapy, other than the affect-focused dynamic strategy.

Also, some therapists could reasonably object that Kristin's tears might deflect the client away from his own sadness. However, it feels that moments of meeting like this are rare enough and always form crucial crossroads in the treatment, so the therapist needs to remain alert for these privileged times and take them where she finds them. She can't pass them up. Maybe Kristin's tears startled the patient, although there's no evidence of that. They mark clear proof of her involvement, and this probably trumps all the other choices that the therapist might make at this important time. We've learned by now that "moments of meeting" hold great importance and that they always have a strong paraverbal motif. Often they mark a turn in the road.

We close this chapter with a brief report on another intense paraverbal connection, although in a very short, less-developed treatment.

VIGNETTE #5—A CO-CONSTRUCTED NOW MOMENT CASE

Five years ago in a particularly brief therapy, I, Jim, treated an African-American couple caught in an excruciating crisis. The therapy started slowly enough—Mr. A, a careful, diffident 45-year-old lawyer brought his wife to treatment because her spending habits threatened the family with financial ruin. He earned a modest salary, and his wife, far less, as a part-time retail worker.

Raising two teenage daughters would have strained their budget under any circumstances, but Mrs. A's behavior introduced a particular stress. A colorful, exuberant lady in her mid-40s, with a definite ADD diagnosis, and perhaps a bipolar one as well, she bought clothes and accessories for herself and for her family at an alarming rate. Many she returned to the store, but many remained at home.

Her husband regularly became furious at her overspending—apparently, the only instances of his losing his temper with her. I focused on the wife's angry sense of deprivation. The buying, apparently, felt like recompense for childhood disappointments at the hands of her apparently remarkably cold mother.

With only a little encouragement, she mentalized and grew more understanding of her constant need to purchase supplies of love and also of her husband's anxiety over the expense. I needed to walk a fine line not to criticize Mrs. A but to still help her regulate her habit. When she accepted the need for self-regulation, on her own, the spending and the marriage settled down.

Then tragedy struck. Mrs. A received a diagnosis of advanced, usually fatal, GYN cancer. Rushed to surgery, before the anesthesia took hold, in her inimitable style, she led the medical team in joining hands and praying for world peace and for healing for her and for each critically ill patient in the hospital. The cancer soon returned, and we all had to accept that her death approached.

These last few meetings represented as difficult an emotional challenge as I've had in my career. I found the image of the two young, about-to-be-motherless girls, almost unbearable to allow to mind, imagining this tragedy befalling me and my own children. I assured Mrs. A that she could call me at any time, 24 hours, 7 days a week, to respond to any crisis that the family might have.

In what turned out our next to last meeting, Mrs. A reported on a conversation with her 13-year-old daughter, who understood her prognosis. The girl asked, "How will I know that you're still watching after me?" Mrs. A replied, "You'll feel a light touch on your shoulder and look around.

You won't see me, but I'll be there looking out for you and knowing how you're doing."

I can barely write these words 10 years later. At the moment, I fell way out of role and burst into tears. Mrs. A reassured me that if I felt this situation too much to bear, I could call her at any time 24 hours a day. I saw them only once more. She did die. I offered her husband and children continued counseling, but they never came back to me. They did, however, meet with other therapists in our system with whom they had had prior contact.

Mr. & Mrs. A, in their family crisis, represent the extreme I'll ever face. I do not make a habit of crying with my patients, but I feel more free to do so now. Mrs. A contributed to making me a more open, responsive, Level 3 relational therapist. Here we see this very spontaneous, somewhat disregulated, zany, warm woman influencing the therapist and leading him toward new behaviors at least as much as he influences her. An obvious "now moment" befell us. Little insight feels involved. The participants synchronize in their open selves. Something has shifted inside both of them—implicit relational knowing marks the gateway to internal change. Mrs. A became free of her compulsive shopping and realistically accepting of her impending death.

Alternative approaches

Recently, 72% of therapists have reported crying with patients (Blume-Marcovici et al., 2013). Interestingly, male and female therapists in equal proportions, and older and younger counselors in equal proportions, have shed tears with their patients. The reader could easily ask whether my unintended intervention supported the client or detracted from the treatment. Of course, I had no choice. I tried to hold back my reaction, but I couldn't. This certainly represented a personal transparent action on my part.

So discussing different approaches feels a bit theoretical. The client, Mrs. A, immediately helped me and told me as a joke that I could call her if I felt in crisis. A treatment should never focus exclusively on the therapist, of course, but I think she felt some relief in turning away from her tragic situation and attending to me.

In addition, she could have no doubt that I cared about her and responded to her terrible predicament. An atmosphere of new openness did characterize the rest of that hour and the next one, so the "moment of meeting" set up implicit connected trust between us. Once the therapist has broken into tears, of course, the atmosphere in the room does become more trusting and open for all parties.

The reader might also wonder whether I mentioned my unusual behavior to the client later in that hour or in the next one. I didn't. In this case, she had an awful lot more to worry about than her therapist crying at her session. If she queried me, I certainly would have opened a dialogue about the tears.

Usually these moments stand for themselves in a human way, and neither the patient nor the therapist feels much like talking about them more. In some cases, this probably represents a mistake and the patient would gain some further exploration of the moment. I might have asked Mrs. A if my crying had upset her, but it didn't seem to. Her mind was elsewhere.

Transference/counter-transference, Control Mastery issues, and observations about attachment

This represented a very intense, very brief attempt at crisis intervention. We can't miss the Unconscious World II issues of anger and loss engulfing Mrs. A. The client's fear and sadness were expressed largely paraverbally in her facial expression and voice tones, and I responded to her likewise paraverbally with a calming concerned, accessible voice and with open bodily messages using my hands and palms held out and arms open.

In terms of transference, Mrs. A treated me as a more understanding person than her mother. Before her illness struck, she was able to take in my belief that she could curtail her incessant shopping. Her tragic medical situation provoked powerful protective counter-transference feelings in me—no surprise—which I obviously directly communicated to her.

In terms of attachment, Mrs. A had an ambivalent stance. She seemed hungry and to want a great deal from the other but then to back off. This was enacted by buying a great many clothes and then returning most of them (but not all) to the store. After only a few sessions, she did use her mentalization to quiet this pattern.

I think she came to the therapy with a negative hypothesis that she was a greedy and poorly controlled person. Her mother told her that so repeatedly. The understanding that she found in our few sessions helped her defeat that hypothesis, that she was not an abandoned insatiable person. She could relinquish her compulsive need to gather more supplies. She allowed me to pass the control mastery test at about Level 5.5. The key piece that she had cast off represented the repressed conviction that she was a loving person on her own and did not need to shower herself or her family with gifts to prove it. Now she could wholeheartedly accept this positive self view, probably for the first time.

We would have learned much more about this family had the treatment lasted longer of course. Mrs. A paraverbally presented us with an intense, bubbly, over-the-top person. This warmed me up and made me more accessible to her. These extra-verbal qualities certainly played a significant role in her unorthodox treatment.

CONCLUSION

In closing, it seems that very high amplitude paraverbal experiences occur from time to time in everyone's practice. However, the therapist usually doesn't have the chance to plan his or her response in the most constructive way. It all just happens, really fast, and we fight to comprehend it later. "Life must be lived forward, but must be understood backward"—Kierkegaard.

This chapter suggests that crucial paraverbal material may arise very early in the treatment, that is, why does a successful architect speak with such diffidence and self-criticism? Right away we need to start watching carefully for these paraverbal mismatches. The Architect's under confidence does not reflect his realistic achievements and generous self.

Second, at some point, we may encounter "moments of meeting," which will almost certainly be accompanied by a preceding, strong nonverbal introduction from the patient's side. We can spot this buildup of feeling if we're alert to it. The two participants then might step out of role and join together. This will carry great importance for that client and for that therapy. When once such an intense nonverbal exchange has taken place, the treatment and the client seem lastingly different. Don't waste a good "now moment"; respond with your full self.

These "moments of meeting" occur when the client and counselor meet as open people, and the patient contacts and embraces the center of his self, with the therapist as helping companion and co-voyager . Then like the Starving Musician or the Architect, he is now able to start on a new path, after which he may never feel the same, providing later growth-promoting experiences that reinforce this positive direction. Once is probably not enough (Wachtel, 2011, p. 121).

We can also find another meaning here. These high-amplitude, paraverbal engagements usually don't repeat themselves in a treatment and may not even occur in a lot of therapies. Is a counseling experience without "now moments," a less successful one? Probably not, it turns out that many now moments remain unconscious in any case (see Pally, 2002) and 80% of those with brain events stay unconscious. The general atmosphere of the therapy, meeting by meeting, perhaps seems the crucial variable (Bohart and Tallman, 1999).

The striking material in this chapter suggests a further possibility as well. An extra-verbal system may underlie a great many far less dramatic therapeutic interchanges. We could track the paraverbal network through a complete session or a series of sessions. If we're to understand the real significance of the nonverbal connections in therapy, we need to discover how this extra-verbal relating appears in much lower amplitude, more every day, subtle interactions. The gradual development of the implicit relational knowing bond may take a central role. This subtle growth and connection could become equally important in the therapy, and in the client's life, as the unmistakably intense confrontations we've just studied here in Chapter 4. We take up this possibility in depth, in Chapters 5, 6, and 7.

Chapter Five

Tracking Paraverbal Connections

Full Sessions

We'll continue our study of the extra-verbal system but this time focus on less intense interchanges, however, on those that develop through a full session of therapy.

We discuss two videotaped cases in depth. One treated by Jim D. in Chapter 5 and the other a published interview conducted by Paul Wachtel, PhD in Chapter 6. We present these two pieces together because they're both 50-minute individual meetings, and studying them side by side allows us a broader perspective on the paraverbal interactions of client and counselor.

JIM AND THE COURAGEOUS ORPHAN

We'll start with an evaluation in which I participated during 1989, a tape that I've studied repeatedly over the last 25 years and still find beguiling because one could follow any number of productive directions with this young lady.

Our client, Sally, a 22-year-old college senior, needed to find a new therapist since her counselor, one of the post-docs in our training program, planned to leave the department shortly and had only met her once or twice. Otherwise, she had had no previous treatment.

Sally readily agreed to a videotaped consultation, as part of her search for her next therapist. We'll soon discover that she also needed to process a central traumatic experience, an agenda for which she probably also unconsciously sought the meeting.

Sally and I begin

As I entered the room, our bespectacled young lady sat attentively but almost without expression. She wore a simple, informal, nearly drab blue blouse and grey skirt. She used no makeup that I could detect. In other words, she dressed in the undergraduate and graduate student uniform of the 1980s, very plainly, very simply, without frills or adornment. She was perhaps 5 foot 3 inches tall and slender. She looked small as she perched on her chair to my left. She wore her short, light brown hair parted in the middle, and she had clear pale skin. She hunched over and peered out at me through her ample glasses.

At first, Sally did not appear depressed but forlorn, almost shrinking into herself. She seemed to nearly blend with the woodwork. Following Ogden and Fisher (2015), her tentative posture might hint at previous trauma or at least fearfulness. She seemed to attempt to look smaller than her actual size. We'll find out that Sally's personality was strong despite her physical habits.

I stood perhaps 3 or 4 inches taller, certainly heavier. Back in the 1980s, I still wore a dress with shirt and tie. I sat and took notes at a small desk, really a shelf, between us.

Our taping area felt cramped. A mounted camera craned down, and to include both of us in the frame, we had to sit close together, huddled around the tiny wall-mounted desk. Our knees rested probably 3 or 4 feet apart, tight quarters.

We started. Sally sat at a 45-degree angle to my right. At first she looked to the side and down toward the floor, not maintaining eye contact. However, she spoke easily, and I quickly grasped that she was bright and articulate. Her artful speech aside, we both seemed to begin the meeting with at least normal levels of social anxiety. We'd just met; neither of us felt at ease.

Both of us understood that we'd engage in a one-session consultation to assess the level of her depression, to formulate a treatment plan, and to start the search for a new therapist. As a secondary goal, we'd agreed to produce this tape that I could use in teaching my postdoctoral students. Despite the odd setting, with its cameras and wires, and the somewhat unusual contract between us, after a few minutes, we both seemed to put our initial hesitancy aside. We got down to work. (In what follows, we present verbatim dialogue, somewhat edited to conserve space.)

SEGMENT #1: MINUTES 1 TO 10

Jim: Tell me what brings you in.

Sally: (looking down at hands in her lap—voice soft) I went through, hit a bottom, deep deep depression. It was either kill myself or change—knew I couldn't do it alone.

Jim: (watching the tape now, I realize I've already started to match the slow cadence of her speech and her quiet delivery. I looked directly at her.) You were feeling really bad. How long did that last?

Sally: Really low, three weeks, conscious effort to keep going. (Her labored somewhat lifeless tone communicates how much effort "keeping going" really called for.)

Jim: Sleep problems? (In a matter—fact, low tone)

Sally: No. Fear of migraines, classic time for them to come back. I lost a great deal of weight. (Still quiet effortful inflection)

Jim: How much did you lose?

Sally: Twenty-five pounds.

Jim: Uh huh.

Sally: If I kept losing more, I would be alarmed.

Jim: Appetite went on this one. Did you feel underwater? (Sharp direct tone, colloquial speech, conveys my effort to empathize with her feelings in a non-threatening way.)

Sally: (gaze inclined downward)

Jim: Missing work? (looking right at her)

Sally: No. Work was sanity. (Still quiet, suppressed tone)

Jim: What kicked this off? (encouraging smile)

Sally: (clipped, more rapid cadence) Involved with this man. I was in love with him, two to two and a half years. Since January and February getting along great. We slept together. He chickened out of the whole thing. "I was too strong for him. He had been dominated by his brother, dominated by his father, afraid of being dominated by me" (sarcastic tone), which was fine, but I got pregnant!

Jim: You must have been awfully worried. (slow cadence, low gentle tone)

Sally: Yah I had a miscarriage—made it easier (very low volume, sad serious tone, which I can hardly hear, eyes down at floor)

Jim: Must have felt horrible (soft tone—unconscious matching of speech rhythm with her, direct eye contact) Did you tell him? (still soft)

Sally: I told him. Initially he was fine, supportive. I really didn't acknowledge what had happened. Then later when I really wanted to talk to him, figured he was the one person I could talk to, but he says, "Don't bring that up" (sarcastic, cutting tones—She shrugs shoulders and shakes head side to side in disbelief.) Before the miscarriage he didn't get that I was pregnant with his child. (more sarcastic emphasis) Not really on speaking terms since then (now more animated, serious, decisive, annoyed, tone)

Minute 7 Jim: He really let you down! (leaning toward her, low, serious, very strong tone, matches her faster rhythm but in a much louder voice—We've already entered into reliving an intense crisis; there's plenty of affect in the room now at minute 7.)

Sally: Yes (she starts upright—nods strongly, my powerful inflection has evidently made an impression.)

Jim: When did the depression kick off? (I'm still trying to assess the severity of the depression.)

Sally: (cadence slows—palms down—looks down) A lot of things come back, when resistances are low. Resistance was dirt low. Low tolerance for things that don't justify life, wasted a lot of it so far (head down, then bobs up). Communications with my family really bad. Very close to my brother Jack, he's gone through lots of hard times. He's older. He's 30. He was a junkie, substituted alcohol. Tried to kill himself on his 30th birthday (head down, sad tone).

(Jim nods, grunts "hmmm" empathically—Sally makes eye contact leans a little toward me.)

Sally: When he tried to kill himself, one of the hardest phone calls I ever made. He said "I don't believe you could ever love me. Ten times around the track before I could get to the starting gate, (animated tone and rhythm as she recounts conversation). Someone I adored, admired, worshiped, feeling that worthless, talked to him, listened to him (loud amplitude, emphatic tone).

Jim: You really reached out to him (soft empathetic inflection), when he was in trouble! Then you called him (for support now)? (Sally nods vigorously.)

Sally: (shaking head, speaking with much louder inflection) He told me I was a complete failure, heading down the same path he did. He did it out of love, but I don't do drugs. (chuckles) (I smile too—interchange between us becoming warmer) I'm not a heavy drinker (waves off that idea with her right hand). Father alcoholic, I've seen what that can do.

Minute 10 Jim: Just don't get started. (Jim D, as it happens, has alcoholism treatment subspecialty.)

Sally: Yah.

Jim: When did the depression start?

Sally: Oh depression started about eight years ago! (chuckles—waves right hand to the side)

Commentary on Segment #1

From a paraverbal perspective, in what way have the two participants interacted so far? Because of the room and camera set up, we sit close together.

I glance down at my notes intermittently. She often looks at her lap before she starts a response, apparently to compose her thoughts. As she begins to speak, she then usually looks directly at me, and I at her. Her prosody is often abrupt and business-like, but she certainly uses sarcastic emphasis when she reports particular events, usually interactions with men, that have made her angry. These include, so far, those with her erstwhile boyfriend and with her brother.

Her voice also sounds weighted with sadness, as she speaks about her brother Jack and his difficulties. She shrugs when using her ironic tone, and she waves her right arm entirely across her body from left to right, when she recalls how angry she became at her disappearing boyfriend. This movement almost symbolizes sweeping him out of her life. In posture, Sally remains somewhat huddled in her chair, as if to deny her power.

I sit and scribble but smile with the client, and grunt in empathy, reacting to some of the bad times she reports: the miscarriage, the unsupportive boyfriend, the addicted brother. I look directly at her and often speak in a gentle, supportive voice with slow rhythm, which often matches hers, "That's hard." I'm unmistakably trying to connect, and she's trying also. My posture feels erect but not frightening. My tone is soft but strong enough to unmistakably suggest that I mean business.

Compared to the average therapist, I'm probably more active in reaching toward the patient nonverbally and verbally, but nothing exceptional has happened between us so far.

I, of course, do not plan my bodily reactions to Sally and to her story, but I don't hold back on them either. This marks the way I generally engage: grunts, shrugs, smiles, laughs, steady looks. As my coauthors and I studied the tape, all of us noticed more details of my extra-verbal style than I certainly did at the time. Sally tells an increasingly sad tale of desertion. I badly wanted her to know that I heard her, that at least in this room, she was not alone—thus my guttural responses and exclamations.

Watching the interview more than 20 times over the years, I've noticed two turning points, so far, where verbal, paraverbal and implicit relational knowing features seem to converge in a powerful way. One came at minute 7, when I observed, loudly, almost yelling, "He really let you down!." She started a bit, as if jolted into more intense feeling by my raised voice. It seemed as if at that moment she got in touch with just how abandoned she did feel. I felt we moved closer after that and this probably, in Stern's parlance, represents a small "now moment." She could tell at a visceral level that I got how alone and scared she felt.

A second shift occurred at the very end of the segment when she offered "Oh, depression started about eight years ago." Here she initiated an obvious offer for us to pursue her earlier life, which I, of course, accepted. In the next minute, beginning Segment #2, she responded to my counter offer and began to relate the events of her mother's tragic illness and death. Now she clenched her hands in her lap, looked down, and spoke in the slow rhythm and the low inflection of real sadness.

In Segment #1, Sally and I begin matching speech rhythms; we seem to start to enjoy talking with each other. We, however, may find ourselves about to discuss really important, really upsetting happenings, which will test our new bond. Our relationship has become warmer but certainly not close as yet.

The beginning transference and counter-transference themes may have unfolded like this: I had no sexual feelings toward her that I could discern. I felt moved by her story of loss and of her medical crisis, including her precipitous weight drop and depressed affect. I wanted to support her and to protect her. I did not consciously connect that I had a daughter nearly Sally's same age, but that probably contributed to my beginning affection for her.

She spoke easily to me and seemed assured of my interest. I suspect I reminded her, in some ways, of her older brother, Jack, who apparently usually, though not always, offered her genuine holding and concern. Just barely consciously I began to wonder about the role here of her earlier relationships with men, specifically her father.

Objective measures for Segment #1

Sally

Turning to the Accessibility and Congruence scores, we've just met a young woman who often gazes down at her hands, away from her interview partner, and whose facial expression changes little. We've also observed, however, a young person who sometimes looks directly at the therapist, nods actively, and shakes her head vigorously to emphasize her spoken point.

She chuckles three times during the ten-minute segment, although once incongruently, "Oh, the depression started about eight years ago." Her often motionless posture and frequently inexpressive face seems to balance out her more demonstrably affective tones and gestures that we've just noted, so she receives an Accessibility Score of 3.7 for this segment, close to the mid-range on the 1–7 scale.

Sally's Congruence Score

Although we've already noted an important exception, (when she laughs at the sad experience of her 8-year depression), in her verbal and paraverbal behavior, most of the time, Sally is congruent in speech and movement. When she's describing her frustration and anger with her self-protective, passive boyfriend, she waves her hand dismissively, gesturing across her body and sarcastically imitates his psycho-babble excuses, "I've been dominated by my brother, dominated by my father ..." She's clearly really furious with him. Her Congruence score for Segment #1 falls at the 4.5 level, somewhat above the mid-range.

Jim's scores for Accessibility and Congruence reveal more subtle detail. Jim fidgets, strokes his beard, and scratches on his notepad, but he maintains regular eye contact with Sally, and he acknowledges her pain in an affective fashion both in his verbal statements—"That's hard"—"You must have been awfully worried"—"He really let you down," and in his soft tone and occasional sympathetic grunts. Given his emotional responsiveness, Jim's Accessibility score reaches 4.7.

The therapist (My coauthors rated all my behavior on this tape. I absented myself.)

Jim's paraverbal participation: body posture, speech tone, and prosody appear of a piece with the verbal content of his interventions. His intonation and body language as he leans toward Sally seemed to express what he really feels. We can tell he genuinely wants to respond to Sally. His soothing tone, relaxed attentive posture and steady, direct, sympathetic gaze lead to an above-average Congruence score of 5.2.

(We have as yet no normative data on the Accessibility and Congruence scales, so these scores, we've just offered, represent common sense, face validity assessments only. For example, we have no specific information reflecting the mean trajectory of Congruence scores for a cohort of 30 experienced therapists, or of 30 "typical" psychotherapy patients for that matter.)

What have we learned so far? We've attended the opening act of a two-character play. We can carefully observe the participants working on how to start a relationship. Perforce they sit close together in a drab interview room. They maintain a good deal of eye contact. They have the beginnings of an affective exchange. The remainder of the meeting may not bring more feeling, more meaning, more intense paraverbal relating, but the pattern of moderate to moderately high scores probably indicates that the two people have begun to trust each other. They feel sufficiently comfortable to engage a little more deeply, with their words and their bodily movements. The implicit relational knowing has started. Enough has transpired so far that they may have set the stage for an important interchange later in the hour—but maybe not.

In the finish to the drama, one of the actors, the client, may test the relationship by introducing very important facts and feelings from her past and present. Or she may pull back verbally, and bodily, and not trust the interaction sufficiently to do this. A skillful and engaging speaker, Sally could keep the therapist, and herself, at bay, and continue to the end in her offhand and ironic style, without revealing much more about herself in depth. Does she feel sufficiently connected to engage more deeply with me? We'll see.

SEGMENT #2: POWERFUL
REVELATIONS—MINUTES 11 TO 13 AND 25 TO 36

The second half of the interview took an unexpected sharp turn into a new topic that Sally just introduced as we closed the first ten minutes. What happened the night that Sally's mother died? Sally moved so directly and so quickly, with such great feeling, into reporting this event that after watching the tape multiple times, I'm now convinced that in part, she came to our consultation to discuss, and to start to master, this trauma, obviously a mostly unconscious choice. That night represented the most important moments of her life, a night that would become the initial focus of any later psychotherapy, "a narrative point of origin" in Stern's (1985) phrase.

We start again:

Jim: When you said the depression started eight years ago, you were joking, but it's not entirely a joke …

Sally: (looking down at her lap, slow deliberate prosody, serious tone) No I haven't been happy for a long time …

Jim: (gentle tone, deliberate prosody) What's happening with that?

Sally: (looking down) Where to start with that one (mirrors my words "with that," now head up, direct eye contact). My mother died seven years ago … (slow prosody, much feeling of sadness).

Jim: Were you aware that she was very sick? (gentle tone—I lean a little toward her.)

Sally: (slow, sad, resigned delivery) I watched her die for two years.

Jim: (slow, gentle, holding tone, low volume, leaning toward Sally) When she became very sick, what did you feel? (We're getting pretty open now so I can ask this very probing question.)

Sally: (emphatic serious tone, strong volume) She couldn't die. She couldn't die. We needed her too much. … My high school years sucked (shakes head emphatically). I'm just beginning to come to terms with what happened. (Maybe in part she's coming to those terms at this moment.)

Jim: 15?

Sally: 15 when she died. I have four older brothers and sisters, much older, and one younger brother with CP. We have a big house that once held eight people. When she became sick, I took over more and more of the duties. When she died, I became the natural head of the household! (shakes head expressing resignation)

Jim: (slow, low resigned voice, slow emphatic prosody—I lean forward—I get her imprisonment) There you were ...

Sally: (nods) Father, a doctor, always drunk or not at home, when he was home, he was mostly nasty. (angry emphasis and tone—her father now joins the drama.)

Deleted section

At this point, a twelve-minute segment began, which seemed less affectively and thematically important. We've edited it out of the tape many years ago. In brief, one year after her mother's death, the father remarried. The father has now stopped drinking but didn't do that when Sally's mother was sick. Predictably, Sally doesn't like her stepmother and doesn't like the way she takes care of the house and of her little brother. She has not only lost her mother but also the mother's role with her brother and with the household duties. Now she's free of her domestic burden, but she prefers not to go home.

She describes how her mother quietly, carefully showed her the way to perform the housekeeping tasks and how a strong bond grew between them. She knew her mother appreciated her sacrifice and effort without the mother saying so. Like Sally, her mother didn't complain, but Sally knew how badly the mother needed her help. Her mother bearing her lot silently did not demand that the father stop drinking, did not ask for paid household help, and so on.

An alternative path, which we did not follow, involved Sally's identification with her long-suffering, loyal mother, probably a fruitful direction to take in a later treatment with more time available. The reader-therapist might have chosen to follow the path of the closeness and the horrible loss wrapped in the relationship with her mother. This represents an entirely justified direction. I'll try to show why I didn't take it.

Return to tape at minute 25

As Sally talked further, my mind kept returning to the horror of when she went to the hospital for the last time. Her mother died the next day, leaving Sally with great responsibility and no support. How terrified Sally must have felt; these feelings welled up in me as she spoke. The sorrow from Sally's chest connected with my inner affect, and I emotionally pictured her awful vulnerability, not only having lost her one ally at home but now faced with dealing with her selfish father.

I continued to wonder if unresolved grief at her mother's loss represented the original core of her depression. How could it not? This represented a tempting but ultimately incorrect hypothesis.

Jim: (gently, slowly) When your mother actually died?

Sally: (speaking quickly with a flat tone, as if to dismiss the interchange with the father) My father had a talk with me. "If something should happen, if your mother doesn't make it, this and that." ... (sarcastic tone begins to creep in)

Jim: (sharply interrupts) What? (Empathic intervention, she needs to talk much more about this evening. In my body I could feel trepidation. More bad news lurked just ahead for Sally ...)

Sally: (loud, sarcastic, looks right at me, tone dripping with anger, rapid prosody) I would be "very necessary" at home, not allowed to go away to school, but he'd make sure I'd have a nice car to commute to and from classes with.

Jim: (incredulous—leans forward) What did you think of that message?

Sally: (looking directly at me, outraged dismissive inflection) A bomb ... wanted to go to USC, and root for the Trojans, be a cheerleader. Brother and sister lived out there. But I'm not blond (Jim shakes his head and smiles) not a cheerleader ... (flips her right hand to the side dismissively)

Jim: Good student?

Sally: Yah, too good a student. Didn't want to go to USC.

Jim: But he says you can't go away to school?

Sally: (bitter tone, rapid prosody) Have to take care of brother, have to take care of him and cooking and cleaning (increasingly angry intonation but a defeated one as well)

Jim: (emphatic tone) It's quite a message ... (Jim inches a little forward—looks right at her. He exhales in disbelief, prosody slows and drops at the end.)

Sally: (slow, deliberate, angry, heavy tone—looking at hands in her lap) Felt trapped, why I can't stand being at home, really trapped, really trapped (cadence slowing, amplitude lower and lower—if you repeat a word two additional times, it implies a special meaning for you.)

Jim: (gentle tone) When she actually died, was it a shock?

Sally: (matter of fact) Expected it.

Jim: (gentle tone) Were you aware of being grief stricken at that time? (At this point, I still think she suffers primarily from unresolved grief—silly me.)

Sally: (intense eye contact, slow prosody) Fear, horribly afraid.

Jim: (gentle low tone, slow cadence, I bend my head forward) Afraid of what?

Sally: (questioning tone) What will happen without her? How will things happen? (slow deliberate prosody, relaxes her posture toward me)

Jim: You were 15?

Sally: (staring right at me) Yah.

Jim: How old are you now?

Sally: Twenty two

Jim: (muses) Mother died seven years ago, age 15 ... (I'm considering what is it like to lose your mother at 15, with no other supports.)

Segment #2—Commentary so far

At this moment, for reasons that I still do not fully understand, a vivid, almost lifelike image suddenly came to my mind, of frightened, waiflike 15-year-old Sally, standing in front of her implacably self-centered, much taller and robust, authoritative father. I think this represents projective identification at work. Beyond her words Sally transmitted her victimized state to me through her tone and slumped posture. Apparently, I caught it and could rework it and hand it back to her (see Tansey and Burke, 1989).

We both understood at a visceral level just how desperate her situation felt at that moment, seven years ago. This is evidently how paraverbal relating starts and continues—her body projects a core affect into mine and the transaction remains unconscious, certainly at the start, but then a picture arrived in my head of bereft Sally.

In the dialogue that comes next, I followed up with a question to which I already knew the answer. This threadbare description just above, I think, captures some of what we usually call insight. My realization of the true state of affairs between Sally and her father was a byproduct of the "implicit relationship" between Sally and me that had already developed.

In my upper chest, I could subliminally pick up the feeling of Sally's desperation and fury without her saying it. A great deal of paraverbal relating started now and continued through the end of the interview. Here, we can see that this process of projective communication emerges from a region at least somewhat removed from consciousness and only partly about the spoken words.

We'll see that this introjective understanding likely heavily influenced what then happened in our exchange. This mutual projection may contain elements of both implicit relational knowing, and of transference/counter-transference issues, in this latter space I'm a protective older brother. I identified with this vulnerable, courageous, 15-year-old girl and she, now 22, could confide in me about how trapped she felt on that horrible evening. Our postures once again relaxed toward each other.

Jim: How did your father do then the night she died? (suspecting the worst)

Sally: (sarcastic tone) He behaved wonderfully at the funeral, pillar of strength.

Jim: (looking directly at her, holding, low, gentle tone) Had you seen your mother the day before? (By 1989, at the time of this meeting, my own father had died in 1987 but my mother had not. I knew how important the last presence at the bedside can feel to those left behind, and I asked Sally about it, but this scene of saying goodbye did not seem vitally significant to her. Obviously she had other issues to deal with.)

Sally: (blunt—sad—resigned) Seen her that morning. The night before she decided she'd had it. (matter of fact) She'd had it. (slow emphatic prosody)I waited up for my father to come home. Then I realized he wasn't going to be there for me. (looking directly at me, heavy, hurt, incredulous tone, slow prosody. Her head bends forward toward me.) He just sent me to bed! (shakes her head vigorously and angrily)

Jim: (slow deliberate empathic) There you were …!

Sally: (nods her head up and down slowly)

Jim: (strong emphatic) You were waiting for something …!

Sally: (slow deliberate) We were going to have to do this together!

Jim: (strong empathic feelingful inflection—reflecting disappointment and betrayal, slow prosody, looking directly at her, inclining toward her, low tone almost a whisper) No together … (mirrors her word).

Sally: (direct eye contact) No together (We repeat same phrase with same rhythm and emphasis. Silence falls between us.)

Sally: (She breaks the quiet in an angry, helpless tone.) So frustrating! I was still dependent on him, financially dependent on him, no place to go, nothing I could do!

Jim: (direct, powerful emphasis. I look right at her.) And you hated him…!!

Sally: (simultaneously with me, matching each other's prosody and wording, strong rhetorical, determined inflection) I hated him! … I thought I'm just going to stop! I wanted out, stop cooking, stop cleaning, forget it! Who would do it! (angry staccato rhythm, very loudly)

Jim: (slow, strong, direct tone, matching her rhythm, solid eye contact) I don't know if this is helpful or not, but a couple of things come to my mind (slow, deliberate, "thinking-out loud" tone). One thing is your depression takes the form of just stopping! (strong emphasis, I look directly at her.)

Sally: (slowly, concentrating on my suggestion) Yah, but what do you mean?

Jim: (slow strong emphasis) Just stopping talking.

Sally: (slow cadence, direct eye contact) Yah?

Jim: (direct, declarative tone, constant eye contact) Not sure your depression is reenacting your feeling after your mother died, and you had this confrontation with your father. On the other hand, I wouldn't bet against it either!! (leaning toward Sally, very strong emphatic, almost a shout).

Sally: (direct eye contact—slow prosody, revealing more) Usually a lot of anger goes with this. (deliberate, open inflection—my suggestion about "just stopping" is probably way off, but I'm intensely involved with her dilemma, which she gets. This paraverbal connection with me sets the scene for Sally to break through her defenses and relate her depression to her anger—one of the key "moments of meeting." We're both becoming more passionately present and important feelings are shaking loose for us both.)

(Next for reasons I don't entirely grasp, I experienced a quick lifelike snapshot in my mind of helpless Sally pushed away by her self-protective boyfriend, Mike, an image without words in my head—implicit relational knowing. Desertion by Mike represents her presenting problem. He reappears on cue in my unconscious. I then quickly drop the idea of the present depression as "just stopping" and connect the abandonment by her father, and by Mike, as nearly identical psychological traumas.

I have received projected information from Sally, and evidently I have accurately enough reworked and transmitted back to her that Mike and her father represent two faces of the same character in the internal tragic drama of her life. Now our paraverbal implicit selves have joined, and through the remainder of the meeting, we continued to work on the same wave length, sometimes finishing each other's sentences, using the same physical gestures and voice pitches.)

Jim: (direct eye contact) Yah Mike did what your father did. I'm pregnant. I need to talk to you." He says, "well I'm out to lunch"! (sarcastic tone)

Sally: (incredulous emphasis, she speaks in a parody of Mike's voice during the exchange. Now she and I have both spotted the key affect—anger at abandonment, and we're completely engaged.) I didn't even tell him I was pregnant. How could I trap him? Wanted to talk to him, no … (sarcastic)(pause)

Jim: You need the man. You're there! You need to talk! You want to talk! He drops out on you, somewhat like your brother Jack did? (My right arm gestures out toward Sally.)

Sally: No, Jack's different I called him back, and I yelled at him! (emphatic, fond intonation—She can stand up for herself with certain important men, probably those of whose love she feels sure—Jack represents an important *exception* to her pattern, (see Wachtel, later in this chapter). The question of which men are safe and which are not, would have a major focus in a later therapy.)

Jim: (emphatic tone) So he responded to you?

Sally: (emphatic, laughs, shakes her fist. I have shaken my fist previously twice in this interview and am about to again.) Yah.

Jim: Different type of man (emphatic). But Mike and your father are similar. (Leaning toward Sally, at last I catch the crucial affective meaning.)

Sally: (slow prosody, greater awareness coming across her face and in speech rhythm—she leans closer to me.) I never really connected them, but they are similar! I guess they are the same!

Jim: (very strong emphatic tone, nods head, shakes fist, almost yelling, directly engaging her gaze, leaning forward) I strongly do connect them!

Sally: (Immediately nods vigorously up and down, makes direct eye contact and sits straight up. This represents a "moment of meeting" between us.)

Sally: (slow rhythm, thoughtful tone) Yes, what kills me is I find myself again in the situation. ... I do self-destructive things when I get very angry, be it losing drastic amounts of weight, which can't be good for you, take things out on myself, things that I know are bad for me. (Sally speaking very quickly and actively expressing herself with an excited emphasis—she's learning something—she's introducing new material, which validates what we've just discussed. She now has had time to study my words, but also my paraverbal posture and tone, to develop sufficient trust to tell me everything. She realizes now that she's about to start another self-destructive relationship—puts hand out in front of herself, palm up conveying openness to the feeling). Or just involving myself in things ... there's this guy at my office, who takes cocaine, self-centered, just about the biggest asshole ...

Jim: That I've ever dated? (Evidently implicit relational knowing in action, Jim picks up the direction that Sally will take and completes her thought.)

Sally: (sadly nods "yes" at me)

(The twelve-minute segment ends. I suggest that she arrange for a course of short-term therapy in our department with a recommendation from her departing therapist or that she could directly call me if she wished and start with me. We warmly shake hands goodbye. She offers a Duchênne smile, which immediately catches my gaze, and I respond in kind with my own broad smile. I'm deeply touched by this courageous young woman and by her story.)

Discussion of Segment #2

The close of this interview seems to explode on the tape. Sally and my relationship moves so quickly into a strong intimacy here in Segment #2—what happened? Our guesses run as follows. Within her unconscious Sally had struggled with heartbreaking abandonment for almost half her life. First her beloved mother becomes mortally ill and two years later dies, and then that same night her father makes his narcissism and indifference cruelly obvious.

Since Sally started her story with the description of the desertion by her boyfriend and quickly followed that vignette with a report of her brother Jack rejecting her as well, (a rupture which she and her brother, it turned out, soon repaired), abandonment themes kept going through my mind. It took me a while to get it.

As the second segment began, I guessed that she perhaps had repressed grief over losing her mother when so young and vulnerable, so I asked specifically about the night that her mother passed away. It became dramatically clear that, although Sally retained much sadness over this terrible loss, a stronger feeling burst out, fury at her exploitative, irresponsible father.

I connected this to her identical rage at her self-protective, boyfriend. She agreed and made the diagnosis herself. She framed the mechanism of her depression by telling us, "I become self-destructive, when I get very angry (at self-centered abandoning men), be it losing drastic amounts of weight ... or just involving myself in things that are bad for me ..."

Sally's statements complete the dynamic formulation and summarize the story of the spoken words. However, our mutual paraverbal messaging: her tone of voice, the prosody and punctuation of her delivery, my matching speech rhythm and tone with her and the reciprocal changes in body language, and posture of the two of us, all deepen our grasp of what has just unfolded. The extra-verbal details make our exchange come alive.

In our first ten-minute segment, Sally revealed something of her intimate life, with the sometime boyfriend, and then she told the story of an immediate pregnancy and miscarriage, but her usually monotonic delivery, often interrupted eye contact, clipped businesslike tone kept me at a safe distance. When I clarified and emphasized, "He really let you down!," Sally's body started upright, and she nodded vigorously.

Three minutes later, I mildly confronted her by suggesting that when she joshed that her depression began eight years ago instead of two months ago, it seemed "not entirely a joke." She again sat up straight, paused, looked at her hands in her lap and started the heart breaking vignette of her mother's death and her father's desertion, the key sequence in the interview.

In slow, strong, deliberate emotional tones, she let it all out. She went inside herself. How betrayed she felt by her father on that fateful night of her mother's passing, which changed so much for her. She lost both her mother and her father on the same evening. Psychologically she became an orphan that night. She later responded in clear agreement when I suggested that her boyfriend had let her down in the same way, as had her father, and that this present desertion precipitated her depression. It seems likely that she became depressed in a similar fashion after the devastating talk (or non-talk) with her father. "He just sent me to bed!"

At several turning points, I support her to tell me more important facts: How did her father act the day her mother died? Could she ask for his help? She could tell from my tone and bodily message that I really wanted to know, and she actively let me into her affective life. The implicit relationship that we constructed became the platform for our later important exchanges.

Alternative strategies

By now the reader has, no doubt, thought of other ways to approach Sally and her story. The perhaps ambivalent identification with her mother marks a promising pathway. Sally's mom did not stand up to the father and his self-centeredness apparently, and Sally has had trouble finding her own independent identity away from manipulative men.

On the other hand, an Affect Focused therapist Kristin Osborn or Leigh McCullough, for example, might already have halted the interview and actively concentrated on Sally's anger exclusively, clearly Sally's major dynamic issue. Either choice could have worked well. I followed my preconscious images—I spontaneously visualized Sally exploited by her father and furious at his self-involved actions. This paraverbal introspective method is the one I use to guide me, but this does not render it the preferred approach on all occasions or for every therapist.

Mutual regulation

Sally and I worked together as a pair—on our mutual and self-regulation. We quickly began to settle down, though each with our own self-protective, self-soothing mannerisms. Sally looking down at her clasped hands in her lap, I scratching on my pad and wiping my glasses.

Sally slowly, and often jocularly, relays her experiences. I smile at her and sometimes join her with a chuckle. She's a woman on guard, after her many desertions, but my gentle tone, my grunts of recognition, my matching of her head nods and speech rhythm, my smile, and my attentive body posture, as well as the content of my interventions probably reassures her.

She resolves to tell me the whole story. Our dance steps unfold: She will slowly reveal more about herself. I will support her with short emphatic phrases, "You must have been very worried!." She then tells more, goes deeper inside. As the momentum shifts toward self-disclosure, I push her hard, and she willingly responds. Jim: "Mike did what your father did" … Sally: "I guess I never really connected them, but they are similar. I guess they are the same." Jim: "I strongly do connect them!" (Jim waves fist.)

She tolerates and uses the breakthrough. She then finishes the interview by telling us both that she has found another self-involved irresponsible man, this time at her office, to whom she's attracted and who will predictably break her heart one more time. I've learned to follow her lead, wait for her to divulge her next deeper, more personal, thought, and then move her even harder at the end to keep up the momentum. This rhythm represents the beginning of the experience of implicit relational knowing between us. We've found a way to work, to cooperate, and to regulate each other.

The Scoring profiles: The ATOS

To gather more quantitative evidence about the trajectory of the interview Jim, Kristin and Susan scored all the tapes using the ATOS introduced in Chapter 3. Because Jim participated in this interview, we dropped his numbers and used Kristin's and Susan's only. According to our measures, Sally showed great advances from Segment #1 to Segment #2 in the following categories: Insight, Motivation, Arousal, a new view of Self, and a decrease in Inhibition of 20 points, all of which predict success in short-term psychotherapy (see Bhatia et al., 2009).

Jim's scores on the companion therapist measure, the ATOS Therapist, likewise dramatically increased from Segment #1 to Segment #2: Insight, Motivation, Arousal surpassing level 50 by the end of the interview. The participants were evidently moving in a coordinated, more and more affective direction—an indication of positive progress.

Accessibility and Congruence Measures: Segment #2

Likewise, the Accessibility and Congruence ratings for both Jim and Sally reach much higher levels in the closing segment. Sally's Accessibility score moves from 3.7 to 6.0 and her Congruence score from 4.2 to 5.7. On the seven-point scale, these numbers for the closing section of the meeting, indicate a shift toward significant openness and affective transparency. (We, as yet, do not have sufficient samples to establish the psychometrics of the scale, but this direction in the hard numbers from Segment #1 to Segment #2 seems clear.)

Jim's Openness and Congruence Scores also increase from Segment #1 to Segment #2. Accessibility moves from 4.7 to 6.2; and Congruence elevates from 5.2 to 6.2. He expresses strong feeling toward Sally and her story, and his intense, sympathetic tone of voice and empathic body language demonstrate that he really means what he says. Sally has apparently brought out the best this therapist has to give. His openness, authenticity, empathy and encouragement for Sally to express and hold deep adaptive feelings, without fear or shame, move toward the top of both scales. In Schwartz's terms, he's unconflicted and "self-led" in Segment #2. Both the client and the therapist have changed here.

Counter-transference and transference themes

Unconsciously Sally probably reminded me of my daughter and her friends: quick, funny, intense, snappy and just finding their way in the world. I'm not sure how Sally experienced me, of course, but I certainly felt protective toward this petite young woman, huddled next to me, telling a story of unjust desertion. I felt like putting my arm around her and warding off the bad things and the bad people.

If the therapy continued, my need to help and to guide her, a much younger person, and her need to feel respected and taken seriously, by an older man, probably would have framed the transference. I had few sexual feelings for her. I admired her spirit and her bravery to soldier on with so little support. I felt her a bright, insightful person, a good companion with altruistic values and a strong sense of humor—all of these counter-transference feelings would come in to play, if the therapy proceeded.

Control Mastery Theory

Sally's Test: Does this man, Jim the therapist, care about her valid relational needs and her mission to stand up for herself against important males, or will I abandon her also? This represents Sally's Negative Hypothesis; "I'm worthless; I'll be exploited." Maybe if I didn't pursue her earlier losses, it would have proved to her that I didn't really care about the whole history of her pain, but I did strongly want to know about these people lost to Sally—the mother who died and the father who turned away.

Assured that I did care about what had gone on, in present time and before, and supported by my tone and body language, Sally lets me pass the test. Like her brother, Jack, I'm a man worthy of at least some trust. She will confide. Sally then lifts her businesslike rather flat, clipped tone, makes more eye contact and lets us both experience how much she has suffered from her mother's loss and her father's lack of concern.

Through the interview she learned more about controlling her depression and self-hate and mastering and focusing her anger. Sally watches me to gauge whether I will disrespect and ignore her, (her negative hypothesis) or show her that she has a right to her angry feelings and support her to express them. After I prove different from her unconcerned father, she tells me the real story, from age 13 on, with plenty of feeling. Our interaction disproves the negative hypothesis. She's not dismissible—the judges arrived at a control mastery score of 7/7.

The Core of the Interview

Sally initially presents herself as depressed and somewhat bewildered, but she transmits enough strength toward Jim to allow him to identify with it and project a more powerful Sally back to her. "You hated him" (You're not weak; you can stand up for yourself against self-serving intimates!). By the last few minutes of the meeting a new object, strong Sally, begins to appear. She takes a different direction psychologically.

Any psychotherapy student, younger or veteran, probably has noticed that Stern and Beebe's" central argument seems substantiated by this video. A paraverbal choreography of implicit relational knowing grows in tandem with the conscious verbal interaction of the pair. A pattern of increasing implicit fittedness and mutual regulation takes form in the meeting.

We see two worlds unfold together. In one Jim and Sally come to a heartfelt, understanding, in words, of what has befallen her, complete with insights into how unconscious conflicted anger leads her toward depression. However, simultaneously entwined with this new knowledge, we nudge closer to one another in prosody, language, body position and particularly in eye contact. There's plenty of evidence of Unconscious World I, without words, interaction here. We both have a developing affective meeting of closeness, which leads to an inside change. Sally feels recognized. She sounds stronger by the close of the meeting. Stern's idea about implicit relational connectedness gradually introducing growth appears validated.

When these two universes meet, the new verbalizable knowledge and the implicit relational connection, the "now moment" comes upon us. We both unmistakably, personally, realised the depth of Sally's exploitation and how deeply she hated her father and other men who have taken advantage of her. We shared this breakthrough insight in words and not in words—our "moment of meeting." The implicit relationship supported us to move closer together and to share the intense feeling that led the interview toward its power. Jim—"You hated him" Sally—overlaps "I hated him!" Or later on, Sally—"They are the same!" When the paraverbal signs deepen the words and the affect something therapeutic is likely afoot (see Wachtel, 2011, p. 121).

The counselor must not forget the continual stream of the nonverbal engagement. It happens whether he overlooks it or not. We can only pay attention to one of the two universes at a time, but it looks as if the therapist needs to check back with his body to make regular readings in the paraverbal space and to pick up the images just emerging from his preconscious.

He or she asks herself such questions as: How close do I feel? Is the client moving toward me? Am I deeply moved by something she said, or do I feel a distance in my body? Where is the implicit relational knowing thread heading now? What pictures appear in my mind as she talks? Do these reveal new ideas to me, beyond this verbal conscious dialogue in which we're engaging?

Sally and I could make this connection. The moment of meeting when Jim and Sally both realized how deeply she disrespected her father, contains new concrete facts. It's marked, though, most of all by the paraverbal signs that we exchanged—mutual outrage, togetherness, and surprise at how well we understood each other. Without this extra-verbal "click," the hour would feel more flat and intellectualized. Ignore the bodily and voice tone messages and you lose much of the therapeutic life. These body signals provoke reciprocal images in patient and therapist which direct the path of the minute by minute treatment. This is perhaps how psychotherapy works.

We've begun to notice that the first dominant paraverbal impression often frames, at least the rest of the hour, if not the rest of the therapy. My initial extra-verbal reaction to Sally suggested that she might take a deferential accommodative stance to a man. Although we learn quickly that she has many strengths as well, the theme of the meeting revolves around the fact that she has become exploited by her father, her boyfriend Mike and now she's about to start a relationship with a narcissistic man at her office. Her paraverbal message of apparent vulnerability offers a strong clue to the later central issues in this session and probably would in subsequent meetings.

Anticipating Paul Wachtel's presentation next, we might start to wonder what "cast off" part of Sally's character could become an important focus. We've learned that she "puts aside" "loveable strong Sally" to seek interactions with self-centered men in which their needs always come first. This "missing strong piece," plays an important role throughout Sally's narrative today and, no doubt would, in any more extensive treatment.

POST SCRIPT

I found Sally a tough, inspiring, young woman and a pleasure to connect with. I wish I could have seen her again and started a therapy with her, but her insurance changed and she had to leave our clinic panel.

I also wish I had more aggressively pursued her right after our interview to help her get settled in another setting. Ultimately, after I finally realized she had left our organization, I found her phone number and called her two years later for a follow-up to our interview. She recalled our meeting very clearly. She lived locally and told me that she had functioned fairly well in the hiatus, had no repeated depression, worked full time, but did not seem to have a steady romantic partner and had not sought more psychotherapy. Sally is 48 now. I would dearly like to know what has become of her in the intervening years, and I'm trying to locate her now, without success so far.

In Chapter 6, involving a different patient, a different therapist with a different plan of action, will we find a similar implicit paraverbal coupling? Our first example here in Chapter 5, feels interesting and supports our hypothesis, and Sterns," of the centrality of "implicit relational knowing." One case does not provide sufficient evidence, but here in our work with Sally we do observe a nonverbal platform underlying a successful psychotherapy interchange. In Chapter 6, we'll learn more about the range of extra-verbal communication, in a meeting between two new participants.

Chapter Six

Integrative Relational Psychotherapy

Louise Tries to Find a "Place in this World"

Paul Wachtel, PhD

We negotiated with Dr. Paul Wachtel for permission to include an analysis of his tape with Louise (Wachtel, 2011) because Dr. Wachtel's video, reproduced in his book *Inside the Session*, seemed to illustrate a number of the themes that we're trying to explore in our own work, although he begins from a different starting point. Dr. W agreed to include his tape in the project, and likewise we received permission from the American Psychological Association to quote several pages from that meeting.

PAUL'S GRASP OF PSYCHOTHERAPY

We'll summarize Paul's theory of therapeutic action, in as close to his own words as possible, and then begin to examine a verbatim example of his work, with a young woman, Louise. We encourage readers to view this video themselves—(American Psychological Association, Series 1. Systems of Psychotherapy 2007—www.apa.org/videos/series1.html) and to read his book cited above.

In the pre-interview discussion with the series host, Jon Carlson, EdD., PsyD, Dr. Wachtel briefly describes his sense of Integrative Relational Psychotherapy. We'll précis that discussion. Paul, trained as a psychoanalyst originally, but began his theoretical work by attempting the seemingly unlikely integration of behavior therapy with psychoanalysis (Wachtel, 1977).

Paul feels that psychoanalysis and behavior therapy, although very different on the surface (What are the origins of neurotic difficulty? What is the technique to alter those difficulties?), both offer us valuable views of human behavior. Psychoanalysis studies conflicted thoughts and feelings and behavior therapy—problematic actions toward which those inner conflicts propel us.

In his theory, Paul notes first that behavior therapy uses "exposure" as its cornerstone. Many dynamic approaches, as well, employ exposure to the sources of anxiety—usually conflicted feelings and inclinations—as a central technique, although they call it something else, like "working through." Exposure lies at the center of Paul's theory of therapy. It's exposure to the feelings arises from inner conflict upon which Paul focuses, as we'll see in a minute. Leigh McCullough and Kristin Osborn likewise use exposure as the central mechanism of their Affect Phobia Therapy—see Chapter 3 of this book.

Second, the concept of "vicious circles" represents another building block of Dr. W's theory and technique (Wachtel, 1993, this videotape 2007, 2008, 2011). Our assumptions about our interpersonal relationships, that is, "I'm no good; I'll be rejected," lead us to behave toward others in ways that influence them to respond back toward us in a self-fulfilling manner. "I act obsequiously toward the other, and he or she does dismiss me as a nonentity, just as I had always feared."

Dr. W feels that these original negative preconceptions start to form very early, often in the relationship with parents. These circular patterns conform to learning theory principles, for example, continued encounters with negative stimuli lead the subject to withdraw in discouragement. We just stop trying. To our ears, this central idea of "vicious circles" sounds akin to the "negative hypothesis" formulated by Sampson and Weiss, described in Chapter 2. We'll find out more about these repetitive self-defeating patterns, as we read further in this commentary and watch excerpts from the tape.

The circumstances surrounding the Wachtel video offer us a unique opportunity for further exploration because Dr. W has published a book, cited above, which offers us the verbatim record on the interview with Louise. We can gain an unusual perspective by reading Dr. W's direct comments on his meeting, as we watch the tape. We cite multiple references to the 2011 book, when we describe our own, line-by-line observations of excerpts from that interview.

As Paul concludes his 2011 monograph, he offers us a clear précis of his therapeutic approach, constructed during 40 years" experience integrating the psychodynamic, the behavioral and the experiential schools.

Dr. W enunciates his four principles of action:

> Central to the therapeutic approach illustrated in these transcripts is a set of ideas and procedures that intersect and overlap substantially enough that they are not fully separable but rather constitute different takes or perspectives on

a single process viewed from different angles. These different complementary takes include:

a) Attending to the anxiety, guilt or shame that have led the person to defend against, or cast aside, certain thoughts, feelings, wishes and experiences of self and other, rather than viewing these defensive efforts primarily from the vantage point of resistance or evasion.

b) Helping the patient to overcome that anxiety, often through methods that combine the behavioral concept of exposure with empathic identification and articulation of the rejected self-experiences (overlapping considerably with what is often referred to as interpretation, but approached in a different spirit);

c) Affirmation and validation of the experiences that the patient has felt were unacceptable and;

d) Enabling the person to make room for and reappropriate feelings that have been cast out or cast aside as dangerous or objectionable. In what follows, I use these ways of viewing the therapeutic process extensively in discussing the sessions and what transpired, but the reader should bear in mind that these are not four separate conceptualizations but alternative, and largely overlapping, ways of talking about the same process and much the same attitude. (Wachtel, 2011, p. 235)

We'll return consistently through the chapter to this interesting summary of Paul's orientation to therapy, which he has just offered us.

Dr. W encourages us to become didactic when necessary, to build on the patient's strengths (p. 244) and to offer "attributional" statements, underscoring what the patient already knows or has already done well. He points out that the working alliance provides a laboratory of a constructive empowering relationship for the client and also acts as a catalyst for the growth-promoting experiences of therapy: facing one's self, experimenting with new behaviors and so on (p. 247). All these objectives have the ring of exposing the patient, little by little, to the sources of his or her anxiety, but also encouraging and accepting the client and not blaming him or her in any way.

Paul strongly argues that change in the therapy office does not ipso facto translate into changes in daily life. The therapist and the treatment must encourage the second just as strongly as the first. "For many therapists, if we promote insight or bring about modifications in the patients "inner world", behavioral change will follow in due course. I'm skeptical that this happens very often" (p. 252).

He explains that he does focus on the here and now relationship with the client, though not in every session, and he does self-disclose events from his personal life from time to time. He acknowledges that on this illustrative tape, which we'll study here, he does not follow either course because the meeting doesn't represent an ongoing therapy, and he will not meet the client again in the future (pp. 255–257).

Wachtel's theory of therapy, of course, drastically summarized here, feels disarmingly simple, but we find his grasp of the field deep and profound. He has mastered the theoretical landscape, from behavior therapy to psychoanalysis, and his suggestions for unraveling the "vicious circle," and for helping to reappropriate "cast-out parts" of the self, seem clinically solid and well put.

It follows that if facing the sources of anxiety and accepting devalued aspects of the personality represent the center of the treatment, then an open and supportive verbal, and paraverbal, therapeutic atmosphere must accompany that treatment for it to gain maximum effectiveness. We'll see how Paul establishes this therapeutic context.

PAUL AND LOUISE—THE TAPE

Setting the scene

This 45-minute video of professional quality shows many facial close-ups and presents us with Paul Wachtel, probably in his late 1960s on the left. Louise, a blond Caucasian woman, whom we later learn grew up in Sweden, age 27, is seated across from him on the right.

How does the pair appear together? As a study in contrast—a slight man, Paul dresses in a simple blue blazer, button down blue shirt, and tie. His gentle voice rarely rises or drops in amplitude. Several features, however, dispel Dr. W's unremarkable self-presentation. He's very active verbally but not necessarily with fully spoken language. He regularly mutters: "uh huh, uh huh," or "yup, yup," or "oh yes, I see yes, yes." The patient can have little doubt that Paul listens to her word by word.

Dr. W, in his 2011 book, explains at length the function of his "uh huh, uh huh" response to Louise.

As I read through this portion of the transcript, I see that at this point I am doing a lot of acknowledging and affirming of Louise's experience ("uh huh," "yeah") in the midst of her articulating what she has to say. (At this point she's discussing friendships with peers.) I think I was sensing the intensity of Louise's feeling here, along with her feeling of *vulnerability* regarding how safe or acceptable it was for her to be expressing these feelings, and as a consequence, I was *implicitly* lending my support to her struggle with these issues (emphasis ours). Therapists are rarely aware consciously of saying "uh huh" or some variant to a greater degree at some points in the session than in others. More often we are aware of some shift in the intensity of our listening and our engaging, perhaps of *leaning forward* in the chair or *making eye contact* in a more intense way that says, "I am with you on this. I hear what you are saying." Such *noninterpretive interventions* are a bigger part of what contributes to the success of the therapeutic effort than was appreciated until recently (all italics ours; Lyons-Ruth, 1998; D. N. Stern et al., 1998; Wachtel, 2011, p. 161). (In this one sentence, Paul comes close to anticipating the focus of our book.)

We can add that we'll soon see that Dr. W interjects his "uh huh," or "yup," almost ceaselessly as he speaks throughout the tape, not just at specific points of intensity. He's connecting in an unmistakable, noninterpretive way without full words or sentences. Moreover, Dr. W's hand movements accent his many verbal punctuations. He gestures regularly with his hands and arms as he speaks—often beginning with his hands wide apart and then bringing them close by, as if to capture the two sides of a conflict and then to show the synthesis of that conflict as his hands slowly approach each other.

Paul's facial expression changes little, but he usually projects an understanding, benevolent, slight grin. His eyes twinkle and crinkle at the corners, indicating that this man has offered many Duchênne smiles in his time. Dr. Wachtel's countenance, like his dress, and his interpersonal style seem quiet and composed but warm, benign, respectful and inviting.

The patient Louise, attired informally in light grey sweater and black slacks, is an attractive, blonde, young woman with mid-length hair parted in the middle and drawn back, and creamy Scandinavian skin, but she projects a restrained facial expression. Louise, communicates in her second language of course, though she speaks with little discernible accent. Her monotonic voice and her almost motionless face and body, initially leave us few clues concerning what deeper feelings she might have about the difficult and sometimes traumatic events that she'll soon describe.

Clearly, if Louise's countenance changes at all in the interview, this shift might carry great import about her inner state at that minute. In fact, Louise warmly smiles four times in the meeting. We think each represents a "tell," a moment of breakthrough, into her true self, a self that she's willing, for an instant, to share with Paul and with the viewer, but for no longer, until the final minutes of the meeting.

We'll give the reader a summary of the first 34 minutes of the interview and then intensively discuss and score the final ten-minute segment of the session.

LOUISE: THE FIRST 15 MINUTES—A PRÉCIS

In her characteristic style, Louise responds to Paul's opening question, about what brings her to the consultation, with a matter-of-fact description of her struggles with her in-laws, to whom she has not spoken in the previous 5½ months.

Eight months before the interview, Louise's father died of cancer in
Sweden. Louise traveled home to Scandinavia for the memorial service and
to comfort her mother. She then invited her mother back to the United States
for a month, from Thanksgiving to Christmas.

She felt her in-laws, who live locally, ignored her loss with few comfort-
ing cards or phone calls. To exacerbate this apparent callousness, her sister-
in-law and mother-in-law arrived unannounced at her house during this
Thanksgiving to Christmas mourning period and confronted her about her
lack of attendance at family events in the previous two years. The in-laws did
not know this, but Louise's mother was still staying in the house when these
emissaries arrived.

One of the striking aspects of Louise's whole story appears that few live
males inhabit it. We discover later that Louise's father lived as a profoundly
ill man and died prematurely just as our narrative begins. Louise, an only
child, makes no mention of brothers-in-law or uncles—and her father-in-law
passed away some seven or eight years previously.

She describes her husband, Ken, as her supporter and as a peace keeper. She
usually speaks of him in friendly and appreciative, but not three-dimensional
terms. (Ken is twelve years older than Louise, it turns out, though this draws
no mention on this tape.) Almost all the action takes place between Louise,
her mother, her sister-in-law, and her mother-in-law.

The sister-in-law, in particular, chided her for her lack of family participation, in what to the observer, seem insensitive words delivered at an unfor-
tunate time. Louise understandably felt "violated and hurt" and "so hurt that
I felt like running through the streets screaming. No one cares that my father
died."

Louise feels her husband was caught between her and his family. Showing
considerable maturity, she wants to mend the breach with them in case she
and Ken later have children. At the time of the interview there appears just
the beginning of an inter-familial détente. Her mother-in-law has contacted
Louise about the difficulties, and some discussion of the family conflicts may
soon start.

Louise clearly wants support and instruction from Dr. W, and from her own
personal therapist, about how to proceed with the in-laws. This represents
her presenting complaint. She experiences her original family as one with
great distance, at least from outsiders, and her husband's as one with "no
boundaries." She senses her older sister-in-law, Denise, as the family leader
who calls the tune. Again male voices seem almost never heard. It isn't even
clear if Denise has a husband. Wachtel clarifies, "You have a different vision
of what family is (than they do). You want to talk about it and say who I am,
and what I'm like."

MINUTES 15 TO 24—A FURTHER SUMMARY

Here Louise continues to describe her feelings about her sister-in-law, "But she's just such a bully. She just reminds me of those people when I was little that hurt me and she just stirs up all these childhood things within me."

Paul with one of his characteristic physical moves beckons Louise toward him with his right hand as if to say let's talk, "Tell me a little more about these experiences as a child when you were bullied."

In the next several lines, Louise recalls the female peers who bullied her as a child and now the in-laws seem to do likewise. However, as the discussion moves on, it turns out that Louise has close friends too. "I have a handful of friends that are really good friends, now." ...

Paul: Right, you actually have achieved what you hoped for.

Louise: Yes, now yeah. (flickering but genuine congruent grin—her first smile).

At this point, Paul observes the following:

The video reveals that Louise broke into a glowing smile at this point. It was an important therapeutic moment, in the sense that it evoked in her, and on an affective level, a sense of herself that was different from the way she usually sees herself and that it contained a sense of possibility that also felt new. This sequence is also an example of the value of the therapist's being as attentive to positive developments and positive ways of seeing the patient and her life as to pathology.

Therapeutic moments of the sort occurring here are unlikely to be Hollywood-style moments of a single, life-changing event. They are incremental and cumulative, and almost always must be multiple, not singular. Nevertheless, they each have real significance. The therapeutic experience occurring here differs in a number of important ways from the "moments of meeting" described by the Boston Change Process Study Group (Lyons-Ruth, 1998; D. N. Stern, 2004; D. N. Stern et al., 1998) but it has in common with their conception a focus on change brought about through the evocation of an affective experience that alters the patient's internal process rather than change being brought about primarily through insight. (Wachtel, 2011, p. 90)

Paul presages the theme of our book once more.

Louise continues to talk about not trusting that her friends would stay with her. Perhaps she's disposable. She then introduces the idea that she's "sensitive." After a brief discussion of this topic, Paul responds "Right, I mean being sensitive isn't a war crime." (This represents a prototypical brief, very supportive, very precise, Wachtel intervention. It promises to lead to an affective self-realization.)

Louise then returns to describe the conflicts with her husband's family and observes that she does feel "solidly connected" with her husband, but she's afraid that he will "cut his family completely out of his life" because she and the in-laws have such conflict. He then will resent her. They apparently have "big fights" each time they go to see his family. She continues by saying that she's trying to compromise.

A précis of what we have read thus far:

We've now reached minute 24, the middle of the interview. Louise still seems somewhat defended during this episode and communicates relatively little through her voice and body movements with the exception of the moment when Paul observes that she has already gained a circle of good friends; and Louise joyfully agrees. In addition, she offers an adult wish to repair the conflicts with the in-laws so that Ken will not lose his family.

Paul interacts with Louise, with acute attentiveness, but also calmness. His regular "Uh huh, huh" and responsive hand gestures communicate that he's with her nearly word for word; but he's in no hurry.

We've had one possible breakthrough around the close friends issue, but for the most part, we have only possible clues about the sources of Louise's deeper conflicts. The second half of the interview may bring important new self-knowledge or maybe not. At this point, the ultimate success of this meeting remains in doubt.

SEGMENT #3: MINUTES 25 TO 34—A SUMMARY

We'll discover whether Paul's active, supportive, verbal, and paraverbal, interventions so far, will lead Louise toward more openness and new learning in the next ten minutes of the interview and then again in the final segment.

Louise now begins to introduce the topic of her wedding, which took place in the mid-west and to which no guests were invited. Her husband's family understandably felt left out and put out. We observe a new important theme emerge. Will Louise stand up for herself?

She explains that her mother could not come to the wedding because of her father's terminal illness, so she didn't want to include the in-laws either, but she continues that she wanted her wedding day just with Ken and herself. She adds that she had planned to have a second ceremony with the two families at a later date, but apparently she never communicated this to Ken's people.

Paul: (hands out to the side) Uh huh, uh huh. So this was a special time for you and it was a time that meant so much you wanted it to be for you and not to make other people happy. (slow gentle tone, slow prosody)

Louise: Uh huh

Paul: (slowly, carefully finding the right words) That sort of, the importance of being able to take a stand that this is for me, this is not to make other people happy, that sounds like there must have been pulls in your life to make other people happy, that made you finally ... (Dr. W has spotted an important "vicious circle," here. What appears like oppositional behavior on Louise's part, may represent a reaction to earlier times when she had to give in on every issue to her family. "Take a stand" represents a brief, supportive, accurate defining Wachtel intervention delivered in his open tone and his gentle manner. Here, Paul "validates" an important step of Louise reappropriating a formerly rejected part.)

Louise: Oh, I'm a huge people-pleaser.

Louise then offers an extended passage describing how she had given in to her in-laws.

Paul: (Hands to either side at shoulder level—slow supportive tone, direct eye contact) ... where your mom and dad, where you were a people-pleaser with them too? (Paul gently, neutrally suggests the possibility that Louise stands up to her in-laws so strongly because she gave in to her mother so often. He has spotted a major part of Louise's core conflict, a part that she has "cast-out," and she realises it immediately.)

Louise: Absolutely, yeah.

Paul: Tell me about that, and how that happened (pp. 103–105).
(Having found a man she can trust, Louise begins to confide her whole tragic story. She will go inside.) When she was eight her father had a near fatal stroke. He partially recovered but could never again read, write or speak. He lived as a half person in need of constant vigilance. He and Louise seemed like brother and sister and he the younger sibling. The mother, under nearly intolerable stress, forbade Louise to speak of these troubles outside the family.

At one point, under this great strain, the mother, without a word, abandoned Louise, then age 14, and the father, in France and returned to Sweden incommunicado for two weeks. The father had a medical crisis, an unstaunchable nose bleed, and Louise desperately sought medical care for him in a country where she did not speak the language—remember the father can't speak at all.

The mother returned but Louise never mentioned the incident until ten years later. She did not "take a stand."

Paul: And so when you were feeling this is gonna, about the wedding say, this is gonna be one of the first times in my life where I'm not taking care of everybody else, where I'm really able to just say, "I've got a place in this world, too." (p.108; This is delivered with volume and force, a signature Wachtel intervention, precisely summarizing Louise's dilemma. This is an attribution. Paul explains ...)

In stating out loud for her "*I've got a place in this world too*" I was helping her to give voice to an experience in a way that facilitates both her self-understanding and her ability to represent herself more effectively with Ken's family. This giving voice to the patient's experience, articulating what we have heard the patient say but doing so in a stronger or clearer way, is one of the most useful things we do as therapists. ... Because I'm presenting what I'm saying as simply a restatement of what I'd heard *her* say, it can still feel like hers, even though it was put in words that she has never quite used. This is an aspect of what I've called the *attributional* dimension of therapeutic work ... thus, the aim of these comments, is at least twofold—to help Louise better understand her own motives and experience and to help her find a way to communicate with Ken's family about what had happened. (Wachtel, 2011, p. 109, all italics by Wachtel)

Louise: Uh huh.

END OF SEGMENT #3

Commentary on Segment #3

This section represents a key one in understanding Louise. She and Paul have just encountered Louise's traumatic background in excruciating detail. Louise at age 8 experienced her 48-year-old father suffering a debilitating stroke from which he only partially recovered. He learned to walk again but not to read, write or speak, not to communicate. Evidently he suffered severe and irreversible right temporal parietal damage. Certainly he never worked again. As Louise suggested, he felt more like a brother, really a younger brother, than a father. Louise's mother became the omnipotent authority, and the only potential source of nurturance. She refused to allow Louise to speak of any of this horrible trouble outside the family.

We can picture Louise's lonely, mistrustful, vigilant childhood without even siblings to share her tragedy. We imagine the mother, a tough, counter-dependent woman trying to hang on to herself and to her daughter under nearly unbearable conditions.

At least once, Louise's mother evidently collapsed under the stress of her unimaginable responsibilities. Presumably in anger and despair, she abandoned Louise and her father in a foreign city to return home to Sweden, leaving her husband and daughter stranded with no means of immediate communication whatever. As chance would have it, Louise's father developed a serious medical problem, the dangerous nose bleed, which sounds suspiciously like a second stroke.

More tragedy averted, the mother returns but apparently does not apologize to Louise or bring up her two-week absence. She leaves it to Louise to do so, some ten years after the fact. The father, a man with no luck at all, then develops terminal cancer some five or six years before the interview, when Louise is about 22. He cannot attend her wedding and dies eight months before this videotaped meeting.

Because of technical breakdowns in the recording equipment, Paul and Louise completed a second re-taped interview. In that session, we learn that Louise's mother had decided to divorce the father, the *day* before he had the stroke so that now she had become doubly imprisoned! We also learn that the mother, on a number of occasions, became overwhelmed and seriously dysfunctional so that Louise had to take over, give her mother a shower, calm her down, become the parentified child. The mother represents a considerably more compromised and more controlling person than Louise is telling us at this first go through.

Louise's Accessibility and Congruence Scores—Segment #3

Louise does not project intensity, vivacity, or playfulness. She has not had a very playful life after all. The viewer and listener do not conclude, however, that she consciously holds back feelings. Affect really doesn't seem to register very strongly consciously inside her at this point, even though she readily recalls the horrific events of her deprived childhood.

The judges scored her 3.0 in Accessibility and 4.0 in Congruence here. However, we're getting the sense of a more intense Louise beginning to emerge from her more expressionless covered-up self. We can tell by her tone and content that she's trusting Paul more. Except for her husband Ken, who is in fact an older man, she has had little contact with a fatherly figure who could give her good advice. Here she begins to accept Paul as that person. In the closing section of the interview, she may dare to come forth even more, or maybe not, perhaps here at the end of segment #3 is as personal as she can get.

SEGMENT #4: MINUTES 36 TO 46

We quote this final segment verbatim (Wachtel, 2011, pp. 99–120, reprinted with the permission of the American Psychological Association).

Paul: Uh huh. Uh huh.

Louise: So when I'm trying to be my own person and stand up for myself it's like, "What are you doing? What do you think you're doing?"

Paul: Uh huh. So you tried to explain to them.

Louise: Yes. And during the confrontation I "tried to explain" (matches Paul's words) to her. She (her sister-in-law), she, you know, she apologized about

Easter when I was telling her. She's like, "Well, you know, I'm sure you took an hour to eat." I'm like, you know, "I was eating while I was doing my exam. I'm sorry. I don't really think I should have to sit here 2 years later and explain this to you." But apparently I did. So …

Paul: (smiles, right hand circling) You know, one odd thing that occurs to me is that in some way Ken's family lives the way you lived growing up. (slow prosody) (This represents Paul's key intervention linking her family and Ken's family. Louise could never say "No" to her mother either—She and Paul seem to grasp this connection—this "vicious circle" immediately, although it's harder for the viewer or the reader to see it quite yet.)

Louise: (smiles—much more lively) Oh yeah.

Paul: You know?

Louise: Yeah.

Paul: You know what I mean?

Louise: Yeah, I never thought about that. That's a great way of putting it, because that helps me be more sympa, empathetic to them, actually. That's a good observation. (For the moment, at least, Louise shows us a remarkable change in energy, in attitude, in prosody and in animation—an affective change has taken place within. She also expresses some authentic charity toward her in-laws.)

Paul: Yeah, they really seem caught in the same … (hands together)

Louise: Yeah [overlapping—Louise still affirming and responding to what I am saying] (brackets represents Paul's commentary)

Paul: … thing. There's no time to really even have any time to think about "what do I want to do?" (Colloquial tone)

Louise: Uh huh.

Paul: It's what should I do? (Paul's gathering intensity)

Louise: Uh huh.

Paul: How do I …

Louise: "Exactly.

Paul: Yeah.

Louise: It's always you should, you should, you should.

Paul: Right, yeah.

Louise: Family, family, family. (They're making an exciting discovery together now mirrored by their stronger voice tones and rapid overlapping responses.)

Paul: Yeah, right. (Paul offers a series of affirmations of Louise's position, accompanied by hand gestures.)

Louise: And it's like when you married Ken you married the family.

Paul: Right.

Louise: And that is so foreign to me. So foreign to me.

Paul: It's so foreign to you and at the same time it's so central to you. (striking powerful inflection)

Louise: Right, yeah.

Paul: You know what I mean?

Louise: Yeah. "Cause I'm caught in the middle of it.

Paul: Yeah, yeah. And were all through growing up in a way.

Louise: Uh huh.

Paul: I mean you couldn't be, I would even wonder whether some of the difficulty you had with the other kids growing up was because there was some way almost in which you *weren't supposed to* make those connections outside, because you had these duties in the family to this very wounded ...

Louise: Yeah. [stated very affirmatively, as a spontaneous expression in the midst of my sentence]

Paul: ... family.

Louise: I'm thinking, because when you said that, when you said even though that's so foreign to you, that's still always been central. I never, you're right because I always, I was always told to be loyal to the family, and never talk to anybody about my problems. And now I'm like telling everybody. You know, in classes and stuff I'm always sharing and I'm always very open. Because it's like, screw you, I'm just gonna tell everybody, because you told me my whole life I should never open up. (With Paul's support, Louise exuberantly tells us she's stepping out into real change ... Did she emigrate to the U.S. to join a freer more outspoken society?)

Paul: Right, right. So you've ... (gestures toward her)

Louise: So, Wow! [strong affect]

Paul: ... broken out of that. . (gentle understanding tone, hands drawn in to chest as if to emphasize Louise's feelings about herself)

Louise: Yeah, I have, [laugh of almost glee, excitement] (Louise is very involved paraverbally. She's authentically delving into certain ideas and feelings, for the first time, with Paul's support.)

Paul: And they almost like represent what you, what the, the trap you were in for so many years. (empathic tone, slow serious prosody)

Louise: Yeah.

Paul: Sort of like they're *so* familiar. (animated tone)

Louise: Wow, I never thought about it that way, (Facial expression changes, recognition on her face, a really helpful reframe, much more lively now, but she still rarely moves her body.) it makes it easier for me to understand why I'm so, you know, it totally makes more sense to me now. "Cause that's what I've been trying, but maybe it's, "cause they always, I don't know if it's the same, but I always hear that, you know, if you haven't dealt with something it keeps coming back in your life. And I guess I never dealt with that, and that's why unfortunately I have this family to deal with. But if, yeah, I need to face it. I just don't know ... again, it's just working on how.

Paul: (slow, gentle, reasoning tone) Yeah. Well let's think together about how. What would you, how would you *like* to approach them? What would you *like* to say to them? If you, if you had a little room for them to listen, and I know that's not easy, and we can't assume that. But what would you like to say to them? (Reaching toward Louise with his right hand with an open palm as if to communicate "tell us more." This represents an example of Paul helping the client to "consider what she would like to do" in other words, to rehearse acting differently outside the office.) Wachtel, 2011, p. 116

Louise: (aggressive tone) Well, first of all I'd like them to return my phone calls. [smiles]

Paul: Right. That's ...

Louise: I want them to just respect me for who I am.

Paul: Uh huh. (Paul's repeated "uh huh uh huh" makes her feel heard and tells her that he's with her.)

Louise: When I, not just tell me, what to do, but also do what they tell me. "Cause they're like do as I say, but don't, you know, not as I do.

Paul: Uh huh.

Louise: Because, and if I make a mistake or if I say something that hurts you, you know, tell me right away instead of you know, waiting two years to tell me. (more conciliatory tone)

Paul: Uh huh. Uh huh. Right. (gestures toward her in agreement)

Louise: Understand that it's not that I don't want to spend time with you, it's just that I honestly, you know, I ... women who have kids and a job and go to school, I hold them on a pedestal because I could never do that. And I don't know what it's like to have kids, but please don't tell me that, you know, I don't know what it's like to be busy because I don't have kids. "Cause I, I mean when someone says, "Wait until you have kids and then you'll find out." I hate that.

Paul: Right. Uh huh.

Louise: So just the biggest thing is respect. And try and, and when I try and explain to you, hear me.

Paul: Uh huh. Uh huh. (slowly) One thing I'm wondering about is ... I, one thing I understand clearly, and that you've described, (hands stretched to either side) and I, it makes sense to me, that there's a way in which there's this pull from them that you feel the need to resist and that creates conflict, because they want to pull you in, and you want to keep some boundary. But I'm also wondering, is there another part of it that is, (pulls hands and arms together, then places fingertip to fingertip in front of his face, making a sign of integration) that there's something about—after all you grew up in a very small family; (Holds fingers together to demonstrate a small space.) you were the only child, and in a certain sense the family was even smaller because your father wasn't fully there, either—whether there's something about this large enveloping family (makes semi-circular enveloping motion with right hand) that's in some way appealing and attractive. (Here Paul opens the central issue of her conflict, a very important theme. Louise both wants to be in the family but to have autonomy too. (Paul's hands reaching out to either side, as if to say, "How to integrate the wish for freedom and the wish to belong?" His accompanying hand movements demonstrate that he's really involved.)

Louise: Absolutely.

Paul: But maybe feels a little too ... sort of almost like *threateningly* appealing.

Louise: Uh huh.

Paul: You know, like you could get sucked into it because there is something that you could like and could want in it. (moves hands in toward himself)

Louise: Yeah, that makes sense. Because I've always wanted a big family. I've wanted you know, maybe two or three kids. I don't know if that's big, but you know.

Paul: Uh huh. Uh huh.

Louise: I've always, the idea of family, big family like them has always appealed to me.

Paul: Uh huh.

Louise: But that doesn't mean that you know, come over whenever you want, and you know, walk all over my boundaries and that kind of thing.

Paul: Right. (nods up and down—hands out to either side)

Louise: So yeah it makes sense what you're saying.

Minute 44 Paul: Right, right. So it's really not just how do you keep them away, (hand pushes out) but how do you move into the family *while* being respected, (hand motions toward self) you know. And not just respected, "cause that's, that's too abstract. (Dr. W chooses words carefully and corrects himself. He tries to use action words and metaphors which he illustrates with his hands "Keep them away," "Move into," and he makes use of specific, not general phrases for examples) But while being able to say, "There's things I want for myself. And I don't want to be just taking care of other people and living a life of obligation." (like her childhood) (Fingers together making a point as if to emphasize the idea of suffocation. Paul speaks about these choices with great seriousness; he dignifies Louise's dilemma.)

Louise: Uh huh.

Paul: Yeah.

Louise: Yeah, "cause I mean I'm, we are very different, not just, you know, I mean I don't care to cook, I don't care to have, you know, parties at my house.

Paul: Uh huh.

Louise: And you know, I wish that we could just reach some sort of compromise instead of, I mean, I'd rather pay them to not have to cook for them, you know. And I don't, I feel like my house is too small, we're moving, so we're gonna get a bigger house. So it's like I just wish that they would instead of telling me to do this, this is the only option you have, (Louise has had only one option to choose through most of her life. Keep silent about her troubles, give in to authority and carry on—our note.) if we could just talk about some sort of compromise. And they could say well, you know, "We notice that you don't really like to cook so what else do you think you can do?" (Louise here exactly states her conflict. How to get people to notice her and her *individual* characteristics and appreciate her for what she *can do, not criticize* her for not acting like everyone else. No one in her childhood ever sought out her individual wishes and preferences.)

Paul: Uh huh.

Louise: So.

Paul: I'm also wondering, I certainly hear ways in which you're very different. (right hand thrust in front of him to emphasize difference) But I'm wondering is that the part that's a little easier to sort of see, to notice, to feel comfortable with, more than the ways in which you might be similar.

Minute 45 Louise: (Smiles—Louise's smiles usually do not represent deep Duchênne smiles. They're genuine, but they flicker across her face, then instantly disappear.) Uh huh. Yeah, it's always easier to talk about what's different. (But these smiles do represent "tells." They mark important moments of affective breakthrough into her self.)

Paul: yeah, yeah.

Louise: Well we're similar I think, me and Denise are similar because I think she's a very insecure person. And I can be very insecure still. Because she feels the need to control everybody else. I have a need to control my environment too, so I know what's, what's going on to make me feel less vulnerable.

Paul: Uh huh.

Louise: I feel, I think she's the same way. His mom and I are very much alike, too. I mean we, I felt, and it hurts, because I felt we had a really good connection. "Cause she was telling me, you know, she doesn't really, she likes her alone time. And she was not being respected for that either. And she just went along with it, she never stood up for herself. (Louise and her mother-in-law have a connection which may turn out to be very important in resolving these conflicts.)

Paul: Uh huh.

Louise: And I was trying to work with her to help her stand up for herself. And I said, you know, "If you have to, you know, tell them you're at my house. You know, if you want to be left alone, tell them you're at my house. You know, I'll say you're here." So yeah, you know, and his other sister Maria, she's not really that much in the picture. But yeah, I can, I can definitely see, I never actually had to say it out loud, but yeah, I can see the similarities. (Louise now breaks into new material and can see the psychological connections between her family and her husband's family. Paul makes the same point here in the text, when he suggests that: "When the patient elaborates and carries forth the theme of the session via concrete, affectively meaningful memories or experiences, especially bringing up experiences that point in a different direction from how she had previously felt and seen things and that signify a different experience of herself or another person, that is a good sign that something genuinely therapeutic has occurred.") Wachtel, 2011, p. 121. (Many of these signs that demonstrate how something new has happened for the client, have strong paraverbal dimensions, i.e., accompanied by her chuckle and her evident excitement—note ours.)

Paul: (right hand gestures in a circular motion) Well, "cause it sounds like there's a lot to talk about …

Louise: Yes! [interjected in the midst of my comment with almost a chortle of joy] (Louise is much more paraverbally expressive now.)

Paul: … between you, and a lot to share, but because you can get pulled (fingers make pulling motion toward himself) it's sort of hard for you to make contact with those feelings, so it's hard for you to let the warm feelings toward them (hands in front gesturing toward the other person) even emerge because they feel like a threat. And then when that happens it's very hard to approach them. (Louise is looking with great attention toward Paul and he notes (she) "has a look on her face that often seems either joyful or serene" (p. 122)—a much different paraverbal Louise at this point. She's coming into herself.)

Louise: Uh huh.

Minute 46 Paul: You know, how do you approach somebody when you've sort of decided that all the good feelings and the longing feelings I have toward them are dangerous? (hands together)—(by far Dr. W's longest speech of the interview is coming up) You know, so part of the job you have to do in some way is to figure out how to make those feelings, which are not the only feelings, I, I'm clear about that, but make that part of those feelings safer. (Paul gives both sides of the ambivalence their due.)You know, we can't, we have to stop in a minute so we can't go in right now to how to do that. But maybe we can sort of at least end on the note of that (hands in front, moving together, to mark an integration) that's an important thing to do; (dignifying Louise's issue) that in some way, part of what happened is that certain parts of your experience were acceptable and other parts of who you are kind of had to be pushed aside. (Paul's fingers make the integration figure—he's directly referring to aspects of the self which Louise previously "cast aside" but parts for which she can now possibly make room.) (In these lines Paul emphasizes her "job," the idea that she needs to do something different in the future to make things work out better for all concerned. She needs to take meaningful actions outside the office.)

Louise: Uh huh.

Paul: You know, the part of you that longs for more connection felt threatening, because there's also a very real part of you that wants the safety, the comfort, and the self-integrity of being able to make your own choices. But in doing that, the part of you that wants connection got sort of squeezed out. And then it becomes very hard to reach out to them. (Dr. W reaches to one side and then to the other and then squeezes his right hand—both sides of the ambivalence again.)

Louise: Yeah.

Paul: And it's really also a loss for you. (respectful tone)

Louise: Uh huh.

Paul: Because that part of you is just as much a part of you and deserves as much space, as much room. So that's sort of like your, your next task in life so to speak (said in a slight tone of affectionate joking) (This represents the center of Dr. W's theory of therapy—work to re-include the formerly excluded parts of yourself to help you solve the dilemma, the vicious circle, in a new stronger way, in the real outside world.)

Louise: (Duchênne smile, for the first time, using a warm grateful tone) You have absolutely given me so much more insight than I thought was possible in so little time. So I thank you. (Their moment of meeting. Louise leans toward Paul and bows toward him with her hands clasped in front of her) (The surprise ending—Louise actively wants a place in her husband's family but just not to feel suffocated. She authentically does want "in" with this group, a break-through in her understanding. From the genuine feelings on her face, we can see that this represents valid new learning.)

Paul: Good. Well, we worked well together. (Direct eye contact, warm Duchênne smile—warm handshake—These mark the only directly relational statements and unmistakably strong paraverbal moves from either participant in this very relational therapy.)

Louise: Thank you, I agree.

Paul: Okay. (They exchange Duchênne smiles again.)

(As Paul closes his presentation of the interview he emphasizes that the two of them did "work well together" and that all therapy depends on an intersub-jective meeting between a pair that connects. Other pairings might not be so felicitous. He states that the phrase "we worked well together" might be the most important message for her and for the reader (p. 124). Some pairs work effectively, and some pairs don't. We add that the paraverbal interaction feels central to the pair fitting or not fitting. As we continue our monograph, we will have suggestions about how alterations in extra-verbal style might help the client and therapist accomplish this more.)

An unusual meeting comes to a close ... a highly defended patient at the beginning, who understandably suppresses much grief, fear and anger, ten-dencies which put stress on her realistically difficult current relationships, comes out from behind her impassive mask at the close of the meeting. She smiles in genuine connection with Paul. What happened? Why did it happen? How did it happen?

A look at the numbers for the session will lead us to some preliminary hypotheses to apply to these questions.

ATOS Patient—Segment #4: Conflicted Affect = Closeness

The client's ATOS scores show steady increases in Awareness, Motivation, Arousal, all up to level 55 and show a marked decrease in Inhibition. These scores represent a 40% increase from the beginning of the interview. Louise's 30-point difference between arousal and inhibition suggest a positive progno-sis for psychotherapy (see Chapter 3).

Louise's picture of others likewise improves. We imagine that the Self-Image profile tracks in tandem with the Image of Others. As we feel better about ourselves, we recognise the charity and warmth in those around us. In Segment #2, Louise tells us that she understands her in-laws more deeply now and that she can feel more "sympathy/empathy" for them. ATOS Change in View of Others score—60. This marks a 40-point difference from the beginning of the interview. Paul's ATOS Therapist numbers remain steadily over 50 throughout.

Segment #4: Accessibility and Congruence Scores—Louise

Louise smiles rarely. When she does, it jumps out on the tape. She smiles warmly twice in this segment and does so very warmly in the last seconds, "Thank you so much Dr." She does make steady eye contact, but her facial expression rarely shifts, and the muscles around her eyes rarely become active, so it often feels impossible to guess at any deeper feeling she might have. Her flat tone of voice seems consistent with her facial mask and likewise gives off few clues about what might boil within.

She's learned to hide. This could represent a cultural particularity as well. Her accessibility score settles at a 3.5/7 for this segment, despite her breakthroughs in the last few minutes. However, she is certainly more present at the end and responds very genuinely to Paul's suggestion about her wish to become closer to the in-laws. Her congruence score reaches 4.5/7—the highest at any point on the tape.

Therapist accessibility—5.5/7

Dr. W, a modest man in his presentation, sits rather quietly verbally in Segment #3, though less so here in Segment #4, but throughout he maintains steady, understanding, patient eye contact. He obviously takes Louise and her complex issues completely seriously. He does not speak as intensely as Jim D or Kristin, but he animatedly maps his points with his vigorous hand gestures. He's un-self-consciously warm and engaged with Louise. The points he offers about her already having a supportive circle of friends and about wishing for more closeness with her in-laws, as well as separation and differentiation from them, feel authentic and well crafted. In response, Louise opens up with an animation not characteristic for her previously.

Dr. W is clearly a deeply engaged and engaging, thoughtful listener. He radiates an accepting, patient air with his relaxed body posture and twinkling eyes. Louise can take the time she needs to figure herself out. He doesn't push her. Unlike Kristin or Jim, he's not trying to orchestrate a fiery affective engagement with this client, so the emotional vitality he broadcasts, while still very high, falls a little lower than theirs—Therapist Accessibility—5.5/7.

Therapist Congruence Score

Dr. W may not seem highly expressive, except through his hands gestures and steady warm gaze, but he communicates an aura of integrity, dignity, and personal interest. This man is very present. He's really listening and really means what he says to his client: "I certainly hear ways in which you're very different (hand out to the left) but that part might feel more comfortable than with the ways that you might be similar." (hand out to the right). These almost constant hand gestures, emphasize important points and communicate unmistakably how hard he's willing to work. He's literally grasping to understand Louise. He's there for her almost every minute.

When Louise warmly thanks Dr. Wachtel for his help at the end of the meeting, he responds characteristically "Well, we worked well together," (sharing the credit) accompanied by his own warm Duchênne smile. Paul has done thousands of interviews, but this response has no ring of a casual answer. He genuinely means it. He feels they did work well together and that each gained from the contributions of the other. This represents a cocreated constructive outcome and a moment of meeting. Congruence score—6.5/7.

Control Mastery Score

Probably near the beginning of the meeting, Dr. Wachtel senses Louise's apparent forced choice that to belong in her husband's family means to become swallowed up by it. He answers her negative hypothesis by observing out loud that she has some of what she wants now, close friends, (an affirmation of what she's already achieved). Furthermore, if she works carefully to articulate her needs in a nonjudgmental way, she can also maybe get more respect from the in-laws without sacrificing her individuality and genuine human need. It's fine to want both *acceptance* and *freedom*; it's normal. She can work to gain both.

The egalitarian interaction with Paul mirrors this key pattern of autonomy and defeats her negative hypothesis, "You've got to comply to have any place at all." Control mastery score was 7/7. This experience with Paul supports Louise to begin working to change her world view and to stand up for herself in her present predicament. Inclusion in a family does not necessarily mean the destruction of your autonomous self.

The core of the interview: Transference/countertransference

At the start, Louise is probably a little overwhelmed by Paul's seniority and authority and in his counter-transference he can probably feel her vigilance, fearfulness and resentment. Our first paraverbal impression of Louis is that she's guarded and careful. How much she can relax this defense and what she will then discover about herself becomes the theme of the session.

As the relationship deepens, however, he projects back different feelings into Louise and helps transform her rebelliousness into a more mature wish for freedom but also acceptance. By the conclusion of the meeting, she really does start to believe that she can have both experiences that she so badly needs—individuation and inclusion—"A place in this world." She's paraverbally joyful about this possibility.

This represents the Tansey and Burke, 1989, transference-countertransference sequence. The *new object* of a less angry, less intruded upon, more aware and more free Louise begins to emerge. She does not need to "cast off" either her wish for independence or for membership in this family. Louise's Duchênne smile at the end of the interview shows that she and Dr. W have shared a "moment of meeting." He, too, then, steps out of role, and offers her his own very warm, very personal smile and firm handshake. The implicit relational knowing choreography, which has grown through the meeting has led Louise toward an interior affective change little by little. Her Duchenne smile offered at the close indicates that a real shift has taken place emotionally; she appears different on the tape, more alive and happier.

Attachment level

Understandably, Louise is ambivalent with regard to attachment. The support from her mother came at the cost of all of her freedom of choice. She now lives thousands of miles from her mother in a different hemisphere and in a different culture. Paul's serenity, solidity, and interest supplies home base, a beacon of secure attachment for Louise.

She can use Paul's constant self to explore becoming less ambivalent with regard to her own attachments. Relatedness to someone does not imply surrendering all your freedom. First, she gradually reacts to Paul more openly and more confidently and then maybe she can approach the in-laws at a similar level. Paul is in the business of "out-of-the-office" change.

OUR THREE THERAPISTS SO FAR

We've now had the opportunity to study three videotaped interviews from three capable, experienced, but at first glance, quite dissimilar therapists. They differ in age, gender, and theoretical persuasion and in this way represent a cross-section of practitioners, albeit a very small sample. Paul made his tape in his late 60s, Kristin in her late 30s, and Jim in his mid-40s. Paul takes an "integrative relational" approach, Kristin an "affect focused" and Jim an "object relations" direction.

However, the three hold important characteristics in common. They seem to undertake, and to largely succeed at, several therapeutic tasks simultaneously.

(1) They look for the telltale clues germane to their theory of action. Paul scrutinises the dialogue for a "cast aside" sub-self, which may be a central issue for Louise. She wants to belong to this family, the new insight, but also to feel free within it. This "forgotten" sub-personality reminds us of Schwartz's internal family theory (IFS), in which parts have become managed by or dismissed by other parts—see Schwartz, 2004.

Kristin looks for one central conflicted affect and eventually finds it, the Starving Musician's grief and loneliness, Jim searches for Sally's unresolved, past object relations trauma and discovers it in her tale of serial abandonment by men. All three counselors know the kind of theme they seek, and they don't miss it when it appears. They are masters of their particular conceptual approach.

(2) Each client presents the counselor here with a paradoxical affective conflict. Louise desperately wants "in" with her husband's family but also freedom from them. Sally helps Jim realise that it's not simply loss that has led to her depression, but it's conflicted anger, turned inward, that represents the path to unravel. Kristin sees in the moment that the Starving Musician is not principally angry with his wife but desperately grieving the losses associated with internalizing his anger/assertion (which he learned from his mother) by denying his joy of music and closeness to appease his wife.

Our three therapists deftly tease apart these complicated conflicts to discover the required focus. To do so they demonstrate remarkable attention for specific emotional detail and they know how to assemble the pieces as they cowork with their client.

(3) How do these counselors move apparently so quickly to discover these central conflicts?—by proceeding deliberately and by becoming humanly involved. We suspect that they imagine themselves in their client's position and draw experiences from their own personal lives to expand their understanding. Otherwise, how could they rapidly, so skillfully grasp the complex issues that we observe on the tapes? For example, Paul, as he listens, unconsciously, may have delved back into his early life and recalled a time when he himself craved belongingness in a family but also freedom. This helps him connect with Louise's story whose life, in every other way, feels so different from his own.

Jim can remember a time in his early history when he, like Sally, felt subjugated and powerless. One reason that these counselors seem to work so fast is that, consciously and unconsciously, they recognize the dilemma of which their clients speak.

(4) Our therapists seem to realize that they ask a lot, emotionally from their clients. They, the therapists, must come through with their own psychological

commitment to the process. According to Paul's theory, Louise needs to recognize a "cast off" crucial part of herself in order to move forward. However, she has put aside that issue for a very strong reason. It represents a primary dilemma for her; can she "take a stand" with her powerful, controlling but desperate mother? If Louise begins this courageous exploration, then Paul must become a nonjudgmental, respectful, gentle, open partner in this journey of affective experience. Otherwise, it will never start.

For Sally to relive her loses in isolation, Jim must offer her his genuine, enthusiastic encouraging therapist self for Sally to dare to move back into her traumatic past, to go inside. Kristin must join in sadness with the Starving Musician for him to realise the extent of his loneliness and sorrow.

(5) This implies that the counselor not only has a well worked-out theory and technique of therapy, but he or she literally becomes a part of that treatment as well. It's hard to imagine Affect-focused dynamic therapy without a jovial, warm, encouraging counselor like Kristin becoming one with the approach.

This, in turn, implies that descriptions of the counselors" particular extra-verbal ambience need to appear in our textbooks. They rarely do. Obviously, there's no correct interpersonal stance for the therapist. Each needs to present his or her own authentic affective self, but we're discovering what we lose, if our picture of that therapist is not included in our understanding of the treatment.

We need to study and report on how we, our colleagues, and our students, actually behave verbally and nonverbally as therapists. What is our paraverbal imprint? How does our client, in return, respond to our extra-verbal relationship offers? This represents the data usually overlooked, but Bohart and Tallman (1999), for instance, have also recognized this problem.

The implication that the therapist literally embodies the treatment unavoidably carries significance for the therapies we provide and attempt to teach. We could ask our students many questions: Physically how do you feel with this client? What aspects of your inner self and your body movement, do you notice get expressed, as you two interact? Bohart and Tallman (1999), suggest similar modifications in their approach to training. This outlook also suggests questions that we could put to ourselves, as we practice: "Why do I smile so little with this client? That's unusual for me." Does my full self feel involved with this patient now or am I distracted by other "parts" from my personality? In other words in Schwartz's language, am I "self-led" at this moment?

Chapters 4 and 5 have implied that a spectrum of therapies from the Object Relations approach to Affect Focused Dynamic and Relational work, offered by therapists of different ages, genders, and educational backgrounds, all seem to rest on an "implicit relational knowing" platform.

Second, this underlying universe often reveals itself through the paraverbal exchange between the therapist and client. If we miss the nonverbal details such as smiles, excitement, and changes in voice tone, we'll miss the role of the Unconscious World I. The implicit relational bond slowly sets up the change process inside Louise. She's a little more trusting, a little more open, a little more able to allow Paul's reframe about the in-laws, to enter her psychological map. Third, we can begin to track the development of these extra-verbal patterns quantitatively and qualitatively. As we study this new perspective further, we might discover profitable experiments we could make in our therapeutic stance.

Next, in Chapter 7, we'll enlarge on these ideas about paraverbal relating when we apply them to couple therapy meetings.

Chapter Seven

Couples Therapy

Its Paraverbal Dimensions

In this chapter, we'll study a couple's videotaped interview that Jim undertook in 1985. We'll explore the data for paraverbal clues about why this meeting turned out in so curious a way. We'll also make full use of our quantitative measures in terms of the Accessibility and Congruence Scores and the ATOS and Control Mastery ratings.

Couples therapy adds a layer of complexity to the proceedings because the pair communicates nonverbally with each other as well as with the therapist. The paraverbal messaging between the members of the pair almost always carries important meaning.

Never more so than with Nancy and Ed, an unusual twosome, who despite many individual strengths and a good measure of mutual respect and affection, had lived in conflict, nearly constantly, for their 35-year marriage. I saw them in consultation, 30 years ago, at the request of their therapist of three years. Linda S, LICSW, a long-term colleague of mine at my former hospital clinic, found herself stymied in her efforts to help Nancy and Ed break the pattern of their chronic rageful arguments.

NANCY AND ED: THE VIDEOTAPE

Setting the scene

Linda, a social worker with 30 years of experience, known in our Psychiatry department for her caring attitude and great patience, felt committed to, but frustrated, in equal proportions, with this couple. She found them so appealing in some ways with their bright creative minds and in their apparently sincere motivation for change but also so imprisoned in their life of blame and counter-blame and nearly endless fighting.

Two years prior to our interview, Nancy and Ed had separated for one year. Now reunited, for 9 months, they battled far less violently but only slightly less often. Linda felt tired, discouraged, and wondered whether more treatment might help or whether a second and final separation seemed a more realistic course for this disputatious pair.

A lot appeared on the line as I came through the door to meet Nancy and Ed, for the first, and as it happened, for the only time. Would this interview catalyze a shift in their style of relating, so that they could gain more peace and satisfaction, or might this therapist and this consultation, go the way of so many similar efforts by my predecessors? What if I found myself ground under by the apparently relentless bickering of this struggling couple?

We had agreed that Linda would join us in the room, though not to participate, actively, in an effort to avoid complicating the exchange. Augmenting the tension of the meeting, if that seemed possible, in addition, we arranged that our consultation team of six colleagues would observe the session from behind the two way mirror. We planned to break twice from the 50-minute interview, so that Linda and I could adjourn to the next room for ten minutes to gather suggestions from our sequestered coworkers.

In the second half of the hour, this group could tap on the mirror as a signal to us to interrupt again for a third consultation with them. This last phase of the plan nearly led to disaster because a very trying meeting became highly emotionally charged, leaving me with my hands absolutely full. At that moment, the team began tapping, and finally banging on the mirror, to offer their help, which I, under enough pressure already, felt forced to ignore—so much for prior arrangements and good intentions.

I entered the conference room, distinguished by wide windows at one side, and by a large, rectangular table around which we sat. Linda, Ed, and Nancy positioned themselves on one side, by the window, and myself at kitty-corner a few feet away, facing the other three participants. The observing team arranged themselves behind the two-way mirror built into the wall at the far side of the room. Linda had briefed the couple concerning the consultation plan, including the presence of the observing team. They seemed at ease, particularly since Linda (mother? big sister?), whom they clearly liked, joined us.

At the time of the meeting, I was 41, a veteran of 10 years of marriage myself, and Linda, my colleague perhaps 50, was married some 25 years. She and I found ourselves in the slightly strange position of consulting to a 55-year-old couple whose marriage had lasted 35 years. I, the "expert," was the youngest in the room by a decade at least, and I felt it.

To start I knew only that Nancy and Ed, together many years, had endured chronic fighting and had had a one-year separation but had reunited a few months previously. Linda also told me that they had two children, (both boys in their 20s), each with a different degree of hearing impairment. As we'll see the children, who with their medical issues must have contributed additional stress to the marriage, curiously drew only two lines of mention during the entire interview. The action in this relationship, as we'll see, swirled around Nancy and Ed, with their children apparently far less involved.

Both members of this couple were petite, neatly and informally dressed, well spoken, and attentive. Ed, a slender, wiry man, wore thick glasses, and had a full head of bushy salt and pepper hair—a physical characteristic that later took on particular significance—as we'll find out at the close.

The pair hardly appeared hostile, war-weary combatants. Nancy made consistent eye contact with me and occasionally with her husband. She smiled several times during the session and chuckled at different points. Ed, the more serious, perhaps humorless and standoffish, did look at me from time to time but almost never at Linda or at Nancy.

Ed sat behind a large notebook on the desk in front of him and often looked down to write out his observations, though he never shared these ideas. I immediately felt Ed on guard against me, probably against the other participants in the room and maybe over the idea of the consultation in the first place. He seemed prickly and mistrustful, though by no means overtly hostile. My own defenses went up toward Ed, as soon as we shook hands, and stayed up for the first two-thirds of the meeting, although gradually I felt them relax. Ed appeared vigilant and skeptical, not a promising first impression for a high stakes couple's meeting.

Nancy, more plump and even shorter than her husband, wore thick glasses and had a short plain haircut. Her somewhat worn blue blouse and blue skirt in their drabness did not match her ebullient personality.

I wore glasses, a blue shirt, matching tie, and grey slacks. Linda looked neat, bright, and professional in her stylish glasses, graying hair, and blue dress and white sweater.

This interview, which would later take dramatic turns, started innocuously enough, although our preamble thus far makes clear that important paraverbal impressions already hung in the air.

I offered that since I had some couple therapy experience, Linda had asked me to consult about their frequent disagreements. (Before we started, I had three questions in mind, which I think Linda shared, but we did not communicate these to the couple or to each other. We wanted to begin with an open agenda, but we clearly wondered. (1) What in the world did these fights mean between Nancy and Ed? (2) Why did they apparently never stop and (3) What held this couple together, despite these regular battles?

Segment #1: Minutes 0 to10, (This represents a verbatim account, somewhat edited to economise space.)

The interview started:

Jim: Would you tell me a little bit about how it is that you get into arguments with each other?

Nancy: Do you want me to start? (glances at Ed sitting beside her)

Ed: Okay. (Ed looks straight ahead and then down at his hands.)

Nancy: So when you've been married as long as Ed and I have ... it's easy to just push a button ...

Jim: How long is that?

Nancy: Thirty five years, not sure if you want to count the one year I left?

Jim: No, beginning to end, beginning to now. How old are you now?

Nancy: I'm 54.

Jim: So you were married when you were 19!

Nancy: Yes, just 20! (direct eye contact with me) There are a lot of times when Ed and I disagree on a procedure, a routine, a household task. He'd like to do things his way. I want to do it my way. Neither way is wrong. (a strong clear voice tone)
(Ed looks down at his hands, with a furrowed brow, and begins to write almost furiously in the large notebook in front of him. He does not look at anyone in the room but concentrates on his pad. It's almost as if he feels alone.)
The arguments don't start when we disagree. The argument starts when I agree! (Nancy points at me for emphasis.) If I continue to insist on my method, then I have to explain the reason, justify it and all the rest, and it's easier to say, "Forget about it." I think he feels guilty for having pushed. We fight over whether I should have stood my ground! (With her hand gestures Nancy seems to diagram the fight in front of her on the table pointing first to one side and then to the other. She smiles, has consistent eye contact and connects well with me.)

Jim: Is that the way you see it, Ed?

Ed: (looks at me and then points toward me) Yup! That's true. She gives in when she shouldn't. We've gone over this many times. I say she doesn't know how to compromise! She thinks compromising is giving in completely! She gives in. I get mad. I've said it to Linda. (glances at Linda for one of 2 or 3 times in the interview) I'm a designer by training and by action! There are rational solutions to problems! We need to find the right way of doing things! We've got to!! (powerful delivery, looks directly at me) Just in the normal way of talking, I hurt her feelings. I don't even know they're hurt. Then she says something that hurts mine maybe. Until I was practically coming here, I didn't even know my feelings were being hurt! (loud, clear voice, deliberate prosody, somewhat confused facial expression)

Jim: (emphatic tone) People fight when their feelings get hurt! It hurts to have your feelings hurt! It makes sense.

Ed: (nods and looks at me) One of the things ......

Jim: Can I interrupt for a second? (with authentic questioning tone)

Ed: Sure (readily agrees to my interruption—some beginning alliance established?)

Jim: Does she strike you as somewhat irrational? (questioning tone)

Ed: (smiles) Good way of putting it (alliance starting with Ed?) Understatement!!

Jim: (I sweep my arm across my body for emphasis) She should have stood her ground, but she didn't!!

Ed: Not the way to solve a problem!

Jim: She doesn't go about it right! (rapid prosody and emphatic tone)

Ed: (nods) Yah!

Jim: Now this is a sort of an off-the-wall idea (I use a self-effacing apologetic inflection, trying to communicate to the tightly wound Ed that I'm not a threat to him.) ... When she acts like this, does she remind you of anybody? (questioning tone)

Ed: No.

Nancy: Yes.

Jim: I'm thinking of anybody from your childhood? (I make an immediate move to their personal histories, which follows my theory of couple therapy, relationships from childhood are repeated in marriage. See Donovan, 2003.)

Ed: I don't know. She's thinking of my parents.

Jim: I was thinking of a parent.

Ed: Definitely doesn't remind me of either parent. (emphatic tone, looks at me)

Nancy: (looks at me) Ed's parents lived with us for four years. I was there. I was the housewife with the kids (one of only two references to the children in interview). Ed's mother frequently backed down. Her husband was very assertive, aggressive. She'd say, "This is not important. We won't talk about it," and she wouldn't! (Ed looks down at his pen.)

Jim: (to Ed in a gentle tone) Did your mother act that way with you too?

Ed: (glances down) I don't think so. (says quietly)

Jim: Pretty tough pattern (empathizing with Ed). Woman gives in, but has she really given in? (questioning tone) What is actually on her list for me to do now?

Now that she's been so nice to give in? Is that the way you feel when your wife gives in? (looking directly at Ed)

Ed: What happens is that she gives in at so early a stage and then she resents it—a day, a week, a month later, I'll hear about it! (Loud emphatic tone)

Jim: Yah Yah (empathetic inflection)

Ed: I haven't had a chance to be what I want to be, a decent person! (This represents Ed's "preferred view of self." He seems conflicted about the fighting and doesn't want to keep it up, but he apparently doesn't know how to escape the pattern either.)

Nancy: Oh you're a decent ... (pats Ed's arm affectionately—I missed this paraverbal cue, and I should have called attention to it because it was a sign of closeness between the two, at least from her side.)

Jim: (loud emphatic emphasis—communicating how frightening Ed's position feels) Putting your foot into a trap! Just a question of how long before it clicks shut!

Ed: No, no thought of that. This thing can be worked out! It's got to be!! (Ed moves his hands up and down in a parallel pattern in front of himself twice, and then he looks at me as if to emphasize how crucial it feels to change the pattern.)

Jim: Maybe this isn't helpful at all (again self-effacing apologetic inflection to calm competitive defensive feelings that Ed may have), but what I'm thinking is that it's not just a question of two people arriving at different ideas. I think there's a lot behind this! You're feeling I'm going to hear about this later!

Minute 6 (Jim's on the wrong track here. He thinks it's the structure of the argument that's the issue, that Nancy gives in, and Ed feels guilty and then snaps at her. I'm completely incorrect as we'll see. Jim's alliance building with Ed, though, possibly supports later dramatic outcomes.)
It feels terrible if someone's agreeing with you, but you know you'll have cold water dumped on you later! (loud voice, empathetic tone, how scary Nancy's stored up resentment might feel to Ed?)

Ed: Probably some of that. (Tentatively agrees, although his inflection and slow prosody indicate that he isn't really convinced.)

Jim: I think that's what makes you angry!

Ed: Some of that, some of both, (still tentatively—He doesn't really buy it.)

Jim: I have no corner on the truth, if I can get something right (Colombo) ... (These represent alliance building moves. I'm not confronting, correcting or competing with my highly defended sensitive client. This sentence in the dialogue just above may become one of the most important in the whole interview. "If I can get something right ..." We're building a way of working, (an implicit relational knowing), even though my rational grasp of the problem, my hypothesis that the trouble starts when Nancy gives in, later turns out to lead down a blind alley. It becomes clear that the real significance of the arguments, runs in a different direction. At this time, I'm only partly consciously aware of making these alliance building moves.)

Minute 8 Ed: Yah (nods his head, looks at me. Ed smiles at me for one of the three times that he smiles at all in the meeting. He has softened slightly.)

Jim: Brothers and sisters? (I sense a dead end in my exploration of the meaning of the arguments in present time. In fact, I don't understand why they fight so much as adults, so I change course and search for clues in their families of origin.)

Ed: Both oldest children with much younger sisters.

Nancy: Compounds the problem!

Jim: Well maybe it does. (Ed keeps looking at me.) (to Ed) Your parents?

Summary: The last two minutes of Segment #1

(For the next two minutes, Ed describes that he was always treated as an adult by his parents and didn't feel pulled into their frequent conflicts.)
(End of the first ten-minute segment)

Discussion of Segment #1

We're ten minutes into the consultation. We had hoped that our questions and clarifications would have led to a lot more engagement than has actually unfolded. We have learned certain things though. We have a couple married a long time, 35 years, less a one-year separation, apparently committed to each other, but who argue constantly, seemingly over trivia.

They're parents of two early adult children, virtually never mentioned in the remainder of the interview, for reasons we need to ascertain. This couple married very young and seems to have fought almost continually from the wedding day onward. Our husband, Ed, an intense man, seems strongly motivated to understand the meaning of the fights—"We can figure this out—we've got to!"

Two problems enter the picture almost immediately though. First, despite his apparently sincere wish to improve communication and to stop the fighting, Ed takes a hyper-rational isolated stance to focusing on the dilemma. He's working by himself here. He shares his careful analysis of the problems, but he never asks his wife for her opinion, glances her way only twice in the segment, and never touches her. Ed either takes notes, looks straight ahead or down at his hands, or he fixes me with his stare. (This paraverbal data is crucial to the tone and experience of this interview. Ed has clear motivation, but he's distant from everyone in the room except perhaps me.)

His apparently protective description of his parents introduces a second difficulty into this not-so-easy first ten minutes. We grasp right away that Ed's parents fought incessantly probably the way Ed and Nancy battle. We learn in Segment #2 that Nancy's mother and father argued continuously also.

I assumed that this couple's struggles bore some direct relationship to the chronic parental conflict of the earlier generation, but Ed denies this emphatically. He explains that his mother and father bickered a great deal though never about him or over him. His family of origin has now slipped somewhat out of bounds for discussion. Where can we take this exploration next?

For my part I'm treading water as fast as I can. I notice in the first minute that Ed sits with a rigid scowl behind his notebook that forms a mini-barrier in front of him, about 2" high. I guess that he could easily feel threatened by, and competitive with, a younger man, PhD in hand, who's an "expert in couple treatment" and proposes to tell him what's wrong with his marriage. Nancy smiles warmly and bubbles with a friendly voice. She's the more inviting of the two by far.

I feel right away that I will have to put maximum effort into assuring Ed that I will not humiliate him or dazzle him in front of the two women and that I will not praise his wife's insightful participation. I begin to take a strongly egalitarian, even self-deprecatory stance with Ed. "Now this is sort of an off-the-wall idea" ... "If I can get something right" ... I hope Ed will receive the message that he has little to fear from me—again, a mostly unconscious choice on my part at this time, but I'm reacting to Ed's implicit relational prickly stance.

Even this early, we can predict that control mastery issues will loom large in this interview. Ed needs to feel reassured that he can lift his defense of withdrawal and hyper-rationality before he will fully participate. He has to sense that I will not judge him pejoratively. We'll see how this plays out. If he can clearly receive this paraverbal message from me—my nonconfrontational, modest, almost deferential tone, could prove a key intervention as we continue. The verbal content certainly hasn't helped us much as yet.

Accessibility/Congruence Measures

Ed's Numbers—Accessibility Score—2.3. Ed subtly leans away physically from his wife. He occasionally inclines toward the therapist. He shows little range in speech rhythm and tones, some facial movement and one smile. He seems to convey "I'm possibly accessible, if you can contact me in just the right way." He holds his head down, his arms down, his palms down. He makes little eye contact with anyone. His body language feels closed. He looks a great deal at his pad and concentrates on note taking. His hands are usually together, and he slouches into the chair.

Ed's congruence score is 5. His body language does seem to communicate what he really feels, which is that he's on guard and that he shrugs off many emotions, save for a strong wish for improved relating with Nancy and his frustration about not achieving it. He strikes us as somewhat angry and confused but mostly flat, he's quite inaccessible, his body language does not lie. He's congruent with the distance and rational perspective that he takes in this first segment. He's isolated in physical message and in speech tone, but he's certainly not overtly angry at this time.

Nancy's numbers

Nancy's Accessibility Score differ markedly from Ed's. She shows 4.9 on accessibility. She makes direct eye contact, her hands move in rhythm with her speech. Her tone of voice has considerable variability. She smiles and chuckles. Her body seems relaxed. She turns with her arms open toward her husband, and once she touches him affectionately on the right arm.

Her Congruence Score of 5.2 communicates that she's expressive, and that her body language matches the tone and content of her speech. Her presentation in Segment #1 is of a more than average, socially engaged woman. Both her paraverbal scores exceed "4." We're quite sure that her outgoing, orientation communicates how she really feels inside, although she too, must have her share of anxiety about this interview and its outcome.

Jim's Accessibility and Congruence Scores: (Jim absents himself from all the ratings of his behavior throughout. For these we rely on the other two judges, Susan and Kristin.)

Jim's paraverbal accessibility score is 5.8. He shows open body posture; he leans toward the clients, maintains direct eye contact, smiles, chuckles occasionally, expresses with his tone that he empathically appreciates the difficulty of their situation, and he mirrors their verbal prosody. His body language congruently reflects his words, for the most part. He seems to reach out to his clients. His posture is open, arms away from his body. His tone is soft and compassionate, his prosody slow and expressive. He reaches toward the clients with his hands inviting them to talk—congruence 6.2.

So by the end of Segment #1, we have a therapist verbally and paraverbally inviting his new clients to join more with each other, and with him, and to experience more closeness and maybe more sorrow as well. This therapist begins to model openness for the couple, but he can only take this a little way on his own.

Nancy seems quite expressive in her speech and in her body postures. On one occasion, she's playful and physically affectionate with her husband. She does hang back though. We don't know Nancy very well by the end of the segment. It's as if she's not sure how far forward, into the session, Ed will come, and she's cautiously watching, reacting to his lead.

In Segment #2, we may see Ed express a wider range of feelings and some closeness to Nancy, but if he doesn't, it's hard to see how constructive the consultation can become. We actually know almost nothing about why this couple fights so much, other than that she gives in too quickly, and that his parents argued all the time also. The therapist has worked hard to forge a beginning alliance with Ed; my labors have apparently brought little fruit as yet.

Now on to Segment #2—will Jim's receptive verbal and paraverbal approach help to break through to his clients in this next ten minutes? Will either Ed or Nancy, on their own, initiate a push toward deeper feeling, toward going "inside," and draw a clearer, more revealing, picture of their conflicts?

SEGMENT #2: MINUTES 11 TO 20

We'll summarize this second ten-minute excerpt. Here, Ed and Nancy describe the relationship between his parents. They lived with our couple for the last four years of their lives. They had little money to support themselves independently. Apparently, they bickered extensively over minute issues such as: Did his mother write too many letters? Ed states that he didn't like his parents arguing so much but that he didn't feel guilty about it or pulled into their struggle.

Comments on Segment #2

Segment #2 mostly replicates Segment #1. Of course, we're exploring small continuous sections of just one consultation session, so we probably shouldn't expect any immediate shifts in the action. Ed maintains his rational exploration of the marital arguments, with the further description of his parent's fighting which apparently, in a parallel form to Ed and Nancy, seems to have marked their entire relationship from the start.

Jim works hard to connect with Ed who, usually remains withdrawn, involved with his own thinking, his own body and his own notes, sometimes looking at Jim but almost never at his wife or at Linda. He self-touches, and self-soothes, by rolling his pen in his fingers and by clasping his hands together in front of him and looking down at them. He slumps in his chair as if to pull into himself and away from the others in the room.

Ed comes out of his shell a little with Jim but usually shows a frequent faint scowl or frown on his otherwise expressionless face. The tightness of his facial muscles constantly communicates his intense concentration and frustration, but following Ekman (2003), the taut cheeks and mouth and clenched teeth could imply anger as well.

Jim has concentrated on building an alliance with Ed since, from minute one, he seems the more standoffish, the less available, the less engaging and engaged member of the pair. Jim has observed in the past that in couples" treatment with a male therapist, if the two men get locked in even a slightly competitive struggle, it always retards, and often destroys the work. He tries hard to avoid this muddle. The pattern of mutual regulation in the interview seems striking: Both Nancy and Jim, very separately, and with very different methods, try to reassure and support Ed to relax and join in more. Will this lead to Ed's greater involvement?—so far not so much.

Unfortunately, as the readers have no doubt noticed, we still don't know much more about the meaning of the fights between Ed and Nancy than when we started. We haven't broken through to any new understanding of their exchange that might point to a path toward change. We're also not kindling very much intimacy between them.

Jim is forming a hypothesis that Ed fights because he feels constant, unstated pressures from Nancy—as he probably did from his parents originally—a reasonable enough trial balloon to float between them, but it picks up little breeze. We haven't heard Nancy's story about her early life or her perspective on the couple's conflict as yet. We will in a minute, but if she cannot, or does not, help us with a deeper understanding of the marital conflict, this consultation will pretty quickly find itself spiraling downward.

Paraverbal ratings

The paraverbal openness and congruence scores reinforce our general impressions of this second segment.

Ed: Not much change here, Ed has little expression on his face though his chiseled brow may indicate hostility, but toward whom? He maintains some eye contact and has some animation as he speaks to Jim, but almost none of either when addressing his wife. He speaks to Linda only once. He usually holds his palms down and leans back or slouches in his chair with his chin down, apparently bespeaking some emotional withdrawal.

Ed seems to use his pen as a self-calming instrument, looking at it and occasionally chewing on it or poking himself lightly with it. He holds his arms rigidly to his side but occasionally lifts them and makes an unusual up and down chopping movement in front of himself to emphasize his thoughts, as if to mark each separate idea with a different chop. Ed has below average accessibility in his segment—2.5/7.

However, Ed's body language, tone of voice, and prosody apparently remain congruent with the thought and affect he expresses verbally. He offers a clinical, rational, rendition of the facts as he sees them. His tone, rhythm of speech, and his facial expression fit that almost businesslike communication. He's congruent within this limited presentation of self. His facial expression and habitus seem to reflect his relative isolation from his companions. What other feelings, particularly more loving, more connected ones, may Ed have buried inside? As yet we have no clue. Congruence: 5.1

Nancy

On the other hand, Nancy has a paraverbal expressiveness score of 5, matched by a congruence rating of 5—not very different from her profile in Segment #1. She's still moderately expressive, and she's much more animated than Ed.

She makes frequent eye contact with both her husband and with Jim. She turns to Ed with arms and palms open. She smiles and speaks in an involved feelingful tone, which expands upon her verbal presentation. She occasionally makes rapid movements with her hands, which probably indicate her anxiety. Nancy's body language remains congruent with her affective and verbal narrative. We see no grimaces or tightening of the lips or jaw, which would tell us she's much angrier, or much more troubled, than she expresses verbally. She participates in the trialogue in a positive, friendly, though not markedly open way. Her bodily movements and facial expression remain consistent with this.

Now at least half way through the interview, neither Nancy nor Ed has introduced much sign of anger, nor despondence or heartbrokenness, all of which seem quite surprising, considering their long conflict-laden relationship and one significant separation.

Jim's expressiveness

(All Jim's scores are rated by Susan and Kristin only) Jim, as the consultant, is obviously less on the spot than either Nancy or Ed. He participates with relaxed body language, arms and palms open, his verbal tone is gentle and explicit, appropriately sometimes louder and sometimes softer, prosody varied, depending on his point. His tender inflection expresses his growing concern for each of the couple—"is that something you feel around the house a lot, nameless guilt or maybe named guilt" delivered in an empathic, and slow cadence, as if Jim can feel Ed's discomfort and confusion.

Jim's open arms, smile, and eye contact fit with the message of inquiring and caring that he sends verbally. His expressiveness and the congruence in his body language all go well beyond the range of everyday social interaction. He seems to communicate, "I'm trying to understand. You can explore this with me. You don't need to feel afraid or judged in here." Jim's accessibility score is 5.5 and his congruence score is 6.0. I was not fully aware, until I watched the tape several times, of my strongly expressive style here.

We can already see that if we miss the paraverbal information on the video, particularly Ed's bodily communications and Jim's welcoming tones, we'd lose half the meaning of the meeting. Why does Ed need to live within fortifications, and what lies behind this barrier? Based on this paraverbal reality, the therapist must take strategic precautions as he approaches Ed, or this difficult consultation might easily lead Ed to move away further.

THE FIRST TEAM CONSULTATION

At the break, Linda and I walked next door to discuss matters thus far with our consultants. The observers did not feel comfortable with the meeting to this point. In fact, there was considerable anxiety in the room. They reacted strongly to Ed, and suggested that he shielded himself with his pen and his notebook and that he appeared hostile and uninvolved. They doubted that at this rate, we would ever learn much more.

The team's concern reflected their reaction to Ed's severe facial expression. At close range, I could catch a faint smile from him once in a while, which my coworkers couldn't observe at their distance. They felt he looked truculent and threatening. Unlike the watchers, I didn't have a strong response to Ed's apparently harsh demeanor and authoritarian tone after the first few minutes. Having grown up with commanding men, and to some extent embodying one myself, I felt Ed a challenge but no frightening adversary.

SEGMENT #3: NANCY'S
STORY: A SYNOPSIS: MINUTES 21 TO 31

When we returned to the interview room, after this seven-minute consultation break with the team, I asked Nancy her understanding of the arguments, and she responded with a description of her sad childhood and marital story, which shocked me, as well as apparently the other observers. We didn't analyze that segment of the tape in order to economize space and time, but I can offer a précis. I have retained my notes, and it remains a clear sequence in my mind.

Nancy grew up as the oldest child, of two, of another chronically warring couple. Her father struggled trying to keep his heating and air conditioning business alive, threatened by stiff competition. He reinvested all his money into this concern and borrowed heavily from Nancy's mother as well, who had a successful career as a school administrator.

Both parents drank at an alcoholic level. Nancy admired and protected her father but hated her mother. Nancy contracted a serious childhood illness and spent one year in bed at age 6. She fully recovered, but as she grew older, the conflict with her mother worsened. The mother beat her. At age 12, Nancy told her mother that if she ever touched her again, she would kill her. "It wasn't very nice, but I meant it, and she never hit me again."

Nancy went to college and almost immediately met Ed. After she left her home of origin, the parents quickly divorced. Apparently, Nancy had provided a bridge between them, though a rickety one. Nancy married Ed during college, and her father died of cancer the next year.

At the time of the interview, Nancy's mother still survived, and Nancy regularly visited her. She had a distant relationship with her younger sister. Nancy and her mother remain in a conflicted, mutually dependent, angry relationship. Over the years of Nancy's marriage, her mother has contributed financially to their household, but still there was little love lost between the mother and Ed and Nancy. Ed describes his mother-in-law as a "hostile bitch," one point on which Nancy and Ed wholeheartedly agree.

Nancy went on to reveal that she and Ed had had violent fights earlier in the marriage. Twice Ed had affairs with other women, while away on business trips; his infidelity apparently became the focus of these earlier pitched battles. Some of these led to physical violence. Ed punched Nancy, and she apparently hit him back. They had various courses of treatment with several different marital therapists, the last one of whom advised them to separate "before they killed each other." Nancy did leave for one year but has now returned for the past 9 months and implied that they got along better now.

After listening to this eleven-minute piece, the marriage seemed more troubled than I and the observers had originally thought. We had now learned that Ed had a history of infidelity and physical abuse toward Nancy. She returned some of his violent attacks as well. As she told her story, Ed said little. From one perspective we learned that Nancy had found in Ed an assaultive partner to replace her angry mother. Why she needed to do this, remained a mystery.

THE SECOND BREAK WITH THE TEAM

At this point, we went next door for our final consultation. The team seemed taken aback that these proper, highly educated, diminutive, gray-haired grandparents, could savagely hit each other. They had little to add except that they predicted that Ed would remain highly defended for the rest of the interview. They felt worried about what would happen, if he relaxed these defenses and directly burst out with his anger.

The observers had become frankly frightened of Ed and likewise had begun to despair of any constructive outcome for the meeting. At this point, I started to see the team as a less helpful ally. They had a negative assessment of this interview, and burgeoning antipathy toward Ed but no constructive suggestions. We returned to the interview room distinctly on our own.

To begin the last phase of the session, I knew that although I might have fashioned a beginning alliance with a problematic character, Ed, I had not helped any of us grasp the arguments more deeply. Furthermore, nothing had happened to reassure me that this couple had learned anything from our meeting thus far that might help them curtail their destructive interaction when they went home. Neither did they seem to be in more intimate contact with each other. At the present moment, this had all the earmarks of one bust of a consultation.

SEGMENT #4: MINUTES 32 TO 42—AN UNUSUAL CLOSE

Jim: We've been talking with the other people. There's a great deal of hurt in this relationship (gentle holding tone—looking directly at each of them). Both of you have been wounded for a long period of time. It's painful to hear about, and it's ten times more painful to live (sad tone, slow prosody, enunciating each word. I'm intently looking back and forth between Nancy and Ed.)
I think what I would do, which sounds kind of corny, I would schedule periods of time to talk, 45 minutes to an hour, go out to dinner alone once a week. In these conversations, I would emphasize some of the positive things that keep you together. One of the very painful things about your history is that the two sets of parents fought, all the time, and now you fight all the time. These facts are related! (emphatic exclamation, I bang my hand on the table)

Nancy: Sure they are!

Jim: It's crucial to figure out why this parallel exists! The negative is being emphasized in this relationship. It's very important to stress the positive too. (strong slow prosody—palms held outward—meeting their gaze) There are many positive things that take place between you. You're both very smart interesting people! You have a lot to say! You've shared a lot of experiences!

Ed: Some good ones too!

Jim: (Strong tone) Yah! That's right! It's crucial to emphasize these or else life just becomes a sadness. All we say is how rotten we get along. (Jim's cadence slows, and his voice sounds sad.) The most important thing is to try to understand these arguments. (Jim gestures outwardly with his hand and with his pen to emphasize the point.)

I've been at this a long time, and I know they have a function! (slow prosody, powerful inflection, direct gaze)

They mean something. It may not be to relieve pressure. A couple of things come to mind. Perhaps this is a way of being passionately involved. You're both excited! Do you find you can be passionately involved in other ways? (strong tone—this idea represents my unconscious reaction to the paraverbal distance between the couple)

Nancy: Ed is very reserved! (Almost on cue, Ed looks down and toward the floor.)

Jim: That gets him out of his shell! (smiles)

Nancy: Causes a tension! (chuckles loudly)

Jim: This is just a hypothesis, (self-abnegating tone). In the marriages you observed, the people didn't pay a lot of attention to each other. This was a way of ... getting some attention, to fight.

Nancy: Maybe in Ed's family. In mine they were all very close and passionate in hundreds of ways, really in love, right up until the day they got a divorce! They just couldn't stand each other! (She looks at Ed and reaches out to him with her right hand. This move poses the question: Do Nancy and Ed have the same kind of marriage as her parents, passionate but filled with conflict?)

Jim: (sad tone) Very hard to deal with this. (slow emphatic prosody) How could you be in love and not stand for each other? I know it happens. But maybe the function is getting Ed to put down his books and his word processors and stop and pay attention? (very serious tone)

Nancy: Not sure might be part of it (still only a little movement as yet. We haven't struck a nerve. I'm working hard, trying everything, but not making much progress. My tone has begun to sound a little desperate.)

(pause)

Jim: Another function may be the opposite, keeping people at a distance (Team begins to tap on window.) If you fight, you keep the other one on their heels.

Nancy: I'm not sure about that?

(Pause—No further response from either of the couple)

Jim: Okay what I would do. I would meet with Linda for three times. (I want to give them some plan for the future, because I'm acutely aware that we're running out of time in the present.) I'd meet with her three times in two week intervals, if that's possible, and concentrate solely on the issues we've spoken about in the last five minutes. If you get progress, great. If you don't, I would reassess. (very serious tone; Nancy and Ed both intently look at Jim, almost frantically asking for some lifesaving advice. The atmosphere in the room has just changed dramatically. This has become serious business now. Both members of the couple feel alert and involved, something important may happen, but we're about to end this consultation. This marriage could fail and soon.)

Jim: What do you have on your minds? I'm really interested in everyone's ideas. (making direct eye contact with both Ed and Nancy, spoken in slow, very serious, respectful tones—The observing team now begins to tap steadily on the window, which continues through the rest of the interview)

Ed: (Talking very slowly and seriously and looking down at first, but then his head pops up. The head bob represents a "tell." Now he's really in contact with his feelings, for the first time today.) Your assessment, that's very interesting. (slow prosody, self-questioning tone) In outside relationships, I look from the outside, I guess, from the outside looking in. It looks like I am reserved. In all my outside relationships I'm enthusiastic, bouncy.
Somehow I got the idea in a close relationship, showing that too much would not appear right. I want to say "I love you" quietly, because I mean it. (Ed shows some mentalisation here; he's wondering about his behavior and about his feelings and how he appears to others.) (A look of surprise and revelation appears on Ed's face. He bangs his hand down on the table. Recall Ed slapping the table for emphasis once at the beginning of the meeting, and Jim banging the table three or four minutes earlier in this segment. Nancy looks at him wide eyed, and he looks at me. For the first time words akin to "I love you" have entered the conversation.)

Jim: (very strong tone) If you're too spontaneous, it looks like you're not serious?

Ed: I don't want it to look like it's not real, but it's absolutely real! (slow, intense, prosody, emphatic tone)

Jim: (loud insistent tone—direct gaze at Ed) The feeling I'm getting is that you can't be yourself at home! With other people you can be but not with your wife!

Ed: Yah!

Jim: (Both Ed and Nancy still look intently at me, and I speak very slowly and rivet them with my gaze.) Nobody can feel good about that! You need to be the same here as there! (emphatic)

Ed: (very surprised inflection) I never felt bad about that before. (Sits straight up. This represents a "moment of meeting" between Ed and Jim. They agree that his bodily message does not represent his true feelings. This is also an example of Mentalism in Fonagy et al.'s (2001) terminology. For perhaps the first time in his life, Ed is realizing what affect might register in someone else's mind in reaction to his behavior.)

Jim: (very emphatic, but warm tone) Need to feel comfortable at home!

Ed: (looks up, cartwheels his hands) Comfortable the way I was acting but seeing I might look reserved.

Jim: Someone looks reserved, you feel it's me! (rapid prosody, emphatic tone)

Ed: It's really me, but it never bothered me before. (Nancy looks closely at Ed.)

Jim: No your wife feels he's reserved. He doesn't care about me!

Ed: Yah! Yah! (loudly—overlapping)

Jim: (loud strong insistent tone) She's going to do things. She's going to rattle your cage!!

Ed: Yah, Yah !! (very loudly—overlaps me, nods up and down, the tell again, moves whole upper body—another moment of meeting)

Jim: It's going to get rattled!!

Ed: Yah! (pause) (very emphatic)

Ed: (musing tone) Very interesting … cause other … how to … (Observing team banging on the glass by now.)

Linda: (gentle questioning tone—her first words in the consultation) Where do you see the problem? (Linda looks down and then at Ed.)

Ed: The problem is how to bring this enthusiasm home? (a remarkable insight—looks at Linda for the second time in the interview)

Jim: Yah, you've got a lot of enthusiasm, important to bring it home! (mirroring Ed's words, very loudly, very strongly emphatic presentation, now I'm almost yelling, fixing Ed in my gaze.) Sounds like you really do love your wife. You can say it in an exciting way! Not just "oh you know I love you." (Jim speaks in a slow, garbled caricature for effect.)

Ed: (looks down, sounds sad for the first time, speaks in a slow serious cadence) The only time I address it that way, now that I think about it, has been in fights! (inflection of mystification at his new knowledge)

Jim: Fight allows you to do something which you can't do otherwise!! (very loudly)

Ed: It forces me to do it. She forces me to do it! (a strong affirmation of Nancy, very powerful verbal emphasis. Note the paraverbal expressions in Ed's breakthrough—"enthusiasm" forces me to "do it," "yah yah." Ed's intense affective state and obvious excitement at his new understanding indicates that real change may be afoot—see Wachtel, 2011, p. 121).

Jim: (gentle low tone) Forcing you to tell her that you love her. Just tell her, and you won't have to fight! (strong advising inflection)

Nancy: Wouldn't that be simple? (loud ironic scoff)

Jim: It's the truth! I'm not being simplistic; it's the truth! (loud, emphatic enunciation, looks at both of them)

Nancy: (laughs—looks at me) I told him that a long time ago when we first got married. But he got terribly mad at me, and I had to stop.

Jim: (points at her) Okay but don't say, "I told you so," or anything like that. We all have to come to our own realizations. Any of us know only a small bit of the truth here. (confrontative but gentle emphatic tone, looking directly at Nancy) (Ed looks down and scratches on his pad, but doesn't look at Nancy.)

Jim: It's the truth. It will work!! (Team smashing on the mirror now, creating an almost comical din in the room.)

Nancy: (She looks fondly at Ed, who looks down at his pad.) I have to tell you about the (toy) cat, (a very affectionate loving inflection), that Ed brought me back from a trip. It's this beautiful two foot long cat, about a foot high with huge eyes and the most glorious big tail (She outlines the size of the cat with her hands.) It's orange, and I put it on the bed and everyone who sees it, thinks it's real. It's a fabulous little creature. (She looks at Ed. Nancy's free association to the cat, to new material, confirms that our grasp of the meaning of the fights is correct. Nancy's reference to the cat is full of feeling and takes the interview to a deeper level. Serious change feels about to occur from her side [see Wachtel, 2011, p.121]. The fight kindles passion between them and now she spontaneously talks about her fondness for Ed and her joy over his gift. At about this moment I realize that Ed looks like a cat with his bushy hair and small face peering out beneath the fur.)

Jim: Maybe Ed is giving you himself? (gentle soft tone, slow prosody, catching Nancy with my eye)

Nancy: (laughs, looks at me) I certainly treasure that cat. No one touches it but me. (She smiles and giggles and looks at Ed. Ed is the cat.)

Jim: (soft holding tone) You treasure him too.

Nancy: Of course I do! That's why I'm here! (strong affectionate tone)

Jim: (supportive but insistent emphasis) Tell him!

Nancy: I told him. He got mad at me (chuckles). I used to when we were first married. He kept telling me to stop. I had to stop. (Ed curtailed the intimacy early on, a tragic legacy from his original family.)

Jim: (strong emphatic but gentle tone) Try it again, we're different. We all grow up! (try a different kind of mutual regulation.) (slow cadence, gentle, firm, encouraging inflection—Ed looking down.)

Nancy: All right (loving tone, leans toward Ed. She mumbles "well Gee." She reaches out to her right and affectionately rubs Ed's forearm. He stays looking down at his pad.)

Jim: Okay, go on from here! (encouraging, emphatic, upbeat tone)

Nancy: Yes.

Jim: Okay Ed?

Ed: Yes, very interesting, I thought about this a long time ago … I couldn't figure out how to do it … still not sure (amazed questioning inflection and facial expression)

Jim: (strong upbeat) Just try, got to do it for yourself Ed, okay? (very encouraging tone) … Well gee (Jim repeats Nancy's phrase—we're on the same wave length.) I'm glad you came by. I hope you got something. I feel good, I think you did get something! (a warm, relational, Level 3 therapist expressing his own personal feelings)

Nancy: Thank you! I feel we got something. We have a good shot. I'd hate to move again besides … (chuckles—rubs Ed's arm again).

Linda: (offering broad Duchênne smile, stands up moves toward Ed, Nancy, and myself, shaking our hands)

Nancy: (warm Duchênne smile—gentle, very sincere facial expression—stands up, offers her hand to me—firmly shakes mine, which I return to her, accompanied by my own Duchênne smile.) Thank you very much.

Ed: (offers his hand to me, Duchênne smile, warm but also still a touch wooden) Thank you. (I reciprocate his grin and handshake. Linda joins in with her own warm handshakes again … smiles all around.)

Comments on Segment #4

What just happened? In a ten-minute burst, this consultation, previously a circuitous, disappointing, even somewhat scary, project has blossomed into an intimate coming together. Four people part, grasping hands with warm smiles and leave the room buoyed in optimism and in genuine warmth.

The turning point in the interview comes from Ed, when he's seemingly struck by lightning—read a moment of meeting. For some reason, he realizes that the fight forces him to leave his cave of withdrawal and intellectualization and become personally involved with his wife. The whole tenor of the session then changes, and all of us become more open and exchange warm gazes with each other, accompanied by Duchênne grins and physical hand touch at the close.

Previously I had no idea how Ed came to his new insight, and naively presented it to my fellowship group, simply as a surprise ending. I did not feel embarrassed over my lack of understanding of the crucial interchange because all the other observers, over the years, seemed as mystified by Ed's sudden breakthrough as I did. But now I get it. I think.

First of all, Ed appears, to all who have viewed the tape, as the least sympathetic character in the piece. He slumps his small wiry frame into the chair. He has large glasses and a shock of long, grey, curly hair that obscure some of his facial expressions, of which he honestly seems to have few in the first place. He looks intently at me, down at his notebook or straight ahead, almost never at his wife or Linda, his therapist of three years. He often seems to glare. He smiles only twice and usually speaks in a gruff, determined, sometimes frustrated and irritated tone.

As our interview unfolds we learn that, in the past, Ed has repeatedly hit his wife—(she apparently has returned punches in kind) and has engaged in infidelity. Ed obviously does not seem the ideal couple therapy candidate, and no one, certainly not I, would ever guess that in 45 minutes he would allow himself a possibly life-changing revelation.

As the years continued, and I watched the tape with class after class, the "act of God" explanation of Ed's sudden enlightenment began to strike me as less and less satisfactory.

I realized that, from the start, I had paid special attention to Ed. As soon as I walked into the room, shook his hand and looked him in the face, I sensed his guardedness and his possible rancorous stance toward me, and perhaps an inclination in him to respond aggressively or dismissively.

At the time, I felt vaguely consciously aware of these concerns. In a preconscious state (implicit relational knowing), I planned a response toward a client whom I, from minute one, viscerally reacted to as a challenge. I realize now that the talented prickly engineer/designer Ed reminded me unconsciously of my older brother with whom I had developed a similar nonthreatening style.

My nonconfrontational approach toward Ed, led me to adopt, unconsciously, an existential stance for my interventions. I imagined what Ed, from inside himself, could or couldn't dare to say or to hear. I carefully moved forward accordingly. I spoke in a gentle, often minimizing, self-deprecating tone, using modest collaborative phrases, "this may seem like an off-the-wall idea" … "If I can get something right" … "We all have only a small corner on the truth."

As ingenious as this method may appear in retrospect, I could not have spelled it out at the time. I never did discover Ed's specific underlying fear, I doubt he knew it himself, but I did help to manage his resistance. I also now realize that I had an unconscious identification with Michael Balint and behaved in the same noninterpretive way with Ed in which I imagined Balint approached his patient in 1972, the Stationary Manufacturer.

Watching our tape carefully, we've discovered what a verbatim, unembellished, case transcript could never tell us. Ed looked down at his lap, at his notebook, straight out in front of him or at me, almost never at his wife or at Linda his female therapist. His eyes kept returning to the other man in the room.

Control Mastery

Ed wanted something from that man. We doubt that his father was that encouraging man. Ed smiled twice in the session both times at me and laughed once after I had said—"Does your wife seem somewhat irrational?" Using control mastery terminology, we can put it that Ed tested the therapist hoping to reject his negative hypothesis, that I would devalue him. When I seemed to stand next to him and to empathize with his dilemma, I supported him and did not humiliate him. I passed the test.

This hurdle cleared, Ed could lift his defensive withdrawal, "reserve" and realize that he only felt energized and open around his wife, after he fought with her. We imagine, though with no evidence, that sexual relations, more intimacy, probably followed some of these fights. Control Mastery score for the interview reaches 7/7.

To approach constructive change, all players in the system needed to move in the same direction, in this case toward the new positive affect that Ed introduced. Their mutual regulation then took a sharp turn. Ed's openness led Nancy to relax her cautious defensiveness and to look at him, speak to him, touch him affectionately, and recall lovingly the toy cat that he gave her.

At the close, the space seemed to fill with buoyancy and friendliness, ironically all at Ed's initiation. Ed set in play a paraverbal breakthrough that for the moment, at least, dramatically decreased the distance in the room. We each now permitted ourselves much greater openness, warmth and optimism, stepping out of role and engaging in a mutual "now moment" at the end.

This represents an implicit relational knowing therapy at its foundation. Ed and I rarely exchanged supportive words directly until the close, but unconsciously he warmed up to my extra-verbal self and I to his. We clicked, and he allowed his positive paraverbal self, his openness, and his enthusiasm to almost magically appear.

My tentative interpretation, regarding the fights leading to greater intimacy, sparked him off, but his trust and comfort with me, developed earlier, allowed him to fully participate and to openly accept some of my ideas. This mutual cooperation transformed the consultation. Our implicit relational knowing led to the final "moment of meeting" in which all four of us participated so joyfully.

Ed "softened" in Susan Johnson's terminology (1998, 1999) and allowed the development of intimacy to grow with Nancy. In Paul Wachtel's terms, it appears that embarrassment may have caused Ed to cast aside many of his tender feelings for Nancy and only the intensity of the fight allowed them to come forth. Ed and I shared a "moment of meeting" about his genuine need to express love. Then Nancy shared a "moment of meeting" with me and with Ed describing Ed's present of the toy cat. However, the depth of Ed's response to the cat story remained unclear.

By the end of the meeting, we all stepped out of role, smiling and warmly shaking hands. I had known this couple only 45 minutes but felt like hugging Linda, Nancy, and even Ed. This warm ending reflected the "moment of meeting," which had just taken place for all of us. Of course, we require verbal content in any interview, but the paraverbal shifts, mostly Ed's, cracked this case open.

The ATOS scores

The ATOS and ATOS Therapist measures, at the start, registered for Ed in the high 20s for Insight, Arousal, Motivation, and Inhibition and for Nancy in the high 30s. But by the end of the meeting, they both reached the 60 level for Insight, Arousal, Motivation, and decreased Inhibition as well as New Learning about Self and Others. This trajectory marks a positive outcome for the session and predicts productive psychotherapy in the future. The 30-point decrease in Ed's Inhibition score feels particularly important.

On ATOS Therapist Jim's ratings in promoting Insight, Motivation, and Arousal moved from the low 40s in segment 1 to the middle 60s here in segment 4, describing a more intensely involved and clued in therapist.

Paraverbal profiles

Ed's numbers

The Expressiveness Scale for the segment explodes upward for Ed to 5.7 on openness and 6.0 on congruence. He moves toward the therapist and toward his wife, at least verbally. He makes direct eye contact with Jim and has an unmistakable look of astonishment (he's not the only one) and excitement, when he realizes the function of the fights. These encounters force him to become more intimately involved with Nancy. He acts spontaneously. His face opens and he muses "very interesting." Ed's intrigued response takes him way beyond normal social openness and congruence.

However, ominously perhaps, his behavior toward the others lacks much of a paraverbal interpersonal dimension; he does not reach out physically to Nancy or look very intently at her or at Linda. His openness remains primarily self-focused and focused somewhat on Jim. He has made a momentous personal discovery, but it stays singular. He's warm toward the therapist, smiles and offers his hand, but he remains somewhat removed from the other players.

Nancy's scores

Nancy's paraverbal numbers, not surprisingly, also reach their highest level in Segment 4, 6.0 /7 on openness and 6.2/7 on congruence. She leans over and strokes Ed twice very affectionately. She speaks in a tender tone to him, "Oh gee" … "I treasure him." Her body relaxes in comparison to Segments #1, #2, and #3, and she chuckles frequently. She smiles, and laughs when she's happy, and grins broadly when she describes Ed's special gift of the cat. Her facial expressions clearly match her affects of affection and relief, when she and Ed reach greater closeness.

Therapist's paraverbal scores

In this segment, Jim's ratings on paraverbal openness and congruence, predictably reach his highest levels for the meeting, 6.2/7 and 6.3/7 respectively. He makes direct eye contact, expresses a wide range of affect with his voice, and holds the clients with a gentle tone. Sometimes he exhorts them, "This will work!," and strongly encourages them "Got to do it for yourself, Ed!."

His tone emphatically enhances the message of his words, well beyond any normal social interaction. He's congruent in his presence: smiling, closely attentive, waving his arms when encouraging, or carefully and warmly, observing the couple with a direct curious gaze. He authentically expresses genuine concern, "I'm real interested in everybody's thoughts here." At the end, the couple warmly reaches back toward Jim. He's moved a step further out of role and become very personally involved.

I doubt we can account for the denouement of this unusual meeting without Stern and Beebe's Unconscious World I—implicit relational framework. Ed, mostly out of his awareness and certainly out of mine, became gradually more in sync with me, in a wordless way, and finally suddenly could drop his defensive distance, much to the amazement of all the participants and all the observers, including myself. I think Jim's paraverbal warmth and acceptance toward Ed and positive reaction to his positive reaction to Ed's shift in stance, made it possible for Ed to take strong initiative in this segment.

He began an unmistakable "moment of meeting" with Jim and the others. At last, he authentically wonders aloud why he has such difficulty expressing intimacy with Nancy. The implicit relational knowing bond imperceptibly has grown between Ed and myself. An affective shift begins to take place in him. He will allow more of his feelings to reach consciousness. He takes a "U-turn inside" (Schwartz, 2004). I take a personal action and suggest that the fights allow intimacy. He matches my action and yells out a few lines later, "She forces me to ... "; the implicit bond has gradually influenced Ed to take a new direction. This suggests that the change process in individual and couple therapy may follow similar paths.

Transference/counter-transference—Ed

In terms of a Tansey and Burke sequence, Ed projected his mistrust and frustration into me. I tried to modify it and to project a feeling of more optimism warmth and acceptance back toward Ed. He moved closer to me and felt more liked and protected. By the end of the interview a new, expressive, even loving Ed suddenly appeared to everyone's surprise. A subliminal process started in Ed as his positive transference toward Jim helped him feel safe. Then under time pressure, he blurted out, yes the fights "force" him to become intimate.

Nancy's transference journey seemed much shorter. She projected a friendliness and openness into me, I amplified it and returned it to her and gradually, a more and more affectionate Nancy appeared, to finally tell us about the cherished cat that Ed had given her. Paraverbal elaboration accompanied all of these transference developments in both Nancy and Ed—Nancy warmly grins as she describes the cat, and so on.

Linda's holding presence supported the other three of us to connect with our congruence, even though she spoke less than 2 minutes during the entire hour.

POST SCRIPT

This tape recounts a startling breakthrough in a single consultation session. My postdoctoral fellows, other previous observers, and probably now you the readers, may all wonder what became of this couple after the interview. Did Ed's sudden realizations support the pair to develop more intimacy or, at least, more peace in their relationship? What has been the long-term significance of a single session, moment of meeting?

Three years after the taping, I called Linda, their couple therapist who by that time, had relocated to Maine. She reported that Ed and Nancy continued to see her, weekly or biweekly, after our session together, until she left the state about a year later. Their fighting did markedly decrease. They also took a quiz about couples" relations in the Atlantic magazine and seemed to gain more understanding of their interactions from this.

Ed did not talk a lot more about his love feelings with Nancy, but he did approach her with good works. Nancy pursued her painting. Ed took time out from his work to build frames for her and a sales booth, which they transported to fairs and flea markets, so she could display her creations. The couple definitely seemed happier and more calm. The corrosive recurrent arguments faded, as did any violence. Linda told me, "It's not happy ever after, but it's happier ever after."

But then Linda departed Massachusetts. In retrospect I think Ed and Nancy required a kindly, supervising, parent object—a therapist to hold them on a quite permanent basis. This would allow Ed to continue having semiconscious breakthroughs into his needs and wishes for intimacy, to no longer push them aside.

For reasons unknown, they did not seek me out when Linda moved, and I didn't know she had left. Apparently, their relationship then slowly self-destructed. Ed pursued other women and Nancy developed a severe drinking problem, which she may have had, mostly hidden, for some years previously. Recall her mother, too, had alcoholism. Ed left the home, lived with another woman, then a second, then a third. The cast-off part for Ed represented his loving self; he could not consistently reengage with it.

I followed up with Nancy by phone in early 2010. She sees an experienced therapist in our hospital Psychiatry department. At age 80, she now has serious medical problems. She remembered me warmly; her cheery voice tones sounded exactly the same. She remained fond of Ed despite his desertion. She feels protective of his reputation and didn't want the chapter to expose him as a flawed person. Nancy, perhaps to her detriment, loved, forgave, and protected this damaged, but sometimes tender man, as she did her tragic father.

What happened?—Back to the paraverbal scales

Ed's lack of general interpersonal, extra-verbal availability, despite his psychological openness at the end of the interview, might predict the eventual outcome of the marriage. This poses a serious question for our project, which we have to address further, as we try to deepen our understanding of psychotherapy. Can a single flash of knowledge, a "moment of meeting" and connection, overcome a lifelong protective character positioning? Probably not, by itself, but coupled with continual long-term therapy it might, gradually, cumulatively.

If we just read the verbal report of Ed's moments of clarity, without any paraverbal videotape data, we would have little idea that in the actual couples meeting on the tape, he rarely touched his wife physically, or addressed her in any affectionate warm way with words, glances or bodily movement.

Despite the promising end to the interview, the predictor for the eventual destructive end for the relationship might reveal itself only in Ed's distancing paraverbal behavior through most of the tape. The average of his accessibility scores is only 3 across all the segments, which perhaps foreshadows the future of an eventual loss of intimacy with Nancy.

Attachment issues

The attachment themes lead us toward another way to understand Nancy and Ed's eventual separation. Recall that this was actually their second separation. They had been apart for one year previous to the consultation. Nancy demonstrated somewhat secure but also anxious attachment as she carefully watched Ed for his first moves. She was well aware of potential danger from both Ed and her mother. Furthermore, it's probably difficult for any couple to exceed in their mutual attachment, the least developed level of relatedness of either of the partners.

Ed certainly showed signs of ambivalent attachment. He also seemed to have an avoiding, mistrustful stance that probably made it difficult for him to maintain consistent intimacy with one person, however supportively she might behave. Recall his previous affairs. We did see that Ed had loving feelings for Nancy, and he courageously offered these toward the end of the interview. Ed and Nancy's 35-year marriage, therefore, certainly had positive phases but also was filled with episodes of destructive conflict, probably mirroring their different attachment positions.

The reader may have observed that socially awkward, isolated Ed who spontaneously offers little eye or physical contact may have demonstrated a mild Asperger's adjustment. We wonder about this, too, but his sudden revelation at the close of the consultation argues against it. He has deep feelings of intimacy, but they're only irregularly available to him.

Possible alternative approaches

Now I would pick up the paraverbal relationship much more quickly than I did then. Nancy touched Ed on the arm in the first segment, but I let this pass without comment. I could have, and should have, asked about affection between them much earlier.

I may have kept too close to my original model of couple treatment. (Donovan, 2003—studying triangles of conflict in the history of the marriage and in the parent's original relationship.) With Ed's help we did uncover the meaning of the fights, but I didn't notice carefully enough, perhaps, what was going on in front of me minute by minute. Many paraverbal responses strongly told me Ed felt reserved and uncomfortable. A gentle, careful focus on intimacy in the here and now consultation earlier, might have improved the intervention.

We would have had to proceed here mostly paraverbally because I don't think Ed could have participated in a direct verbal exploration of his warm, passionate feelings for Nancy, until he very gradually contacted his own authentic loving responses at the end. We imagine Ed absorbed his very ambivalent attachment from his argumentative parents. His consequent defensiveness against attachment (Stern, 201, p. 155) evidently followed Ed all of his days.

In retrospect, Nancy and Ed required a therapist who could provide regular, supportive, soothing treatment over many years. As luck would have it, Linda moved away. The couple didn't seek further help as a pair, but Nancy received long-term treatment after Ed left. Given their different character positions and levels of attachment, consistent therapy over time represented maybe the only possible efficacious intervention.

This therapy would need to address the repetition within Ed and Nancy's marriage of their parents" relationships. What they saw from early childhood was attachment through hostility. Their default choice unchecked, meant to start a fight (Ed) or join in one (Nancy). The therapy would have to focus on the paraverbal atmosphere, created by this pair, which led along a destructive path.

Probably the best clue to Ed's affective state rests in his slouched posture, lack of eye contact, and flat voice tone. He would need to learn to escape this taciturn stance on his own, in some productive fashion, that is, without resorting to conflict with Nancy. Ed's isolation and Nancy's openness clash. Any productive therapy would have to focus on this problematic interaction.

I have noticed that the first dominant paraverbal message between the client and the therapist registers barely consciously but usually offers a sometimes crucial clue to the main theme of the therapy to come. If I study my own mind, I ask, why did I approach Ed so gently from the start? In the short term, the unconscious choice of this therapeutic approach worked, but it came to my consciousness because I registered Ed as so fragile an attachment. This ultimately turned out a limiting factor in the long-term outcome of the treatment. Evidently, Ed could move only so far in closeness.

IN CONCLUSION

As we've worked our way through this chapter we realise, and probably a number of readers have as well, that couple (or family) therapy and paraverbal interaction feel closely entwined. For example, one can readily "take the emotional temperature" of a pair in the first few seconds of a treatment hour, by gauging their facial and bodily responses toward each other. It's as if a couple interaction clearly illustrates most of the features of paraverbal interchange, which we've studied so far.

Couple-hood is all about: eye contact, smiling and being joyful, welcoming or hard and forbidding messages on the face, relaxed or rapid breathing, gentle, physical touches or lack of the same, warm, or indifferent, or sarcastic tones of voice. We can't venture far into couples work, ignoring the nonverbal messages between the two. The paraverbal world is the world of intimacy and for most couples, this language has developed over many years. We need to find our way around in their particular "implicit relational knowing" universe, if we hope to offer them meaningful treatment.

We've just observed Ed's remarkable flash of insight explaining the function of the fights between him and Nancy. But ominously we did not see him follow through paraverbally by affectionately catching Nancy's gaze or touching her arm. We've suggested that this lack of nonverbal communication, even after his genuine stroke of insight about the meaning of the fights, might represent a predictor of the eventual demise of their marriage.

Harville Hendrix, (1988, 2008), the founder of Imago Therapy some 30 years ago, places the couple's "dialogue" at the center of his intervention strategy. This approach enlists many extra-verbal techniques. First, the couple face each other, maintain steady gaze, take three deep breaths together, and then make reciprocal requests to discuss intimate relationship topics: their sex life, their financial issues, possible substance abuse, and so on. Each member speaks uninterrupted for at least 5 minutes. Next, the partner repeats what he has just heard and then they switch roles.

Physically, the Hendrix pairs look directly at each other and the therapist sits somewhat to the side, observing and facilitating the dialogue. The action is within the couple. They keep a steady gaze, and Hendrix emphasizes feelings of fear, safety, and joy within the pair. The dialogue interchanges often focus on shifts in bodily feeling in both members. At the close of the exchange, the couples share a one-minute full body hug. Without directly stating it, or perhaps fully realizing it, Hendrix has evolved a heavily paraverbal approach to couples treatment.

Dr. Hendrix and his group have practiced in this format, for decades, in a number of different countries. There are maybe 2,000 Imago therapists working somewhere in the world today (Hendrix, 2014). He reports strong success with his model, and it represents one of the most widely known approaches today. Paraverbal dimensions play a major role, minute by minute, within it. The principles of nonverbal communication may represent the theory, and couples therapy, the laboratory in which we put that theory into action.

We've learned first that we, or the client, can offer level-1 interpretations of the action. Ed brilliantly points out that the fighting forces his intimate involvement with Nancy. Along a second dimension, at Stark's levels 2 and 3, Jim offers Ed an accepting, gentle object to support his greater openness. Kristin with the Starving Musician, and Paul with Louise, supply a similarly accepting and encouraging object. In the case of all three therapists, this productive stance represents more than therapeutic style. It becomes simultaneously an intervention, not of an interpretation, but of a relationship offer.

What is the next move? The therapist could take further, probably more direct, paraverbal actions, to open the treatment toward more intimacy. In Chapter 8, we'll explore additional possibilities for this broader, therapist, experimental behavior.

Chapter Eight

The Therapist's Body/The Patient's Body

Lessons from the Cases

These videos and case excerpts tell us a complex tale, however, far from a complete one as yet. As we trace the narrative further, strand by strand, we'll gain greater clarity.

Our final exploration will follow this path: First, we'll summarize what we've learned so far. We'll revisit Stern and his Implicit Relational Knowing framework and use it to explore, more deeply, the rhythm of the tapes. When we do, we realize, that we cannot tell where the psychotherapy enterprise starts, in the therapist's body or in the patient's body, but it moves back and forth between as they create a mutually regulating secure bond and as they continue to exchange extra-verbal offers and counter offers. Stern seemed to get it right.

Then we'll consider how we might integrate our verbal understanding of psychotherapy within this paraverbal picture. We'll close this first section by introducing the concept of "presence," which knits together many of the wandering threads we've tried to secure through our story.

In the second half of the chapter, we start to apply our paraverbal observations to a reexamination of the treatments we all offer. What can we, the work-a-day counselors, learn from this project that would help us to understand our task more fully and to encourage us to experiment with particular changes in nonverbal technique that might deepen our approach? We'll offer further case examples here. In other words, after we finish the book, maybe we'll grasp our patients in a rather new way and often respond differently to them. What then might unfold between the two participants?

STERN'S THERAPEUTIC MODEL

It turns out that we can't understand our data, unless we fully see and feel Stern et al.'s position. Let's return to his 2010 book. Then we'll realize, little by little, that his group has, in fact, minutely described for us much of the subtle extra-verbal flow that we just viewed on tape.

In drastic précis, we've learned how the Boston Change Process Study Group (BCPSG) bases their picture of psychotherapy on the analogue of the mother–baby growth-promoting exchange. Stern and his colleagues include many from the ranks of the most experienced researchers in parent–infant communication: Stern himself, Edward Tronick (2007), Beatrice Beebe et al. (2005), Karlen Lyons-Ruth (1998, 2005), and Louis Sander (1998). Directed by the irreplaceable knowledge gained from the mother–baby laboratory, we watch them apply their findings to the patient–therapist interaction.

We learned in Chapter 2, that Stern and Beebe propose that the mother and infant communicate, and mutually regulate, according to the process, which they call Implicit Relational Knowing. In sum, parent and baby, mostly paraverbally, relate according to a format of greater and greater "fittedness," through more and more complex and intimate contact, toward new "higher levels of organization" (Stern et al., 2010, p. 62).

"Implicit relational knowing" begins well before the baby acquires any ability to use language or symbolic forms of interchange. This forum of paraverbal exchange remains active through the life cycle but largely out of the awareness of either participant. It recedes early in its noticeable profile because verbal communication begins to take so emphatic a place in the personal exchange from age two onwards. However, "implicit relational knowing" continues to play on, in the background, within any two person intimate coupling: client/therapist, marital pairs, siblings, close friends. This is the real departure in Stern's unique thinking, the existence and the ongoing influence, mostly out of awareness, of that parallel extra-verbal world. Apparently, it's real in every baby and mother, in every adult closeness and in every psychotherapy session.

Upon further reflection, we realize that (1) intimate communication would have to start with the mother–infant connection and continue to become influenced by that first relationship. That's where we all first learn intimacy. (2) Stern and colleagues did not just speculate about the parent–infant interaction; they built their therapy template on the basis of hard data, hundreds of observational studies in the nursery.

We'll more carefully explain what implicit relational knowing represents and what it does not. Although it remains mostly within the unconscious, this form of knowledge is not dynamic transference and is not repressed for psychodynamic reasons. We've already heard Pally (2000), a neurologist and a psychoanalyst, suggest that 80% of brain events remain unconscious. Implicit relational knowing usually stays within that 80%, unless either participant calls attention to it.

Nevertheless, the Stern group argues that changes in the universe of implicit relational knowing directly, consistently, shape the unfolding of dynamic therapy and probably psychotherapy of any sort. Stern et al. are clear in their position that the process of change takes place largely within the shared implicit relationship (Stern et al., 1998, p. 918). We first encountered the following paragraph in Chapter 2, but it feels so central that it bears repeating in part.

Moments of meeting

This flow of implicit relational knowing, "moving along" in Stern parlance, represents one important parameter of therapeutic exchange and change, but as we also learned, "moments of meeting" can suddenly occur. These times of punctuation, which patient and therapist sense, consciously or unconsciously, as crucial personal transactions, represent the fulcrum paradigm for Stern and his group. We first encountered this paragraph in Chapter 2, but it bears partial repetition here since it's so central to our discussion.

> The key concept, "the moment of meeting" is the emergent property of the moving along process that alters the inter-subjective environment and thus the implicit relational knowing. In brief, "moving along" is comprised of a string of "present moments" which are the subject units marking the slight shifts in direction while proceeding forward. At times a present moment becomes "hot" affectively and full of portent for the therapeutic process. These moments are called "now moments." When a now moment is seized, that is, responded to with an authentic, specific, personal response from each partner, it becomes a "moment of meeting." This is the emergent property that alters the subjective context. (Stern et al., 2010, pp. 12–13)

These flashes reorder the implicit relational knowing state of the client (and of the therapist), which leads to change, often lasting change, in how the patient experiences himself or herself and the other. My "I suck" session with my architect client, marked an obvious "moment of meeting." We both catapulted out of role, yelled at each other, and openly and clearly made known our love and respect for each other. The therapy, my client's life, and to some extent my life never followed the same path after that meeting. Our preverbal selves suddenly emerged and interchanged directly with each other. This release of energy created our startling personal confrontation, an unforgettable few minutes for both of us, a turn in the road.

We interrupt ourselves now to offer three clarifications. First, moments of meeting represent key junctures in therapy, but Stern et al. make clear that they do not seek these breakthroughs alone in the treatment. The continual, subtle, mostly unconscious "moving along" direction toward "fittedness" that the pair takes, also powerfully contributes toward growth. Mother and baby spend the majority of their time together in very important but lower key "going on being" times.

For example, Beatrice Beebe (Beebe et al., 2005, pp. 89–143) offers us a case in which her adult patient, Dolores, after tragic early traumas, emerges from childhood, nearly mute. Beebe concentrates on matching breathing, speech rhythm and tone with her terrified lady. She offers her the attunement of "home base." Beebe "moves along" in the slowest, gentlest possible way. Very gradually, the counselor and the client negotiate a space in which they can talk a little in a calmer and slightly more engaged fashion. This represents an unusual adult treatment that uses, almost exclusively, the extra-verbal techniques of an early childhood intervention. This subtle therapy contains no obvious "now moments" or "moments of meeting."

Second, "moments of meeting" do not come as a bolt from the blue; they express the state of the relationship that has already developed, mostly implicitly, and then move it forward in definitive paraverbal and often verbal terms.

Third, we need to enunciate that "preverbal," "paraverbal," and "implicit relational knowing," for Stern and for us, often overlap but do not represent interchangeable concepts.

Preverbal seems to extend in a fairly straight line to later paraverbal communication. As the toddler begins to master speech, his preverbal behavior blends with, and amplifies, his new word skills, but he continues to express himself paraverbally also. As he grows, "Implicit relational knowing" registers in first a preverbal, and then in an extra-verbal world, since it often remains "implicit."

However, preverbal or nonverbal does not equal implicit relational knowing. This third phrase refers to a special experience, a syntax or rules underlying interaction (Stern, 2010, p. 153). In other words, not everything preverbal, or paraverbal, reflects implicit relational knowing, but we will learn the most about this kind of knowing by studying paraverbal relating. The interpersonal world of speech assumes a larger and larger profile, but the original implicit relational knowing states certainly never disappear. They continue to exist and to develop and to exert influence.

In addition, when my client yelled out "I suck," his paraverbal, implicit view of himself, one that he had held largely unacknowledged since childhood, burst into words. I yelled back my rejoinder with words and gestures: "You don't suck!"—waving my right hand in front of me. His conviction about self, and my response to it, remained *"implicit"* knowledge no longer. They have now become unmistakably explicit and verbal as well as implicit (see Stern, 2010, p. 153).

Similarly, when Kristin leans toward the Starving Musician, with tears in her eyes, and holds him with "I hope you find someone with whom you can give and get love," she's using bodily implicit messages but words as well. "Moments of meetin") can, and often do, include explicit verbal and paraverbal-implicit communication simultaneously.

These elaborations notwithstanding, Stern et al.'s thrust often doesn't feel that clear. What is his theory of therapy anyway? It starts with the mother–baby exchange. The pair interchanges verbally and nonverbally, exploring each other, stumbling toward common ground, supporting and regulating each other, collaborating, sometimes finding moments of close agreement and connection, sometimes not. Then they move toward more complex tasks at an uneven and lurching pace, without any definite end point.

The patient (infant), and to some extent the therapist (parent) as well, gradually internalize these states of greater safety, mutual regulation and clarity. This represents Stern's and Beebe's therapy, one based fundamentally much more on growth-promoting collaboration than on content. The Tronick Still Face video (YouTube, 2007) captures this mutual regulation and attunement between the intimate pair better than can any poor words from us.

Consider Stern's goal in treatment: "increasing the flexibility, range and effectiveness of the patient's adaptive capacities, along with the reduction of the experience of maladaptive behavior and dysphoric state") (Stern et al., 2010, p. 69).

Well and good, but how does this take place? In the Still Face experiment at first we see the holding, direct eye contact, attunement, and delight of mother and baby. The baby (and the mother) internalize a feeling of safety, self-esteem and joy as they communicate mostly paraverbally, cooing and matching facial expressions. This communication is tested when the mother closes down her facial response, but then it quickly returns when she emotionally reconnects.

This implies that at least some of the gain in therapy probably enters through the exclusive, warm, attachment bond. This means that therapist and client reenact, in adult guise, the mother–baby coupling that we see so clearly on the screen. It is the focal interaction in which change can begin to grow. Gradually, mostly wordlessly, something within both parties shifts. The implicit relational knowing represents the medium through which this connection unfolds. Paraverbal interchange, caught on the tapes, offers us direct access to observe that bond as it develops. The "moment of meetin") is an important event but the two participants prepare for its arrival gradually in their deeper paraverbal relating. "Moments of meetin")

are by no means required for gain in treatment but paraverbal connectedness is required.

THE CHOREOGRAPHY OF THE TAPES

With this summary of Stern's translation of psychotherapy, we'll return to an
overview of what the videos and the case fragments can teach us.

Our direct observations and our scoring strategies seem to corroborate
Stern's and colleague's predictions. If we review, from Chapters 5 and 6,
Jim's work with Sally and Paul Wachtel's with Louise, for instance, we can
watch the "implicit relational knowin") universe come to life. Sally, at first,
looks down toward her feet, avoiding Jim's gaze. She speaks quietly and
softly, but she can probably pick up my empathic tone, that is, "That's hard")
(her miscarriage), as we discuss the betrayal that brought her to us, the desertion at the hands of her erstwhile boyfriend Mike.

Just as the first segment closes, Sally decides that she will allow me in
and tell me the whole story. She ends that ten-minute window with "Oh, the
depression started about eight years ago") As Segment #2 begins, she starts to
recall the details of her mother's tragic death and of the heartrending consequences for her. She starts to go inside but only because the implicit relational
knowing already begun, allows her to trust.

Now the final minutes of the interview play out: Sally leans closer to me,
catches my eye with her direct look, and speaks much more loudly and asser-
tively. I pick up my pace, too, and in my turn, incline my body toward her,
talk more quickly and forcefully, finally nearly yelling … "I strongly do connect them." (Mike and her father both deserted her in a time of great need.)
By the close of the meeting, our speech rhythm and amplitude closely match.

We start to "sync"; we speak rapidly and openly. We maintain eye-to-eye
connection, and communicate, verbally and paraverbally, on the same wave
length—Jim: "when you get angry, you just stop, stop talking, stop eating."—
Sally: "When I'm angry, I do self-destructive things." Then we enter into a
"moment of meeting," both of us facing her rage at the series of men who
have left her in the lurch. Once we finish each other's sentence. Jim: "You
needed him (your father) and you hated him." Sally, simultaneously: "And
I hated him." This pattern of exchange between Sally and myself follows
Stern's format of greater and greater "fit." At the close, we each begin to step
out of role to encounter one another as more complete persons. Finally, we're
fully connecting, both in it together, our moment of meeting. We literally
speak the same language in word and gesture.

Paul W's gentle, quiet, steady, reassuring, firmly attuned style contrasts
with Jim's more active, louder one. However, if we follow the flow of Paul's

consultation with Louise, perhaps surprisingly, we come upon the same general motif that characterized Jim and Sally's meeting, despite now studying a new therapist and client pair, very different in temperament and amplitude from Jim and Sally.

Louise, for good reasons, a cautious young woman, initially keeps her distance from Paul. However, Paul, midway in the interview, has moved toward her, relatively silently, in actual words, apart from "Uh huh, uh huh, uh huh." Deftly, in a tone of seriousness, respect and encouragement, he now breaks in and strongly suggests that Louise has already achieved one of her important childhood goals. She has developed a small, tightly knit group of trusted girlfriends, with whom she can enjoy free give-and-take. She can begin to accept an unrecognised resource in herself, her ability to build friendships.

Louise looks and sounds dumbstruck by Paul's insight. She smiles with excitement. At that moment, he's proved himself to her as someone helpful and probably reliable. The pair then start to develop an "implicit relational knowin") interchange in which Louise speaks with increasing feeling and openness to Paul, and he remains gently attentive and responsive. Their exchange differs from Jim and Sally's, in that Louise speaks more and more, and Paul still remains relatively quiet, although absolutely engaged nonverbally. He doesn't push the pace, but Louise has learned that she can expect something valuable from him. She continues to hope for it, to look for it, and to get it.

At the start of the final ten-minute segment of the meeting, Paul offers her a remarkable reframe that suggests that Louise also wants to *join* her in-law tribe, not just to *escape* from it. Given Louise's background of family isolation and secrecy, this new knowledge, which she wishes to admit her husband's relations into her intimate world that she needs them, could easily feel threatening to her, perhaps even repugnant.

However, now she's developed more trust in Paul, a feeling of safety around him. She lifts her defenses (her control) and even welcomes in this new information, which she then starts to master. "Yeah, that makes sense because I've always wanted a big famil") (Wachtel, 2011, p. 118). Louise accepts a formerly cast aside part of herself—she wants a place in this large family network.

Their overall choreography unfolds in a now familiar pattern. As Sally does with Jim, Louise gradually allows her self-regulation to include Paul as her helpful partner. Their synchrony of implicit relational knowing permits each member of the therapeutic duo to feel validated, calm, and free from intrusion. They can unconsciously collaborate and put their whole selves into it.

This represents the operational definition of "allianc") and a paraverbal demonstration of it. Alliance accounts for 22% of the variance in psychotherapy outcome (Norcross, 2002). Louise, who, 30 minutes before, seemed distant and stiff, ends with—"I never knew I could learn so much in so short a time, so I thank you!"—(Louise offers Paul a warm Duchênne smile and bows toward him with hands clasped.) Paul—"Good, well we worked well together."—(He responds with his own broad Duchênne smile and firm hand-shake; Wachtel, 2011, pp. 123–124)

If we consider all the cases that we've explored through our quantitative meas-ures, we track each time, a pair feeling greater and greater paraverbal comfort, mutual regulation and togetherness as the interview unfolds. This development invariably follows a herky-jerky pattern, not a smooth trajectory. Nevertheless, the two participants find themselves far more connected, and engaged at both verbal and behavioral levels, at the end of the meeting than at its beginning.

Stern and Beebe's map of implicit relational knowing captures the move-ment in all of these interviews, sometimes to an almost uncanny degree. On the strength of the paraverbal, implicit relational knowing communication, the therapy becomes a deeper experience beyond any verbal exchange alone. (We need to add the disclaimer that for illustrative purposes, through the book we've studied consultations that turn out well—best case scenarios. Of course, some implicit relationship alliances never constructively form.)

The Stern concepts brightly illuminate the interchange in our cases and exemplify our points about the centrality of paraverbal relating so clearly that it's tempting to center our discussion simply on the extra-verbal transaction for each pair and then to stop our exploration. That's a mistake though. The tapes and cases have more to teach.

CONNECTING THE DOTS

These new ideas about paraverbal relating aside, insight, Level 1, still plays its own pivotal role in therapy. Our original Venn Diagram from Chapter 2 includes many additional dimensions of the therapeutic relationship beyond the paraverbal. For example, in our vignettes and tapes, the counselor and the client discover specific verbalizable themes that stretch back in time and capture quite closely the patient's recurrent life dilemma or "red threa") (Gustafson, 1981). Therapist and client then can, "connect the dot") in the words of our coauthor Susan Rice. When this occurs, the patients depart the meeting with important gains in self-knowledge that they can clearly articulate, which will help keep this understanding alive in their memory as active insight.

However, these discoveries often happen, within an open "moment of meeting," with an engaged, holding therapist. The explicit validity of the spoken insights also contributes a great deal to the power of the experience, in addition to, and reinforcing, the implicit relational closeness. The more cognitive and the more affective find integration. Paul Wachtel suggests, in

Chapter 6, that when these specific, deeply felt realizations accumulate, lasting change in psychotherapy becomes likely (Wachtel, 2011, p. 121).

Kristin and the Starving Musician

In an apt example of connecting dots, Kristin Osborn offers us her iconic interview with the Starving Musician. In distinction to our other therapists, Kristin knows her client well by the time of this meeting, their 8th hour together. Also, having Kristin as a colleague, friend and coauthor helps us to expand the discussion of her tape.

Kristin uses an affect-focused expressive approach with this and with all her clients. At the beginning of the session, she originally developed a plan to concentrate solely on the Starving Musician's *conflicted anger* toward his wife and to help him open himself to those warded off feelings more constructively. This conflicted anger originates from his childhood as he refers to his mother "She taught me to internalize my feelings instead of asserting myself." In this way, she hoped to support him to clarify his crippling, ambivalent, marital relationship—good plan. Midway through the interview, though, Kristin realized that her chosen approach hadn't moved her client, or herself, ahead into much adaptive affect.

When we spoke with Kristin about the action on the tape, as it simultaneously rolled on the monitor, she blurted out "I had this formula around conflicted anger, but I could feel we weren't really getting very far, so I said f... the formula and went with my gut") (the implicit paraverbal choice) ... "You take the term "Starving Musician" to a whole other level. Your not playing music and your not in a relationship where you are giving and receiving love." (Her client tears up; Kristin's eyes fill with tears as well.) Kristin's attunement to her mind and her body told her that she had started on a less helpful path, so she altered her direction toward her client's lonesomeness and away from his anger—paraverbal therapy in action.

Kristin's words capture the new focus: the Starving Musician's grief due to losses associated with suppressing his anger/assertion, like loneliness, rejection, and hopeless wish for loving acceptance from his frigid partner. Kristin adds, "You have so much love to give, and she isn't able to receive and give back your love." The conflicted affect is alonenessgrief related to his inability to set limits in his relationship so he remains true to himself. Kristin sees the pattern, he sees the pattern, we see the pattern. This is a moment of meeting. Kristin provides the crucial Level 1 insight—he's starving, and his wife may never feed him, but it's a discovery delivered within a Level 2 and Level 3 relationship.

Kristin affectionately, affectively, holds her patient and his feelings as they both shed tears over the emptiness of his arid marriage. She connects the dots but does so in the context of her genuine bodily reactions to her client. We can see that it's Kristin's contact with her physical self, which leads her to tear up, that allows her to feel so clearly what's missing for her patient. He's starving for affection. If we leave the therapist's body out of our understanding of the therapy exchange, we consign ourselves to working with only one half, the patient's half, of the unfolding events. We can see that the therapist belongs on the screen too, and in our analyses, contributing his or her verbal insights and bodily responses.

Return to Paul W and Louise

Paul's manner with his patient differs markedly from Kristin's style, but he just as surely verbally marks each way station with Louise. At some point in the middle of his interview, Paul realizes that "My lady doth protest too much." He reasons that Louise feels so deeply outraged by her intrusive in-laws that possibly she's denying her opposite feelings, casting away a part of herself. This new tribe may also offer something which secretly attracts her, in addition to repelling her. Paul suggests that life with her husband's boisterous family beckons with an exciting energy that her own tiny, injured, shutdown family never provided.

At the start of the meeting, Louise feels real anger and mistrust toward her husband's group. Indeed, dealing with their overbearingness represents Louise's stated reason for seeking this consultation interview in the first place. Initially, she clearly could never accept any suggestion that she might want to move closer to this new demanding network. However, 40 minutes later, after testing Paul's reliability and helpfulness, she can follow him as he weaves together the important episodes of her life and offers the possibility that she's drawn to, as well as terrified by, the overly affiliative in-laws.

We can specify the exact point when Louise realizes the full depth of both sides of her ambivalence: (1) her split-off part, which seeks closeness with her husband's family, as well as, (2) her conscious feeling of hot resentment over their meddling (see below). This represents a "moment of meetin") with Paul and a textbook instance of Control Mastery therapy. Louise has satisfied herself that Paul differs from her overbearing mother from whom she always unconsciously wanted independence. Then she can relax her controlling defenses of distancing and projection and begin to master in a new constructive way, her wish to receive a measure of love from this second family but without becoming swallowed up by them (Gustafson, 1981).

Now we see the two dimensions of expert psychotherapy melded into one. Part 1, Paul explains the continuity of her life events for Louise and unravels the red thread of her story. She needs autonomy from, but also closeness with, loved ones. She hears him clearly, "I never thought of it that way before." But Part 2, she could not grasp his message with nondefensive immediacy, if Paul had not first established himself as safe, engaging, caring, and noncontrolling.

In other words, he's an object, distinct from her original family. Insight arrives but embedded within a new, trusting, implicit relationship.

Back to Jim and Sally

Or consider, for a final time, Jim's meeting with 22-year-old courageous Sally. ... The two of us leaned closer, established eye contact, began to match speech rhythms. In the midst of this increasing paraverbal engagement and collaboration, we also tracked Sally's central dynamic conflict, suppressed anger at men who desert her. This idea spontaneously came to my mind, quite possibly because I had become so involved in implicit relational connection with her.

The nonverbal closeness makes the cognitive, Level 1 insight more likely to occur and more intensely true when it does. Together we followed her dots. She chases intimacy with irresponsible men like her father, who inevitably play their part, and desert her. Then she becomes self-destructively enraged—stops eating, withdraws, suffers migraines, gets depressed. Jim: "I strongly do connect the") (father and boyfriend). Sally: "Yes I never saw it before, but they are the same." In a mutually insightful minute, we join forces and create a moment of meeting—verbally and paraverbally. The implicit relational knowing interaction, through the sessions, represents the starting place from which Levels 1 and 2 discoveries gradually emerge.

PRESENCE

For the therapist

"Presenc") lies near the center of our story—the presence of both therapist and client. For the former, we've learned that presence suggests authentic, affective, open bodily involvement with the session and with the client. At the end of the day, our paraverbal scales really measure presence. At different junctures, the therapist unmistakably conveys great interest in, respect for, empathy for, support for, hope for this client. He or she authentically wants to engage with this client now, in this room, about this topic. He prizes the client (Bohart and Tallman, 1999; Greenberg et al., 1993). His body is open to more understanding; he feels this strong interest and preconsciously projects it toward the patient. The client, in turn, paraverbally registers this real concern and can feel her defenses soften.

Presence represents the crucial paraverbal dimension, an amalgam of "Accessibilit") and "Congruence." Our scales register Paul Wachtel's bodily communications, his calm, respectful, sincere interest. Paul's stance feels so genuine that almost any observer, psychotherapy student or not, would warmly react to him. Paul's hands and arms speak for his paraverbal self. They show his struggle to rein the pieces together and explain them in an understandable way to Louise. These gestures are not new to Paul. We can readily imagine him as a youngster expressing his thoughts accompanied by expressive hand and arm movements. This is the way he signals access to his inner self and to his presence.

Recently Geller and Porges (2014) have reported important work relating the therapist's and the client's presence to their polyvagal neuropsychological functioning.They also offer a scale to measure the presence of both participants.

As we've also noticed, however, presence includes more than nonverbal attunement. Words play an important role too. When Paul tells Louise that she wants to feel "I have a place in this world to") words play a role. He captures her dilemma exactly. Given her traumatic, straight-jacketed history, she hangs on by her fingernails to the idea that she has any meaningful "place in this world." Paul actively means this affirmation for Louise, with immediacy and sincerity. It's extra-verbal engagement and kindness, plus the words. (Schwartz, 2004). If Paul were not verbally and paraverbally attuned to Louise, he never could have formulated his summary of her ambivalence toward her in-laws, in so timely and in so clear a way.

At regular intervals, the therapist can assess her own level of "presence." How fully am I in the room? Does my mind keep wandering in an unhelpful way? Do I keep checking the clock? The appearance of such telltale signs will correlate with how present the counselor feels, which, in turn, will influence the intimacy level in the office. A fruitful path of self-inquiry enters, when the therapist asks herself: What disturbs my level of concentration? Do I feel undervalued by this patient? What transference or countertransference themes could explain this? Does the client's defensiveness intrude around every issue or just this particular one?

Here we can see that the therapist is somewhat stuck. She needs to open herself to more presence. Presence starts in the therapist's body with mindfulness. She needs to clear herself of distraction and allow the patient to subliminally enter her conscious and unconscious paraverbal self. What reactions does the patient evoke in me? Do they remind me of something from my past or present? What images arise in my head?

On the night of her mother's death, I imagined Sally's tall, overweight, blustering, red faced, tipsy father looming over her and giving her his cold instruction—"Go to bed." But the patient's presence also helps us to find our own. Sally finally opens herself to me so much that I can emotionally pretty precisely see her dilemma in my mind's eye, and speak it back to her. She helps me get my implicit relational knowing on track. In Schwartz IFS parlance, we both become self-led.

When our presence is open, strong bodily sensations and thoughts readily come to us. We've learned that it's not a cognitive puzzle only. It's the full taking in of yourself and of the other, verbally and paraverbally. Then their body, as well as your own, in addition to their verbally crafted narrative, will give the clues that we can spontaneously register. Do we clearly see the characters in the client's world or do their descriptions fall short of lifelike form? What's left out? We can gently ponder the details omitted with our client. Psychotherapy often needs to deal with the "unsai") as much as the "said." Why is this or that information passed over?

For example, Louise is so very outraged by her sister-in-law, the leader of her husband's family. Does this woman remind her of her own controlling mother? If we follow this approach, we'll mirror the free flowing connectivity of Tronick's mother and baby. A spontaneous, productive path to follow with our client will then emerge. When therapist and client become "self-led," they work creatively together.

The client's presence

The therapist's self draws the client into greater presence herself. Both participants will learn from the meeting to the extent that they can each become authentic, receptive, and lift a defense … no presence for client, no meaningful therapy (Wachtel, 2014). The counselor sets the tone with his smile of greeting, like the mother's first smile to her baby in the morning. So the therapist often goes first, her open face and body posture beget the same stance in the patient's mind and body, but the client needs to follow suit and respond with her own warmth and receptivity, her right side brain response (Siegel, 1999, 2012)

The client feels that introductory paraverbal message of safety and openness from the counselor. Then, as the tapes teach us again and again, the implicit reciprocity of mutual knowing can start. We can track when the client becomes more present. Sally looks directly into my eyes and speaks much more loudly and clearly, at the end of Segment #1 and the beginning of Segment #2. "Oh the depression started about eight years ago (shallow laugh)"—I respond, "That's not entirely a joke."

She then shifts and locks my gaze. "My mother died."—the indispensable fact that we must know to continue. Presence is inevitably mediated paraverbally, then, and depends on both participants. However usually, though not always, the therapist takes the lead. It's hard to imagine a client finding her own presence with a nonresponsive therapist. When the presences of both participants intersect, we discover a key to psychotherapy. Both players shed their defenses and move quickly into a new experience. Sally: "I never thought of it that way before." Many authentic possibilities open. We can now accomplish much more working together, and surprisingly quickly.

When the pair senses serendipitous common ground, that bond of presence comes more easily, but empathy can transcend personal differences.

What exactly does Paul Wachtel intuitively understand about the life of a young girl growing up in Sweden during the 1990s as an only child, with a disabled father? Not much. Nevertheless, Paul reaches across the age/gender/cultural gap with his accepting smile and his ever-encouraging "uh huh uh huh."

Sometimes, overly conscious attention to technique interferes with presence. We've seen other tapes in which the impeccably trained therapists let their skills come between them and their client. They seem to bring an agenda with them and a method to carry out that plan, but the focus on the unique client becomes blurred. Paul demonstrates remarkable interviewing ability; however, the observer almost never notices his technical moves. At the end of the meeting, we try to unravel the mystery of the positive outcome; it seemed to appear from thin air.

CHANGES IN APPROACH

As we review this chapter so far, don't we mostly agree on the teachings from the videos and from the case examples? What's really innovative here? Aren't we just describing "plain old therap") (J. G. Allen, 2013)—two minds trying to understand each other (J. G. Allen, 2013; Fonagy, 2014)? Maybe, but a fuller paraverbal picture of that familiar approach helps us grasp more surely the spoken and unspoken dimensions of the treatment.

Now we switch focus for the balance of our discussion. Thus far, we've reviewed what has happened on the tapes, and in the case excerpts, between the client and the therapist. Given this introduction, a potential shift in the counselor's direction presents itself. We can start to suggest how the therapist might specifically act differently to build on the cocreated extra-verbal experience and to optimise the bodily presence of both participants. This, in turn, will probably deepen the therapeutic relating, as more parts of the therapist and client become involved, more of the unconscious can become conscious. The paraverbal connection, over and over, marks one important access to that unconscious.

Alterations in the therapist's behavior—Four propositions

We've grappled with complicated questions throughout our monograph. At first, we asked if patients and therapists really do communicate paraverbally, and if so, how to characterize that language and take measure of its significance within a given treatment hour. We've made progress on that question. If we can see it on the video, we can score it. Then we can more fully comprehend it, and finally, potentially, we can teach it.

Now we need to ascertain, if indeed, we can teach it and apply our new learning to offer practical guidance to our readers. Specifically, how do I more accurately understand my paraverbal messages and those of my client? How will I know if I'm drawing helpful conclusions about these observations? If I wander off into musings about nonverbal communication, will I distract myself from more crucial dimensions of the meeting?

Since I'm not used to working with paraverbal data, if I venture into this area, do I become vulnerable to serious naive errors? In sum, how do I attempt to increase my presence and the patient's, productively, without intruding on the natural sweep of the interview. If the reader does not already have some of these concerns in mind, we haven't presented our findings in a very compelling way.

We'll respond to these quandaries first, in general fashion, but then quickly move into more involved clinical vignettes.

First, clearly, we encourage the therapists to more regularly observe their and their patient's paraverbal messaging—why does my client look down at her feet when she begins to talk about her brother? Or, the patient says he's less depressed, but his face still has a rigid sad mask. Or, why do I sit so stiffly in my chair and smile so little with this third client? Why do her facial expressions feel so severe to me?

We need to return repeatedly to such points as these and to study their meaning, as we continue our minute-by-minute observations within our "moving alon") work. If we do, we'll pay closer attention to the whole experience of engaging with our client, rather than less attention. In other words, we do not need to worry about becoming distracted from our central task, when we let the paraverbal information in, that activity represents part of our primary goal. Susan, Kristin, and I, admittedly only a tiny sub-sample, never feel so connected with our patient as when we're engaged paraverbally: open palms, direct gaze, matching prosody. Bodily awareness of self and other makes one more involved with the client's story, not less.

I know that when I first interviewed Sally, I tried, in general, to move closer and closer to her congruent feelings, but only after I watched the tape many times, did I recognize the details of my specific approach: Adjusting my speech prosody with Sally's, strongly raising my voice at important times and holding her all the while with a riveted look, for example. Over the years, grasping my behavioral actions more particularly has helped me become a more fully focused, body–mind counselor, able to offer a more helpful experience, hour by hour. I have greater familiarity with and greater confidence in my nonverbal style. If I practiced without attention to my bodily presentation now, I would not recognize myself as a therapist.

Kristin reports a similar change. (After studying her physical signals on the tape) "I'm more comfortable in my own body when I try to bond with a clien") (Kristin Osborn, 1-14-14, personal communication). Kristin continues: "When I check in paraverbally, I feel more relaxed physically and more ready to deal with whatever happens. I'm less agenda drive") (personal communication, 1-23-14). Watching ourselves on video represents an invaluable opportunity, but even without the tape, we and our colleagues can observe how we and our therapeutic partner interchange nonverbally.

Of course, we humans can at times overdo and misapply any technique, including the extra-verbal stance we describe here so enthusiastically. We'll ponder those risks in a few minutes. But now let's study particular cases to suggest how therapists might use their paraverbal awareness to experiment with specific changes in approach, if they so wished.

Four propositions

The therapist could (1) more intensively study *her patient's* paraverbal self and/or (2) increase her grasp of *her own* extra-verbal participation. (3) She could experiment with *specifically* calling attention to, and exploring with her client, that client's nonverbal contribution, or (4) the counselor might start to increase her own paraverbal interventions and *remark directly* on these. If our assumptions here prove sound, following these trails should lead to observable changes in the vividness of the treatment for both participants.

Vignette #7—The Marathon Man

Our coauthor, Kristin Osborn, contributes this report about a young male client, who telephoned in an emergency, suffering from an extreme anxiety reaction, following the bombing at the Boston Marathon on April 15, 2013. In her observations, Kristin emphasizes the many paraverbal symptoms reported by her patient and traces those in a helpful way toward an unanticipated conclusion. This represents a clear example of focusing on the patient's body and on his physical, extra-verbal reactions—proposition #1.

> Our 22-year-old, Latino-American male, an ex-college athlete, waited at the finish line for his runner wife, when the attack began. He was unhurt, but as the second bomb exploded he became terrified for his wife's safety. Using his cell phone, he located her as she ran about a half mile short of the finish. He rushed out to help her and a number of her friends. He also guided several strangers to safety. Clearly he acted in an heroic fashion. However, four days later he became overwhelmed with anxiety and called Kristin in great distress. We relay part of the phone conversation between the two.
>
> MM (Marathon Man): "I'm feeling symptoms I've never experienced before, and I'm terrified. I have nausea, I'm sweating, exhausted, and my heart is racing. I'm staying busy and trying to ignore my anxiety, but I'm feeling worse and wors") (tone of near panic).

In the following dialogue, Kristin, at first, focuses on increasing her client's access to his anger, but then she realizes that perhaps this represents a less helpful path. She actually needs to track his issues concerning self-care and self-compassion.

At the start she asks him to pay attention to the sensations in his body—Proposition #1—Study the client's nonverbal experience. The Marathon Man describes tightness in his arms and chest, legs, hands and throat. Kristin asks if he senses he's avoiding any feeling. He says he thinks he's holding back anger, explaining that he almost didn't go to work due to the fear he would "snap." As he describes this terror of "snapping," his throat begins to tighten. "I feel like screaming, but I can't."

He explains that he's angry, first of all angry at himself for forcing himself to go to the marathon, in the first place, to cheer on his wife.

MM: I didn't want to go, but I made myself go. I knew it was important for me to be there and watch Anna cross the finish line, but now I'm mad. I always feel like the world's about to end. My heart is pounding in my chest, my anxiety is interfering with my life, my relationship with my wife. I'm so upset. I just want to scream! (He never explains why he initially didn't want to attend the race, but perhaps he had anxiety about the pressure from the huge cheering crowd?)

He continues to describe increased tension in his arms, throat and stomach, but he experiences no relief doing so. "My muscles are so tired from being tense for so long. I want to scream, but I feel like I'm dreaming that something bad is about to happen, and I can't get a sound out." (Of course something bad has already happened.)

Kristin used her own visualization to picture that he's feeling anger in his body, but she notices also that it isn't directed outward, as she would expect of true anger. At no point does he mention the terrorists for example. In fact he seems to be more angry with his anxiety symptoms than with the violence inflicted upon him, and his friends, and his city.

The Marathon Man's anger seems directed at himself even though he has survived the bombing and courageously helped others.

Kristin: Are you frustrated with yourself?

MM: Yes I'm afraid if I let myself get really angry, I'll lose it. I'll be out of control fighting so hard. I'll hurt someone. I'm so afraid I'll have a psychotic breakdown.

Kristin's hunch is partially confirmed. He's feeling mad, but the focus is himself, that he'll break down and hurt someone. He mentions no specific external targets. His problem appears that he's besieged by symptoms of PTSD that he can't control.

In a crucial insight Kristin realizes that the Marathon Man seems to feel a general lack of self-compassion, as if he expected himself to respond in a robotic way to these traumatic events. His anger is at his symptoms. He apparently sees no reason that he should receive a measure of the comfort, and of the care, that he has just offered to others.

Kristin decides to challenge his thinking, which is apparently resulting in self-persecution for a crime he certainly didn't commit. "I noticed a high level of self-neglect, refusing to care for himself in a loving way. So I began to understand the problem from an affective perspective." (Here Kristin studies the Marathon Man's nonverbal reactions, but also her own, and realizes that she's uncomfortable with how little self-compassion her client experiences. Right here something about his presentation doesn't make sense. These represent examples of using Proposition 1; studying the patient's paraverbal messages and Proposition 2; examining her own paraverbal sensations.)

"I focused on his anger, once again and asked him to describe what happened in the moments following the bombing. (tracking his paraverbal reactions— proposition #1.) I'm using an exposure intervention. "Pay attention to what was your "behavior."

He described a sensation of calm, even though he was close to both explosions. He chastised himself for feeling terror later, but perhaps he had a good reason to be really anxious. He broke away from this line of thought and said, "I don't think that it's helpful for me to ignore my anxiety. It's okay for me to be scared." (He creates his own breakthrough here.)

He returned to the terrifying experience and described what happened the moment the second bomb went off. "I was focused on whether Anna was okay. I knew I would be okay, if she was okay. I was able to locate her on my phone, and I started running toward her."

Kristin interrupts him and points out how calmly he was feeling in the moment, and how he was able to use technology, common sense, eyesight, athletic ability and adrenalin to confront the situation before him. As an affect focused dynamic therapist, Kristin will naturally gravitate toward proposition 1, studying the client's paraverbal reactions. People talk about feelings, but mostly they experience those feelings in their bodies.

MM: I wanted to scream, but I didn't. I just stayed focused. One of my wife's friends, (inexplicably) sat down on the sidewalk, turned her purse upside-down and started organizing it. I was calm inside and out; I knew it wasn't the time to be emotional.

Kristin interrupts: You were, in an instinctual part of yourself, a protector of your wife, your friends and yourself.

MM: I did a better job than I thought I would. I was organized, and I was calmly looking for Anna. (Kristin asked him to pay attention to how well his body worked, how his anxiety guided him—hoping he would feel some pride for his actions and not castigate himself, only four days after the horrific event.)

(MM concludes by following Kristin's lead:) I did do a good job. My great uncle (a decorated officer in the American Marines, who died last year) would have said, "You did a good job." (validation from a war time soldier) He chokes up and cries, "Everything's okay, I can't push away, I'm feeling I can't push it aside. The bombing was upsetting, of course I feel nausea. I need to forgive myself and not be so hard on myself." He accepts that he had a normal delayed stress reaction—very much like a soldier in combat might.

He begins to sob. Kristin softly repeats to him, "Your uncle would have been so proud of you. He would want you to feel proud of yourself."

MM pauses for air, his voice, now much calmer, stronger and more clear. "The time to be a hero is over, now I need to focus on myself."

Kristin ends the exchange and suggests that he needs to rest, eat healthy food and connect with his friends. He returns, "Comfort, rest, relaxation that's probably the best thing for me to let my guard down now."

Kristin takes us inside the mind and body of one victim of the marathon attack, as he struggles with his own particularized reaction to this tragedy. She offers her ingenious affective exposure intervention, which moves the client from his anxiety, to his anger and finally to his need for self-comfort. She concentrates mostly on Proposition #1—track the client's nonverbal bodily messages but also on her own paraverbal feelings, Proposition #2, as she asks herself, "Why is he not kinder to himself?"

Tracing her client's extra-verbal experience and her own in response supports Kristin to offer an effective verbal and nonverbal, step-by-step, intervention. The paraverbal stance helps her to study the client's communication and to see what's missing. He's angry but not at anyone but himself. This insight is the pivot, which leads to a productive resolution to a difficult crisis.

It's important to follow the paraverbal signs wherever they lead, Proposition #1, and not to help the client suppress them. Although in this case we could hardly miss the bodily metaphors—"panic," "about to snap," "nausea," "scream." If Kristin had tried to circumvent or dissipate the power of these signs, the MM might have felt ignored, his wrenching anxiety passed over, and he might have curtailed the conversation. Without her paraverbal understanding, Kristin might have missed the significance of the Marathon Man's self-critical outburst. This method revealed that the focus of his conflict started with his lack of self-compassion. Kristin implicitly—bodily connects with the MM. His inner self shifts following her lead, he can start to care for himself—their moment of meeting.

The Marathon Bombing represents an extreme, near war-time experience. Nonverbal language in other contexts is much more subtle and confusing. To illustrate that idea, we return to our day-to-day office practice. There we meet a new couple, Jack and Helen. In their treatment, we find it crucial to concentrate on Jack's barely perceptible extra-verbal messages, and on my own reciprocal nonverbal reactions back toward him. After a slow start, this direction allows us to proceed more constructively with this complex man and complicated couple.

Vignette #8—Jack and Helen: Optimal Therapist Activity?— Propositions #1 & #2—Reading the Client's Paraverbal Signs and Our Own—Jim Donovan

Jack, a 65-year-old, mid-level insurance executive and his wife Helen, two years younger, referred by her social worker, came to me two years ago, at Helen's insistence. They both are of Scandinavian ancestry. She wanted to focus on a lack of action, intimacy, and particularly, of appreciation, in their 34-year marriage. "I'm not important to him."

> Jack, a stately man nearly always attired in grey slacks and sports coat, still relates to me somewhat carefully as he enters the office for the couple's twice monthly session. (We meet only at two to three week intervals for the stated reason that Jack feels the couple cannot afford more frequent visits.) Jack generally catches my eye out of the corner of his, smiles momentarily and deliberately takes his seat.
>
> Tall, slender, slightly stooped Jack, looks younger than his age, exercises regularly and appears in excellent health. Jack, verbally, never starts the meeting, ceding most of that active role to Helen. After she begins, he speaks soberly, and unemotionally, but often quite wisely about each topic. His neutrality feels his defining characteristic. At a recent meeting, he enunciated his spare, down beat philosophy of life—"You grow up. You work. You find ways to amuse yourself, and you die." Jack doesn't ask for much. He needs to learn to ask for more.
>
> Attractive, spirited, Helen decidedly contrasts to Jack in her coordinated brightly colored blouse and well-quaffed, tinted, reddish hair. She speaks in a friendly, energetic, hopscotch, unmistakably ADD style. Helen, with considerable edge, regularly verbally pokes at Jack and sometimes berates him over his blandness, his distance and his humdrum routine. "I'm living your life. I'm bored too." So Helen brings irritation to the sessions. For his part, Jack finally pushes back with "Get over it Helen! You'll feel differently in a few days."
>
> She complains regularly about the financial perils of her consulting business and the lack of monetary resources in their couple. Sometimes, they could not appear more different; in their appearance, in their interpersonal styles, in their goals and in their attitudes about money and feelings. She freely spends; he carefully records each transaction and plans for future necessities.
>
> Jack recalls his parents as distant from him and distant from each other. "It was an awkward situation always." His father had alcoholism and depression and remained in the background. Jack worked his way through college but at graduation experienced great career indecision. Feelings of aloneness now closed in on him. He felt terrified not to have a job direction.

Then in his early 20s, Jack developed acute panic attacks, a major sleep disturbance, and recurrent suicidal thoughts. Terrified, he felt he was "having a nervous breakdown," as if he had no solid identity to guide him into adulthood. Could he lean on an identification with his father? Probably not.

Jack found his way to a major local hospital and received psychotherapy and antidepressant medications. Over a seven-year period, ages 21 to 27, he gradually recovered. In his early 30s he met Helen, and immediately fell in love with her brightness and vivacity.

His life followed a much more positive turn then, particularly with the later birth of their twin sons. In the past 35 years he has taken maintenance doses of antidepressants. He reports some sleep difficulty which responds adequately to medication and to meditation. He has had no return of the serious depressive episode.

A strong student, regardless of his emotional distress, Jack attended professional school at night and somewhat, by default, chose a secure occupational path, adequately remunerative but below his level of skill and training. Jack plays it safe. "After that depression, I just wanted a steady job with no pressure."

As I carefully register him paraverbally, I realize that Jack tries, at every opportunity, to manage the stress level of his life, perhaps lest, his depression suddenly return and leave him exquisitely disorganized once again. On a daily basis he carefully deals with his profession, his wife, and his two adult children, trying to keep things in check, rather than to explore spontaneous new thoughts or feelings. "I avoid confrontation." He explains. But why so completely?

Jack seems to suffer from a vague but deep and long-lasting anxiety reaction, subsequent to that horrifying breakdown in his 20s. As if he's, half consciously, frightened every minute, as it is. What if the panic and suicidality should suddenly return in full force?

He loves his sons and feels genuinely engaged with them. He offers them careful supportive advice and major financial assistance, neither of which he received from his family. "I got no feedback ever." He had a restricted relationship with his parents particularly with his father, who, in Jack's narrative, appears only a grey character with almost no personality. Jack says he does not feel lonely now, but in-between sentences his face falls into an expression of stillness and maybe sadness.

By contrast, Helen's parents were intensely involved with one another. They affectionately loved each other and followed two full time careers, as well as an active social life, despite her mother's severe asthma. They went out frequently to socialize and left Helen alone and sometimes unprotected. She feels her father a warmer character than her mother. Her mother's euthymic moods ran the family.

Jack and Helen are committed to one another and exchange some affection and sexuality, but within neutral boundaries. Helen would like more engagement, and particularly more obvious attention and caring from Jack. She actively resents his understated somewhat melancholy distance. She feels: "I don't matter to anyone except the dog."

Our treatment has relieved much of the bickering in the relationship. Jack: "We get along much better now." The sessions have brought them more togetherness, as well, but to develop more intimacy, we clearly have work left to do. What's the plan?

Proposition #1: The first move—read the client's paraverbal communications— I needed to translate the messages from Jack's nonverbal self, which will help me understand him more fully. I realize his reticence marks the first hurdle in this therapy. I further understand that much of the information I can gather about him will have to come through paraverbal channels.

As I take him in, I sense his self-protectiveness most of all. The signs I get convey that he's afraid to make a move physically or emotionally, despite his high intelligence and perceptiveness. He sits nearly motionless and parries his wife's requests, apparently effortlessly, as she turns and twists in her chair and challenges him for more involvement. Also, there's that forlorn, lonely caste to his face.

Jack looks and maybe feels bereft. He wryly smiles and chuckles, but I've never heard him laugh out loud. He communicates little joy. He does not say that he's afraid of losing what he has—money—security—loving feelings, most of all Helen herself. But the image I have of him is of low level, though pervasive fear. Jack's a man enclosed in a fort, mostly unwilling to emerge. He's tentative. He rarely feels fully present.

If we miss his bodily characterologic message of self-guardedness, we miss the essence of this man and of this therapy. What lies behind his wall though, what missing part has he cast off and how might we help him reconnect with it? Jack represents so nonverbal a presence that his body is at the center of the therapy not his spoken words. If we are to understand him, it will come mostly through paraverbal cues.

Proposition #2: We've grasped the message from Jack's self, "I keep on alert," but now we need to take measure of the contribution from the therapist's body, too. Jack's self-girding insularity leaves him one low key, but one challenging patient. He can frustrate us, which increases our chances of making a mistake with him and which limits our ability to develop presence with him. Signals from my own paraverbal self give me suggestions about how to approach Jack and how not to.

In my chest and jaw I feel impatience and the strong impulse to push Jack toward greater reactivity, for instance—"Come on Jack something must make you happy, excited, angry, or scared. Everyone has these feelings sometimes. It's okay to say them out loud."

As I listen to my upper chest messages of some frustration, fortunately, I glimpse the therapeutic error looming just ahead. The counselor can have plenty of feelings of his own to track, but he's not required to act on each of them.

If I followed my first reaction and confronted Jack, even gently, over his apparent docility and distance, I would risk shaming him in front of his wife and me, frightening him more and driving his core self further underground, achieving the opposite of my goal. The therapy office might begin to feel unsafe for him. Jack, then, could feel the need to assert more control and defensiveness but develop even less mastery of his dilemma. He'd withdraw further, as he does when Helen confronts him. He skitters away.

Also I have advanced directives not to push Jack. The referring social worker, Helen, and Jack himself, have told me that he does not wish to change and that under pressure he backs up and could become more resistant and might even leave the treatment. As it stands, he attends therapy regularly, never misses a meeting, and is never late, but he carefully spaces out the sessions. Attendance in the office represents paraverbal behavior. He's committed up to a point.

I need to meditate and stay in an accepting space so that my positive feelings for Jack can grow. I find that I like and respect him. He's overcome an empty early family life and a dangerous depression. He consistently takes a caring and responsible, if somewhat distant, role as a husband and father. He's not uninvolved. I find him on occasion passive, certainly, but smart, interesting, kind and sophisticated about a number of subjects, particularly politics.

I step back from any impulse to question him, exhort him or move to change him. At each appropriate moment I take the opportunity to observe with him places in his life where he has acted softly and skillfully. "You're handling the family finances really well, and you've avoided bankruptcy at some tough spot") ... "Your kids know they can get concerned, sound advice from you, whenever they want it." This echoes Paul Wachtel (2011) speaking to the client's cast off, devalued, hidden, strong points. Jack is more engaged than he seems.

We now know Jack is unconsciously hiding some important part of himself but what part and why? We need to use all our extra-verbal skills to figure this out. Words will help us only a little here.

Jack and Helen feel present for the treatment and to each other. For the most part they now seem closer and less irritated with one another, but their paraverbal pairing often doesn't, and hasn't, fit well together, thus their frequent courses of couple treatment over the past 35 years. Anger still sparks up between them and stays there, unresolved, until Helen, more or less, lets it go. Jack withdraws from the anger quickly. He wants no part of it.

We have not reached their underlying discontent in a constructive way as yet. As they sit with each other, they feel somewhat pessimistic, a little unengaged and a little bored—a little disappointed. This is the usual paraverbal atmosphere they create with me and apparently at home with each other.

Jack and I alone:

By chance two weeks later, Helen is traveling and "by mistak") forgets to cancel their appointment so Jack comes by himself. I excerpt some of our exchange:

As soon as he arrives, I sense something different in my body and in the nonverbal messages from Jack. He's a little more present now to me and I to him. I prompt him, "How are you doing") He answers that he feels that many marriages founder over money and that he has given in to Helen too much in this area. He says that he's sad that he owns no home, and he's almost 65 years old.

Jack: I did that to keep the peace. She's a warm figure. I'm negligent in that area. (apparently)

Jim: "Your father"

Jack: "Yea he just went to the men's club and drank. (father depressed?) It was cold between my parents. Helen's outgoing, less standoffish than I am. I know I've disappointed her") (But he also feels he's sacrificed to keep Helen happy and with him.)

My body perks up at his readiness to talk more deeply. He's perhaps more open with Helen absent. He inclines his glance down toward his feet, but angles his eyes toward me. He seems to give me the signal that I can move for a bit more closeness. (Proposition #1) Inadvertently, I dip my head to look directly at him, with an open, accepting, facial expression (Proposition #2—the therapist studies his own paraverbal reactions).

Jack: We each have grievances. I want a home. She does, too, and blames me, when she gets angry. It's not regular anger; it's total anger.

Jim: Everything but the kitchen sink?

Jack: Yes, I crawl into a corner. I avoid conflict. (Is he afraid of his anger?)

Jim: Your family?

Jack: (his eyes catch mine—I hold his gaze. Propositions #1 and #2: the therapist studies the patient's nonverbal messages as well as his own. I'm zeroing in.) My mother took care of my father. He could barely read or write. Helen's mother bossed her dad (silence), ("Sad Jack," maybe "Angry Jac") registers in my chest—Proposition 2—the therapist studies his inner nonverbal reactions.) Not easy for either Helen or me I guess. (Jack has a downtrodden look but why so discouraged and ashamed? I remark with him that in the marriages Jack and Helen each observed, the woman seemed to direct the relationship. As I picture Jack's sad face in my mind's eye, he looks ashamed, as if he's identified with the father whom he feels had little of value to offer him, so he holds back too. He doesn't know what an active, loving man looks or feels like.)

Jim: I have the feeling that you love Helen, but something gets in the way. You feel this in your body. (Very slowly and gently, soft edge to my voice. I match his prosody and attend to both of our physical sensations. Again in Proposition #1, I study Jack's nonverbal messaging, and I'm aware of my own in Proposition #2.)

Jack: Holding back, my own family was like that. She holds back too. I don't think I have a need for it (closeness).

Jim: Where do you feel this in your body?

Jack: (silence) Lot of rejection. Women before Helen, my own family, caution, get hurt. I was rejected by a woman when I was very depressed; it really hurt. (He probably had suicidal thoughts.) A lot of people don't understand rejection. My own history, an awkward situation in my family.

Jim: No laughter?

Jack: Laughter? There wasn't any (no joy between family members). I had myself in a cocoon for protection. Jack was not recognized in his family, and he still feels that way. (We're approaching the core of his difficulty and the part cast aside. Jack felt love for a brother, for his mother and then for a former girlfriend who rejected him at the depth of his sadness. Now I begin to see that he loves Helen too. He has a loving part, but he's on guard lest he suffer still another rejection, if he's found wanting. His vulnerability keeps him apart. This defense prevents him from getting what he needs and certainly Helen from getting what she needs. He still goes into that cocoon when he feels afraid—a Proposition #1 observation.)

Jim: But you're not as vulnerable as before. You can lift your cocoon or pull it down again when you want to. (His eyes meet mine in recognition. This seems like a new idea for him and he appears to appreciate my support.) You could open up to Helen if you pleased, and then stop, if you didn't like it or if she hurts you.

Jack: She hasn't rejected me.

Jim: I know. So perhaps it's something to try. (He nods.) … Well, we did okay alone together today. (I feel Jack has put himself in my hands a little more—a Propositions #1 and #2 observation.)

Jack: I wondered what it would be like, but it was okay. (Jack feared rejection and criticism in our one to one meeting. It look courage for him to come by himself. This represents a small "moment of meetin") between us. Our implicit relating earlier in the hour prepared for this moment. He feels some of my affection for him, and I could certainly feel that affection returned to me a bit. We exchange warm Duchênne smiles and firmly shake hands as he departs.)

I perceive his body as more open to me in this meeting than ever before and mine to his. I read the wistfulness in his eyes. This helps me with the frustration of his nonresponsiveness. He admits a little more anger, a little more sensitivity to rejection in this solo session, which helps me become more present. I'm hopeful that the low-key "moment of engagemen") that we shared in this meeting will lead to more openness in our three-way sessions. He feels recognized by me.

Propositions #1 and #2 have shown us a possible path. The therapist needs to focus on tiny eye shifts, moments of facial relaxation, changes in speech tone, to approach Jack, since he reveals so little in direct verbal interchange. The therapist therefore can track Proposition #1, but he also needs to follow his own paraverbal responses to Jack, particularly his feelings of affection for him—Proposition #2.

This therapy remains on the edge though. It's unclear how far Jack will dare to explore himself or Helen or me. A month later Jack and Helen have another falling out, over disagreements about renting a new home. This time, however, Jack readily responds to my suggestion and leaves Helen a note saying that he wants to work it out with her and that he cares for her. The couple moves closer and serious conflict ebbs. Luckily they discover a new affordable house to rent, which feels acceptable to both of them. He has reached out to Helen a little more.

A month after that, Jack and I are alone again; Helen arrives late. Jack tells me he has spent two days babysitting his 6-month-old granddaughter. I say, "Responsibility") "A good responsibility." He says with a spontaneous warm grin.

Jim: There's a loving part that comes out when you're with your children and grandchildren.

Jack: I always hug my kids. My mother hugged me sometimes. Up till the 3rd grade things went well. I had friends but hard in adolescence, no real friends. (His mother stopped hugging him too soon and his father never did.)

Jim: Some of that love, some of that hidden away part of you loves Helen.

Jack: I see. (serious tone) Maybe I should work on that do you think? (open genuine questioning tone)

Jim: Does it feel like a good idea?

Jack: Yeah it does, maybe I can do that (tone of serious resolution)

Jim: You'll feel better too. (encouraging authentic tone)

Six weeks later Jack has a cancer scare.

Jack: Helen very helpful, very supportive. I appreciate it … we're closer together (slow genuine serious prosody) … Helen and kids sustain me. (He feels recognized by them, registered by his grateful facial expression, and his open feelingful tone. Jack received minimal recognition at home after the third grade.).

Jack's engagement with Helen is his most authentic so far. We can grasp the central irony of their relationship. Jack loves Helen too much, not too little. She's too important. He fears she'll reject him. By connecting para-verbally with Jack this new image of him comes to my mind. The dimension that Jack has cast aside represents his active loving self. He has felt too embarrassed and too vulnerable to let it show. In his family of origin, he experienced virtually no evidence of directly demonstrated caring; none from his father. Mostly without words, Jack and I rehearsed a little of this male bonding in our one to one exchanges. He did not get paralyzed with fear when we did so. He's a little more ready to reaccept the loving part that he has suppressed.

In our latest meeting, they prepare for a visit from their son and his new girlfriend. They remark that, with company, they often snipe at each other, which never feels constructive. I ask them to face each other, join their gaze and take five minutes each to explore this pattern of mutual undermining. Helen realizes that her anxiety to please can feel overwhelming. Jack grasps that he's frustrated with Helen's frantic activity, and he won't participate. Then Helen feels abandoned. After this exchange, the furthest they've ever pursued this pattern, they sense they've learned something. They now feel more prepared for the visit. "It's a good thing we had a therapy session just before our son arrives."—each grins.

The intimacy that Jack and I achieved in our original solo session prob-ably influenced the tone of these later productive couple") interactions. The initial paraverbal interchange between the two of us has moved the treatment along to more implicit closeness. Jack seems more accepting and valuing of his loving part. In order to make this shift, he's probably borrowed me as the father that he never had at home. I'm happy to oblige. I really like Jack and feel close to him without words.

Looking back at all our cases, we can observe that the critical focus, the missing part, enters early on but it gets expressed paraverbally from the cli-ent to the therapist even though, at first, neither participant can consciously articulate any description of this missing piece. Once he spots it, the coun-selor needs to make a paraverbal connecting response quickly back to the client.

In our one to one meeting Jack offers me his vulnerability. He has a loving part; he fears to show it. He also has an angry part. Helen has squandered their money through poor organization. He's afraid to show that too. Potential rejection is the primary feeling behind the fear of expressing both the love and the anger. I offer back my affection and respect. Unconsciously he real-izes I have received his message and given something in return to him. The alliance joined, we can profitably continue the therapy. We must stay on the lookout for these first nonverbal requests and respond with specific under-standing and warmth where we can.

Helen, of course, brings her own paraverbal challenge. I have suggested stimulant medication that has helped her focus at work, but she can quickly dismiss Jack—"He won't change; don't you see that") Her impatience covers her cast off part, "I want people to stop overlooking me, the way they have my whole life."

The counselor has to take on Helen's distractible verbal self and support her to slow down, organise her thoughts, and study details of her interaction with Jack and take better care of her money—this last a constant irritant for Jack. She needs to feel her sadness over her lifelong lack of attention, first from her mother and now from her husband. Helen moves and speaks incredibly quickly, and he responds much more slowly, verbally, emotionally, and physically. We have to find a way to balance their tempos, but Jack is a more present participant now, and he's a little less frightened of Helen since he feels me as an ally.

PROPOSITIONS #3 AND #4

In Proposition #3, the therapist specifically remarks on the paraverbal language of the client. In Proposition #4, she changes her own extra-verbal participation and draws direct attention to that. Through these two classes of intervention, particularly Proposition #4, the counselor can reach out with her own strong paraverbal messages. It's an experiential leap to make obvious extra-verbal shifts in one's technique. The therapist, now, in Propositions #3 and #4, takes a higher profile in the treatment, often with productive results. We'll learn to gauge these, as we continue with our clinical vignettes. I don't feel that Jack and Helen are ready as yet for Propositions #3 and #4, but consider Peter and Jeannine.

Vignette #9—Peter and Jeannine: Deeper Mutual Enjoyment

This pair, each 58, married some 31 years, have two sons in their 20s. Peter, a slender, alert, humorous man, like his wife, from a blue collar Irish family, has achieved great professional success in mergers and acquisitions. The couple, now semi-retired, each have extensive avocations.

They can afford almost any home purchase, to buy almost any object or to take any trip they choose on the spur of the moment. They do travel frequently for business and recreation. They sometimes seem about to go away or to have just returned. Probably some of this hectic activity helps them avoid issues between them. However, it creates other ones.

We've met for two years, about twice monthly, not more often, because they so frequently are out of town, but our sessions typically last 90 minutes. At the beginning, we usually focused on their disagreements over their use of common resources, on their difficulty sharing, particularly financial means, but also time and intimacy. This represented their initial presenting complaint. Peter has, in a concrete sense, earned all the money, and has a strong interest and expertise in researching and acquiring antique manuscripts. Jeannine has developed skills in organizing events that promote environmental awareness, many of which involve her out-of-pocket expense.

Peter has encouraged her in this commitment but ambivalently. He has no strong interest in this area. Peter makes his choices for his purchases quickly and decisively, but then it remains unclear how much money or time remains available to support Jeannine's projects about which she's less definitive.

Jeannine, a petite, bright, lively woman stands up for her part vehemently in the beginning, but she soon loses steam. Peter continues to add to his collection. This issue of sharing regularly drags the couple down. Jeannine feels her commitments pushed aside somewhat but, at the same time, she reflects that but for Peter, no funds would exist to invest in either of their pursuits. She also wonders if she advocates strongly enough for herself.

Jeannine then moves into an uncomfortable, resentful and distant state— Peter, a generous man in many respects, feels unloved and sexually lonely. In one guise or another this issue of mutuality, and fair exchange, became the central topic from the start.

Gradually Peter, with some encouragement from me, has more genuinely offered Jeannine backing for her events, and some he actively attends. The atmosphere around these negotiations certainly feels freer now—a paraverbal observation. However the couple can still slide backward into withholdingness and distancing, versus openness and shared participation, when they sense that the allocation of supplies seems not just, or easily offered. Jeannine then feels less supported emotionally and sometimes financially. Peter, in a parallel way, sees Jeannine holding back her warmth from him, and then he feels truly alone.

The impasse of how to share and to spend energy, intimacy, time, or money, stymies many couples, of course. Peter and Jeannine illustrate this conflict dramatically. Even in the midst of plenty, where there really is more than enough to fund both of their avocations, the couple can still readily sink into misunderstanding and anger about levels of openness and generosity; whose choices count more?

A depth seemed missing about this core issue. We could discuss the problem dispassionately, but we could never seem to capture it as surely as it required. We often appeared to make real progress, but then the matter would recede and return still unresolved—a bad penny that just would not go away.

Why is this central issue their Waterloo? There really is enough for both. In very different ways, Peter and Jeannine each high-energy, competent adults, inherited a control issue from their families. Peter had a bipolar mother who lavished love on him when in remission, but she expected perfect loyalty and attention in return. Her love came with a price.

In Jeannine's family, women had a lower status than men. The males received their education first. She had to buy her liberation with apparent compliance. In other words, for both, they never experienced unfettered psychological freedom growing up. There were always strings attached. The cast off part for each appeared … "If I give freely, will I get the good things offered back in the same vein. I'm afraid I will lose out. Someone else's needs (mother, brother) will take priority." Neither one seemed quite sure of getting recognized for who they really were and what they really wanted, so they needed to continue battling it out, symbolically, to build and retain their cache of desirable supplies, metaphorically buying a new a manuscript or contributing a hundred thousand dollars to an environmental campaign.

Then, one almost entirely paraverbal engagement, helped the three of us move in a much more productive direction with this crucial matter, than had any amount of previous verbal discussion. We came upon this critical event unawares. When they returned from a vacation trip, Peter and Jeannine offhandedly described a fun afternoon abroad. I pushed the issue, picking up, embedded in their story, and in my paraverbal reaction to it, what felt like moments of real joy between them. (Proposition #2— observing the therapist's own paraverbal reaction)

Jeannine and Peter found themselves in Northern Italy. She, a skilled chef, sought a supply of a specific rare spice that is found only in a particular local town. The flight to leave that evening gave them but a few hours for their hunt. Peter joined in the search …

They followed the clues from shop to shop, using fumbling Italian, trying to describe this apparently unusual substance. They jumped into cabs, walked down winding alleys, struggled to make themselves understood in dingy shops. Time grew short, but the hints of where to look got warmer. They both became more excited. These bodily paraverbal feelings started to fill the room as they related their story. They finally located the right merchant with the right supply. They bought all he had, amounting to only a few dollar") worth, jumped in the waiting cab and rushed to the airport.

They beamed recounting their escapade. They obviously enjoyed the teamwork and the collaboration. Peter handled the taxis and interviewed the shop owners, while Jeannine poked through the dark recesses of the Italian markets. When they finally located their quarry, this capped off an afternoon of fun.

A warm feeling suffused the office. I remarked how happy they looked recounting their adventure and their common involvement in it, using all their sleuthing powers to find the elusive spice. The item had minimal material cost. With almost no money involved, this episode became all about the interaction. In the past, they had spent up to a million dollars on other purchases, often with less satisfaction, and only as a prize for one partner, or the other, not a mutual undertaking.

Jim: "Sounds like you had real fun joining as detectives together with a common goal. You shine when you tell the stor") (an obvious paraverbal direct observation—Proposition #3). Peter and Jeannine readily agreed. This foray has become a "marke") in the treatment, which we refer back to as the "spice episode," a happy time in which both felt really engaged with their adventure, and with each other, and one in which no one's interest held first place—collaboration happened upon them. For both, the "cast asid") part, to enjoy giving, became activated and no longer put aside. No arguments over fairness entered this picture at any point. Each freely became #1 for the other.

The expedition itself clearly represents a highly extra-verbal experience. I called attention to their broad smiles, to their relaxed body postures and to their giggles as they recounted their adventure. They felt giddy together racing from place to place, feverishly searching for their little packages of condiments, representing the joy between them which they often wanted to feel together and which they usually just missed. (Harville Hendrix (2008) emphasizes that successful marriages include "high-energy fun.")

Proposition #3

The therapist actively brought the issue of their paraverbal relating directly into the treatment—Proposition #3. It became real for all of us. These feelings and the positive atmosphere lasted through this session, and regularly we can recapture it; clearly we've made gains in implicit relational knowing.

Just two months ago, they enjoyed another event of great closeness. The previous year Peter had arranged an elaborate destination birthday party for Jeannine, which took much planning and great expense. This year, however, he organized a small family celebratory dinner, which he cooked himself. Both Peter and Jeannine enjoyed this low key, inexpensive, intimate meal more than the gala of the year before. Jeannine said that she could tell how much love Peter had for her, and she felt the same. The mutual involvement and not the spectacular venue made all the difference.

I pointed out that they seemed happier and closer during the second party—not an extravaganza but an intimate dinner at home and an opportunity to get in touch with each other (Proposition #3—calling clear attention to the client's extra-verbal behavior). They could experience their usually cast off part more fully, which allowed them to give and to take trustfully.

If we leave out the paraverbal dimensions of these episodes, they fall flat on the page, flat when recounted in the office and flat in our hearts. If the couple described their condiment search without the drama, the excited smiles, the images of the shabby shops, their obvious exhilaration in their chase, little remarkable feels were left to experience. Jeannine and Peter could have summarized the story in just a few minutes, but the episode here plays in color, not in black and white. Likewise, the tenderness and the intimacy of the second, laid-back, birthday dinner only feels important in its extra-verbal detail, quiet closeness and satisfaction, full selves present.

The therapist needs to stay open to encourage, directly, the couple toward these kinds of richer more joyful life experiences. Without support from the true self of the counselor, the possibilities of the pair reacting to each other with their own authentic selves, will come less frequently into our therapies, and we'll lose crucial impact. Sometimes, the therapist needs to make unambiguous behavioral and verbal contributions. When we as therapists can join in with our full selves, we can spontaneously feel the part that's cast away and introduce it in the room. If we're separated in the presence from our client, these key images are much less likely to appear to us.

Proposition #4

The therapist can also, purposefully or not, introduce his or her own paraverbal, bodily self more fully into the exchange—now she becomes really active and relational. Leafing back through our chapters, we encounter several counselors moving in this direction. Kristin comes to tears as she speaks out the Starving Musician's pain. He's starving for someone to enjoy his music with him, starving for love that his wife can never offer. Kristin accompanies him in his wistfulness with her tearful reaction, Proposition #4—the therapist's full paraverbal reaction.

Leigh McCullough (1997, 2003), apparently, often hugged her patients after particularly harrowing, feelingful meetings (Kristin Osborn, personal communication—2-12-13)—that paraverbal alteration in technique doesn't make mention in Leigh's textbook. When the counselor opens himself or herself to personal participation and puts his or her own emotional life into the therapy verbally or behaviorally, he or she's working in Level 3 relational territory, and in Proposition #4, when he or she reacts within her own self-led paraverbal fashion.

If we return to Jeannine and Peter laughing together as they pursue their spice around the Milan suburbs, we encounter another example of a therapist's paraverbal sharing.

Peter and Jeannine clearly enjoyed their mad dash so much that their excitement and playfulness quickly spread to their bodies and to mine. Their story drew me in. I spontaneously felt in my chest and stomach what fun this careening from shop to shop felt to me. I began to express myself more openly; I spontaneously offered them a Duchênne smile, arms open, palms up, grinning ... "It feels so much better when it's a common pursuit, not just her hobby or just his hobby, which can compete! How much joy you had with each other for just about $40! I can feel it all over the room and in myself. You sparkle when you talk about it."—Proposition #4.

Jeannine, Peter, and I shared the excitement of their expedition as a threesome. I stepped out of professional role clearly communicating my happiness for them with obvious paraverbal messages going from me toward them. The three of us will not forget their Italian foray; it's an authentic experience for all of us now. Since that meeting, the therapy has moved palpably deeper in mutual connection. With the spices, we came upon a moment of meeting and had an extra-verbal flash of where we wanted the treatment to go and of where we can maybe nudge it more surely in the future. The paraverbal moment lead to an affective change inside that sparked more openness between all three of us.

Expression of joy, and all its attendant bodily reactions—smiles, physical warmth, open posture—represent an entirely paraverbal focus. Toddlers feel and express joy in a very similar way to adults. Hopefully, joy can represent a lifelong experience. Searching for joy in any therapy is an important undertaking. It changes the atmosphere in the room sometimes, though not always, quite permanently, a turn in the road.

A more successful attempt at sharing

Recently, we completed an extended session in which Peter and Jeannine faced each other, took deep breaths, and spent 5 minutes each exploring their feelings about the discretionary expenses. Jeannine felt that Peter had no budget, and with the funds left over, he sensed himself free to make repeated large purchases. She felt he tacitly ignored putting decisive limits on his own spending.

Peter agreed that that seemed unfair and explained his thoughts about the allocation of extra resources. He told Jeannine that she had as much right to the discretionary monies as did he. She had not really believed this before. The three of us felt this a new clarification and agreement surrounding their financial decision making. Paraverbal relaxation entered the room. We all felt the beginning of a more genuine resolution here to their recurrent conflict, and I remarked on the feeling—Propositions #3 and #4.

I also realized what I had overlooked previously. When Peter earlier had discussed the allocation of money, the words easily flowed, and his face showed little of the tension that this recurrent, difficult topic might have provoked. Once again the client's initial paraverbal messages points us toward the crucial part cast out, if we can but register that communication.

Peter did not feel ready to take up, authentically, the issue of relinquishing control over the resources. He had not yet connected with how serious a matter it had become in his marriage. I missed the message in his inexpressive voice and face that revealed his subtle lack of involvement. This therapy can only go forward when Peter gives over some control and Jeannine realizes and appreciates that he has done so and for her part, does not take advantage of him. She must feel first in his priority—a paraverbal message of recognition. To give openly, Peter must feel first in her priority that she wants to cuddle and cherish him.

The spice episode helped us see how joyful free giving can feel. We might have moved the therapy further at an earlier time had I picked up Peter's initial paraverbal messages of disengagement over the sharing issue. We've made more genuine progress with that matter in these last discussions.

I've noticed an important shift in the content of our meetings as well. The sharing conflict has receded in the therapy; both now energetically pursue their separate avocations often with strong levels of mutual support. Jeannine can stand up for herself, and she invests more time and money on her pursuits. Peter seems fine with that and engages a little more in her work with her.

The treatment focus has moved on toward matters involving the maturation of their two young adult sons and how Peter and Jeannine can stay intimately in touch with each other in the midst of their sometimes dizzying schedules and home projects. I sense that the paraverbal progress: the smiling, the exchanging fun, have played a major role in helping develop more teamwork and fuller mutuality in their two distinct avocations and in the rest of their lives.

The issue of who gets the lion's share of the resources returns, but we're on a more solid ground to negotiate it. They each have some more capacity to accept what they had previously rejected, a part in each of them that wants to give as well as receive. Each has to face the fear of losing important supplies reflecting important intimate recognition—their missing piece and their great longing. They can't become closer unless they confront that anxiety.

Consider the condiment story without the nonverbal richness though. If we did not plunge into extra-verbal relating, with Duchenne smiles, waving our hands, raising our voices, and laughing, the three of us might have passed by this original story, as just another enjoyable vacation anecdote and overlooked its significance. Something real happened for them in those musty Milan markets, and luckily we did well to follow the nonverbal clues to explore this event more deeply. Peter and Jeannine have a clearer grasp of the feeling of collaboration that often has eluded them but also feels so important to them.

So much goes on when the therapist takes action beyond the words—yelling "You don't suck") or chuckling with the clients over their search for an inexpensive cooking ingredient, or crying with the Starving Musician or supporting vulnerable Jack. If we miss these focusing moments, maybe we risk missing the whole point.

When the therapist participates this way, he or she is, "in sel") (Schwartz, 2004). The counselor allows his whole open person to suffuse the room and join with the open self of the client. Everyone feels more fully present, more real, more creative, and more open to wanting to enlarge their emotional lives with more consistent emotional connection to one another. They can then export these experiences out of the office and into their daily lives. However, the counselor usually leads the way into paraverbal openness. This represents the first necessary condition of effective therapy.

Both sides need to participate; counselor and client spark each other. Proposition #4 converges with Level 3 relational therapy. It does not necessarily represent a higher order, more effective intervention, every time, than do Propositions #1, #2, or #3, but Proposition #4, at the right time, can play its own unique role in the therapy. Here, the counselors become very present in their paraverbal selves and directly remark on their behavioral participation.

Ogden and Fisher (2015) introduced the possibility of a Proposition #5 when they outlined coaching their clients to take, literally, different physical postures during the session. Aligning the spine, and holding the head more upright leads toward different emotional experiences of greater confidence and optimism, as well as different physical sensations. This is an example of a very direct paraverbal intervention—changing the bodily stance to free the feelings versus the other way around. We have not experimented with these techniques, but they represent a natural extension to our emphasis on the Proposition #4 therapist, taking a new nonverbal, strongly connecting stance.

IN CLOSING

In and out of the consulting room, we cannot keep ourselves from becoming paraverbal people; why should we? Therapists have certainly smiled, laughed, and cried with their clients for the last hundred years and probably well before. We earlier noted a recent paper reporting that 72% of therapists report having cried in their treatment sessions with their patients, and that male and female, and older and younger, practitioners do so at similar rates with clients of either gender and across wide age ranges (Blume-Marcovici, Stolberg, and Khademi, 2013). Freud apparently lent patients small amounts of money and directly advised them on life issues (Peter Gay, 1988). Clearly we must listen to our clients words to help us locate their concerns, but what if coequal with that priority, we try to locate their paraverbal behavior, and our own, and exchange with them on that basis as well? Our case reviews have taught us the strength of that approach.

If we take this path, we might discover a quite different therapy. Since we, the counselors, would feel the patient's experience from inside our own skin and respond from inside our bodies to their paraverbal selves; a livelier, more intense and engaged meeting might often come to pass. The client might regularly contribute spontaneous new material, which would then validate and augment this approach.

We're inviting our colleagues, not toward a sweeping new orientation, devaluing the past, their own and that of our discipline, but encouraging them to experiment, in appropriate ways, with these (somewhat) inventive variations in technique that we've just introduced in the discussion of Propositions #1 to #4. We're encouraging them to pursue a heightened awareness toward their own paraverbal messages and toward those of their clients. We're describing a therapist here who's very active at many levels.

We offer the qualifier "somewha") because you, the reader, and we, the writers, realize that, from one lens, most of our findings don't appear startling at all. In a way, we did grasp it all along, although not with full consciousness. When the client connects to us with a Duchênne smile, which we spontaneously return, although we might not use this paraverbal terminology, we get that we've "synce") with each other in a meaningful way. After all the neurologist Duchênne practiced a hundred years ago, and he wasn't even a psychiatrist, he got it.

At this point, perhaps inevitably we start to conjecture about paths our field could have taken, if the pioneers had not begun, developed and almost fanatically defended psychotherapy as a quasi-rational scientific endeavor, built upon the verbal/cognitive Level #1, understanding of psychological conflict (Norcross and Lambert, 2014; Schore, 2014). Through our story, we realize, time and again, that the memorable critical turnings in the development of our profession, have come when Balint or Winnicott or Stern or Wachtel or Schwartz, usually without calling special attention to their revolutionary positions, actively added a new, nonrational, relational, experiential, paraverbal, "in self," dimension to their participation in the therapy encounter.

Balint invites his patient to somersault across the office. Stern clearly and directly states that psychotherapy has an implicit relational interchange at its base and that aspects of the paraverbal selves of both participants never stop playing a strong role in that exchange. We cannot ignore Stern's crucial insight. As they interact, the patient and the therapist mirror, to a remarkable degree, the extra-verbal mother–infant pair. It's about the behavior as much as about the words. It's about the right side of the brain as well as the left (Schore, 2014). It's about the presence of *each* participant, not just one. It's not only about the insight—greater presence leads to more open insight in any case. When we purposefully step into the right side of the implicit relational knowing brain, new, possibly indispensable, discoveries may quickly greet us.

Risks?

What if the therapists alters their style to reflect their bodily experience more openly but then feels that they verge, here and there, on becoming too reactive or too self-revealing? For example, perhaps the patient recalls his or her last bittersweet meetings with his or her late father and quietly begins to cry. Our therapist comes to tears, as well, for a moment or two, as I certainly did, in Chapter 4, with my dying mother of two teenagers.

The therapist might, or might not, call attention to the fact that the two have just shared a tearful experience, but the patient could still leave the office wondering on the one hand, if he upset the counselor, or wondering, on the other, if the therapist had unresolved feelings for her father, which he had unwittingly activated through his recollections of his own dad.

The pair, obviously, could discuss any of these reactions later in the meeting, or at a subsequent one, but maybe the client never mentions the therapist crying. If the counselor registers a paraverbal change in her patient soon thereafter, she could return to their tearful exchange to inquire about its effect on her client. However, not every important experience requires examination. Two people can sometimes just share an event wordlessly.

Further, Stern and Pally have repeatedly suggested that many Implicit Relational Knowing interchanges take place at the level of half-consciousness, probably in the right side of the brain (Schore, 2014). These events unfold, barely perceptibly but nevertheless they strongly support the alliance, as the two continue "moving along."

In the example just mentioned above, the therapeutic pair need not concentrate on their mutual tearfulness. Kristin and her client the Starving Musician did not remark that they both simultaneously cried in the hour. Perhaps the client, so deep in his own thoughts, did not consciously notice Kristin's reaction, but we can see that this sharing of tears, consciously or unconsciously recognized and probably strengthened the alliance in this crucial session. It certainly didn't undermine it.

Of course, the therapist cannot irresponsibly deflect the treatment toward a focus on her own paraverbal affects and behaviors, but "good enoug") contact with her inner state will usually curtail that possibility.

The real risk, here, runs in the opposite direction, that the counselor might shy away from contacting her own, and her client's, extra-verbal messages and thereby their inner selves. Each page of our book suggests the potential loss of cleaving to that strategy. Looking for and exploring our nonverbal participation and that of our companion, probably will lead us more fully, more presently into the interview. We have to explore continually for these paraverbal happenings; there's no other strategy to ferret them out. We need to grab hold of the extra-verbal information that swirls around us both; if not, we may miss much of the new learning of the therapy.

We, perhaps might redefine our mission as psychotherapists more broadly. Our direction actually is to seek, in any way we can, to gain deeper knowledge of Pally's 80% reservoir of the unconscious, including the ever present paraverbal behavior of both participants. We don't have to track every nonverbal motion. That would ultimately become boring for all concerned.

As Stern (2010), Fonagy (2014), and Schore (2014) all seem to suggest, however, we do need to become more and more aware of the client's paraverbal unconscious emerging from the right side of the brain, as it exchanges with our own. Unconscious World I and Unconscious World II both exist. We can explore them each more fully at many levels using a spectrum of methods, some spoken, others not.

If our readers now note their client's extra-verbal messages, and their own, in more specific ways, and call attention to them either behaviorally, or verbally or both, all at an appropriate time, they will operate in a self-led fashion and we've happily succeeded in our mission. There are as many ways to use this book as there are therapists to read it, when they bring the priceless resource of their paraverbal selves into the room.

We can readily integrate a nonverbal focus into our usual way of offering therapy of almost any stripe. The techniques we're describing do not call for us to jettison any present approach and adopt a new allegiance and a new language. We can introduce as much or as little of the paraverbal approach as feels warranted at particular moments, with particular individual clients or couples.

Our method feels like part of an evolutionary step, apiece with other contemporary developments, such as adding the neuropsychological, the attachment, or the sensory motor perspectives to our working view of therapy. The field seems poised to make a paradigm shift forward. As Martha Stark hinted (at a May 4, 2012 conference, in West Roxbury, MA), our next move in exploring psychotherapy will probably lead us to Level 4, treatment beyond the words. Our narrative describing paraverbal therapy suggests one direction toward exploring that new extra-verbal world.

Appendix A

The ATOS Scale

ATOS – 1 Page Brief Overview
ACHIEVEMENT OF THERAPEUTIC OBJECTIVES SCALE- 20 Point Brief Rating Guides 16APR09
The Psychotherapy Research Program at HMS
Leigh McCullough Ph.D., Director

CORE AFFECTIVE CONFLICT: 1) Anger/Assertion____ 2) Sadness/Grief____ 3) Closeness/Tenderness/Love____
4) Positive Feelings for Self____ 4.1) Self Compassion____ 4.2) Self Interest____ 4.3) Self Respect 4.4) Self Confidence/Mastery
4.5)Self Worth ____4.6) Self Entitlement/Deserving____ 4.7) Other _____
5) Sexual Feelings 6) Enjoyment ____ 7) Interest/Excitement ____ 8) Healthy Fear____ 9) Other _____ 10) Unclear ____

INSIGHT OR AWARENESS INTO MALADAPTIVE PATTERNS OF THOUGHTS, FEELINGS, AND/OR BEHAVIORS
81-100 - Excellent recognition of problem patterns. Excellent links to past origin of behaviors. Excellent awareness/insight.
61-80 - Good recognition of problem patterns. Some description of origins in past, linked to present. Good awareness/insight.
41-60 - Moderately clear recognition. On own describes occurrence of maladaptive patterns. No references to past. Moderate awareness/insight.
21-40 - Low recognition. Can see problem pattern only when pointed out by therapist. Little/no elaboration. Minimal awareness/insight.
1-20 - No recognition of maladaptive behavior patterns, or unsure when pointed out. May mention anxiety without reference to pattern. No awareness/insight or resists awareness/insight.

MOTIVATION TO GIVE UP MALADAPTIVE PATTERNS OF THOUGHTS, FEELINGS, AND/OR BEHAVIORS
81-100 - Excellent motivation to give up maladaptive patterns. Very strong discomfort, sorrow, openness to change. Little/no resistance.
61-80 - Strong motivation to give up maladaptive patterns. Strong discomfort, sorrow, openness to change. Low resistance.
41-60 - Moderate motivation to give up maladaptive patterns. Moderate discomfort, sorrow, openness to change. Moderate resistance.
21-40 - Low motivation to give up maladaptive patterns. Low discomfort, sorrow, openness to change. Much resistance.
1-20 - No motivation to give up maladaptive patterns. Ego-syntonic/desirable. "This is who I am." Almost total resistance.

ACTIVATING AFFECTS (VERBAL OR NONVERBAL BODILY SIGNS OF AROUSAL OF MAIN CONFLICTED/ PHOBIC AFFECTS)
81-100 - Full experience of emotion, well-integrated. Full grief, full openness/tenderness/trust, full justifiable outrage, full joy, etc.
61-80 - Strong experience of emotion. Strong affect quickly cut off or sustained but a little held back.
41-60 - Moderate experience of emotion. Some grief, some anger, some openness/tenderness/trust/care, etc. Some holding back.
21-40 - Low experience of emotion. Beginning indications of grief, anger, openness/tenderness/trust/care/joy, etc. Much holding back.
1-20 - Little/no physiological experience of emotion in facial expression, verbal report, tone of voice, body movement. Flat, dull, bland presentation.

INHIBITORY AFFECTS: (VERBAL OR NONVERBAL BODILY SIGNS OF ANXIETY, GUILT, SHAME, OR PAIN
81-100 - Extreme inhibitory affect: e.g., extreme shakiness, hesitancy, vigilance, trembling, anxiety or shame. Extreme uneasiness.
61-80 - High inhibitory affect: e.g., high levels of shakiness, hesitancy, vigilance, trembling, anxiety or shame. Great uneasiness.
41-60 - Moderate inhibitory affect: e.g., moderate shakiness, hesitancy, vigilance, trembling, anxiety or shame. Moderate uneasiness.
21-40 - Low inhibitory affect: e.g., low shakiness, hesitancy, vigilance, trembling, anxiety or shame. Low level of uneasiness.
1-20 - Little or no inhibitory affect. Little or no shakiness, guardedness, hesitancy, vigilance, trembling, anxiety, etc. Comfortable, at ease.

NEW EMOTIONAL LEARNING: ABILITY TO EXPRESS THOUGHTS, FEELINGS, WISHES, OR NEEDS
81-100 - Excellent expression of thoughts/feelings; sense of completeness, balance and excellent results. Great relief and satisfaction experienced.
61-80 - Good expression of thoughts/feelings; slight holding back. Not all expressed, but good sense of relief in speaking up. Good satisfaction.
41-60 - Moderate expression of thoughts or feelings; moderate holding back, but moderate effectiveness. Moderate relief. Moderate satisfaction.
21-40 - Beginning attempt to express thoughts or feelings. Much holding back. A little relief in expression. A little satisfaction.
1-20 - No expression of adaptive thoughts or feelings. Total holding back. No relief. No satisfaction. High end of this rating level: can begin to imagine expressing adaptive thoughts or feelings, wants and needs, but is as yet unable put it into action.

SENSE OF SELF
81-100 - Highly adaptive sense of self; compassionate and accepting of strengths and vulnerabilities.
61-80 - Very adaptive sense of self; much compassion and acceptance, but some self-blame or shame present.
41-60 - Moderately adaptive/maladaptive aspects of self-image in approximately equal amounts.
21-40 - Very maladaptive sense of self, but a little compassion, and a little ability for acceptance.
1-20 - Highly maladaptive sense of self; little or no compassion, awareness, or self acceptance—or excessive grandiosity.

SENSE OF OTHERS
81-100 - Highly adaptive sense of others. Very much compassion/acceptance/trust in others; little or no idealization or devaluation.
61-80 - Very adaptive sense of others. Much compassion/acceptance/trust, but some devaluation or idealization.
41-60 - Moderately adaptive as well as maladaptive aspects; moderate compassion/acceptance/trust, moderate devaluation/idealization.
21-40 - Very maladaptive sense of others, but some compassion, empathy or ability for acceptance; much devaluation or idealization.
1-20 - Highly maladaptive sense of others; Little or no compassion, empathy or acceptance. Very much devaluation, idealization or splitting.

Appendix B

The ATOS/Therapist Scale

ATOS THERAPIST 1-PAGE BRIEF OVERVIEW – 20 POINT BRIEF RATING GUIDES 9/16
The Psychotherapy Research Program at HMS
Kristin Osborn

**CORE AFFECTIVE CONFLICT: 1) Anger/Assertion_____ 2) Sadness/Grief_____ 3) Closeness/Tenderness/Love_____
4) Positive Feelings for Self_____ 4.1) Self Compassion_____ 4.2) Self Interest_____ 4.3) Self Respect 4.4) Self Confidence/Mastery
4.5) Self Worth _____4.6) Self Entitlement/Deserving_____ 4.7) Other _____
5) Sexual Feelings 6) Enjoyment _____ 7) Interest/Excitement _____ 8) Healthy Fear_____ 9) Other _____ 10) Unclear _____**

DOES THERAPIST HAVE AWEARENESS & INSIGHT INTO MALADAPTIVE PATTERNS OF THOUGHTS, FEELINGS OR BEHAVIORS AND CAN HE/SHE COMMNICATE IT TO THE PATIENT?

81-100--Excellent recognition of maladaptive patterns. Therapist suggests a hypothesis and describes problem pattern clearly, notes defenses and anxieties used to ward off a specific feeling, origin of behaviors, and impact. Therapist asks for patient collaboration.

61-80-Good recognition of maladaptive patterns. Therapist wonders out loud about maladaptive patterns, notes defenses and anxieties to ward off a specific feeling, explores origin and/or impact of behaviors, but the therapist is not directly noting their observations or asking for collaboration.

41-60-Moderately clear recognition of maladaptive patterns. Therapist describes occurrence of maladaptive patterns by noting defenses and anxiety, but does not address origin or impact . Therapist does not ask for patient collaboration.

21-40-Minimal recognition of maladaptive patterns. Therapist points out parts of the problem patterns, notes a defense and/or anxieties, but does not explore the origin of the behaviors or ask for patient collaboration. Patient points out problem patterns and therapist validates observations.

1-20-No recognition of maladaptive patterns and appears unsure even if patient points them out. Therapist may mention anxieties or defenses, but appears to have little focus or clarity. Therapist seems to have no or resists awareness/insight even if prompted by the patient.

DOES THERAPIST ATTEMPT TO INCREASE MOTIVATION TO GIVE UP MALADAPTIVE PATTERNS?

81-100--Excellent Interventions to help patient give up maladaptive patterns and replace with experience and/or expression of adaptive affect. Therapist stays focused in the face of patient discomfort and communicates that maladaptive patterns are ego-dystonic and describes potential for change.

61-80 - Strong Intervention to help patient give up maladaptive patterns and replace with experience and/or expression of adaptive affect. Therapist tries to stay focused in the face of patient discomfort, tries to communicate that maladaptive patterns are ego-dystonic and tries to describe potential for change.

41-60- Explicit/Moderate Intervention to help patient give up maladaptive patterns. Therapist may point out cost of maladaptive patterns, but may not point out benefits or vice versa. Therapist seems ambivalent and there is a lack of focus, particularly in the face of patient discomfort. Therapist may or may not communicate that maladaptive patterns are ego-dystonic and may or may not describe potential for change. Patient may do so on their own and therapist is responsive.

21-40- Implicit/Low Intervention to help patient give up maladaptive patterns. Therapist may not explore the maladaptive patterns or point out the cost and benefits. Therapist seems unaware and/or does not communicate that maladaptive patterns are ego-dystonic and does not describe potential for change. Patient may do so on their own, but therapist is not responsive.

1-20-No Intervention to help patient give up maladaptive patterns and no responsiveness if patient tries to do so on their own.

DOES THERAPIST USE INTERVENTIONS TO EXPOSE PATIENT TO BODILY EXPERIENCE OF ADAPTIVE AFFECT?

81-100--Excellent Interventions to expose adaptive affect. Therapist interventions are deliberate, focused, and tenacious, therapist is obviously attempting to assist patient with experiencing adaptive affect.

61-80--Strong Intervention to expose adaptive affect. Therapist interventions are deliberate and focused, therapist is attempting to assist patient with experiencing adaptive affect, but is not trying to help the patient experience more affect.

41-60--Moderate Intervention to expose adaptive affect. Therapist seems focused on assisting patient with experiencing affect and uses effective interventions, but doesn't seem to be particularly determined to find an intervention that may help expose more adaptive affect.

21-40--Low Intervention to expose adaptive affect. Therapist doesn't appear focused or aware of emerging adaptive affect, may even be blocking emerging adaptive affect.

1-20--No intervention to expose adaptive affect. Therapist seems unaware of emerging adaptive affect and offers no interventions to increase affect exposure, may even block emerging adaptive affect.

DOES THERAPIST INQUIRE OR POINT OUT PATIENT'S NEW LEARNING: ADAPTIVE EXPRESSION OF THOUGHTS, FEELINGS, WISHES, OR NEEDS.

81-100--Excellent Interventions Therapist describes observations fully and helps the patient to see new changes he/she exhibits inside and outside the session.

61-80- Good Interventions Therapist describes observations fully, but doesn't explore further to see if patient can see the changes.

41-60--Moderate Interventions Therapist notes changes observed inside and outside the session, but doesn't elaborate or help the patient to see the changes.

21-40--Low Interventions Patient notes the changes inside or outside the session, therapist agrees, and may explore further.

1-20--No Interventions Patient notes changes experienced, but therapist disagrees or doesn't respond.

DOES THERAPIST INTERVENE TO REGULATE INHIBITORY AFFECT? (ANXIETY, GUILT, SHAME, PAIN).

81-100--No Interventions: Therapist doesn't offer any interventions to regulate anxiety

61-80--Low Interventions: Therapist offers interventions, but does not pursue

41-60--Moderate Interventions Therapist offers interventions and seems ambivalent or unsure as to whether or not to pursue

21-40--Good Interventions: Therapist offers interventions and seems comfortable in pursuing

1-20--Excellent Interventions. Therapist offers interventions and seems comfortable regulating pursuit as needed

---

DOES THERAPIST INTERVENE TO ASSIST PATIENT IN IMPROVEMENT IN SELF-IMAGE

81-100--Excellent Interventions Therapist uses interventions to help patient have a healthier sense of self and to be compassionate and accepting of strengths and vulnerabilities and will challenge self-blame or shame.

61-80--Good Interventions Therapist helps patient to have a healthier sense of self and to be compassionate and accepting of strengths and weaknesses, but does not challenge some self-blame or shame.

41-60--Moderately Interventions Therapist sometimes helps patient to have a healthier self-image, but accepts versus challenges signs of self-blame or shame.

21-40--Low Interventions Therapist barely helps patient to have a healthier sense of self, and seems to be encouraging lack of compassion or low ability for self-acceptance.

1-20--No interventions Therapist appears to validate an unhealthy sense of self and does not challenge patients lack of self-compassion, awareness, acceptance, or grandiosity.

DOES THERAPIST INTERVENE TO ASSIST PATIENT IN IMPROVEMENT IN IMAGE OF OTHERS

81-100--Excellent Interventions Therapist uses interventions to help patient have a healthier sense of others and to be compassionate and accepting of their strengths and vulnerabilities with little to no idealization or devaluation.

61-80--Good Interventions Therapist uses interventions to help patient have a healthier sense of others and to be compassionate and accepting of their strengths and vulnerabilities, but does not fully address idealization or devaluation.

41-60--Moderate Interventions Therapist uses interventions to help patient have a healthier sense of others and to be moderately compassionate and accepting of their strengths and vulnerabilities, but does not address idealization or devaluation.

21-40--Low Interventions Therapist does not use interventions to help patient have a healthier sense of others or to be compassionate and accepting of their strengths and vulnerabilities and enables idealization and devaluation.

1-20--No Interventions Therapist does not use interventions to help patient have a healthier sense of self, enables a maladaptive sense of others with little to no compassion, empathy or acceptance and much devaluation, idealization and splitting.

Appendix C

Accessibility Scale

CLOSED → OPEN

Scale Point:

1. Closed:
   Jaw clenched
   Blank facial expression
   No smiles
   Tears if present, are choked
   Nearly silent
   Eyes cast down or eyes closed
   Body and face, often turned away from therapist
   Rigid body
   Hands clenched or palms down
   Voice low, no variability in tone or prosody (rhythm of speech pattern)
   Speaks slowly, voice inaudible at times
   Body scrunched down
   Paraverbal Message: "I am inaccessible, no matter what you do."

2. Mostly Closed:
   Never smiles
   Only a little eye contact
   Palms down
   Scrunched down in chair
   Mostly turned away from therapist
   Arms usually stiff and close to body
   Fidgety or rigid, uncomfortable in chair

Appendix C

Minimal facial expression

Leaning down or back from therapist

Low tone, few words, almost a monotone, often inaudible, slow prosody

Paraverbal Message: "I'm slightly accessible but very unreliably so."

3. A Little More Warmth—less closed

Fleeting Eye Contact

Palms up or down

Mostly slumped

Arms down

Mostly leaning away or noncommitted in posture

Leaning away, but occasionally moving toward therapist

Little range of affect, but an occasional brief smile or nod

Some range in speech, tone up or down, prosody fast then slow, still not many words

Switches physical positions and moves a little bit to express affect

Little facial movement

Jaw clenched then unclenched

Paraverbal Message: "I'm possibly accessible, if you respond to my subtle invitations."

(It's highly unlikely that any therapist would present as inaccessible. However, from now on our descriptions will apply to the therapist's body language and verbal expression just as they apply to the client's. We score counselor and patient separately on each segment.)

4. Normal Social Accessibility:

Some warm facial movement appropriate to the verbal interchange

Palms up or down

Some responsive body movement

Body facing therapist (or client) and rather relaxed

Some leaning toward therapist or therapist leaning toward client

Eye contact 50% of the time at least, for therapist or the client

Different postures but appropriate in relation to the companion and to the exchange

Occasional opening of arms

Some range of affect

Speech, prosody, voice tone more variable and correlated to content

More words

More animated in relationship—both therapist or client

Jaw mostly unclenched

Less rigid posture
Attributes of normal conversation with someone you know but not a close
    friend
Paraverbal Message: "I'm accessible on safe topics."

5. Quite Open:
    Facial movement animated, in relation to therapist/client
    Palms up
    Body relaxed and mirroring
    Leans toward therapist/client
    Expressive speech appropriate to content
    Some smiles
    More active face
    Arms open and relaxed
    Speech tone up and down, prosody expressive and reactive to exchange
    Many more words
    Shows unmistakably strong affect, sad, mad, tender—signs of a spontane-
        ous, not rehearsed exchange
    Paraverbal Message from Client: "I will tell us both some limited secrets."
    Paraverbal Bodily Message from Therapist: "You can confide in me."

6. Very Open:
    Face open and expressive
    Palms up
    Body relaxed, not covered up with arms
    Client leans toward therapist and/or therapist toward client
    Often mirrors therapist in body posture
    Direct eye contact
    (Couple) regularly looking at each other
    Speech expressive in relation to therapist or client or to partner (couple
        therapy)
    Smiles, laughs, tears
    Range of personal affect beyond normal social interchange
    Verbal tone up and down, prosody and volume enhances the exchange
    Much affective expression
    Effort to reveal self well beyond social conversation
    Hands and jaw open and relaxed
    Paraverbal Message from Client: "I am willing and able to tell some
        secrets and express some true feelings."
    Paraverbal Message from Therapist: "I am present as a human being, not
        just as a counselor."

7. Peak Moments in Relating—very open

Tears, intimate sounds of recognition, that is, spontaneous laughter

No censure in room

Client looking directly at therapist and/or therapist looking directly at client

Touching self, touching hands to express affect

Holding hands (couple)

Looking at partner (couple)

Deep expression/whole body movement for either client or therapist

Jaw and fists relaxed

Patient may look startled by lack of control

Voice is warm and tender, where appropriate for therapist or client

Deep range of affect (new insight—new feeling)

Tone up and down, prosody and amplitude punctuate exchange

Sad, mad, loving, frightened affect expressed

Smiles, laughter, tears for one or both participants

Paraverbal Message client: "I am willing and able to tell secrets, and to show strong feelings and vulnerabilities in this relationship with you."

Paraverbal Message therapist: "I'm resonating with you in a deep and personal way."

Congruence/Incongruence Scale

SCALE POINT:

1. Incongruent
   Body and face give opposite message to underlying affect and content
   Laughs when hurt, closed up when expressing closeness
   Palms up, when defensive
   Palms down, when expressive
   Leans toward therapist when highly defended
   Smiles, when angry
   Tears, when angry
   Charming and apparently sincere, when actually manipulative
   Open and expressive in body when chatting and saying nothing of import
   Paraverbal Message: "My body language expresses the opposite of my
      true feeling."

2. Mostly Incongruent
   Body and facial message apparently not related to affect
   No strong expressive trend in face
   Body open or closed but giving no discernible messages
   Body/face/tone/prosody add little to our understanding of content
   Shrugs off emotions with arms, hands, eyes
   Behaves this way, on all of these dimensions, for most of the interview
   Paraverbal Message: "My body language gives you no clue about what
      I'm really feeling."
   Cool and noncommittal when reacting to therapist

3. Slight Congruence

   Smiles a little when happy

   Lifts voice a little when mad

   Some appropriate facial activation around emotional topics

   Arms/hands a little open when topic is important

   Jaw a little clenched when mad

   Eyes downcast when sad, body language as likely to match affect as not

   Congruence off and on, mostly off, little body movement one way or the other

   Paraverbal Message: "You can make some valid inferences from my speech tone and body language but not many."

(From here on, the scale applies equally to the therapist and the client—we score counselor and patient each separately on Accessibility and Congruence.)

4. Normal Social Congruence

   Expression does not discount content, but only moderately mirrors it

   Average social congruence

   Eyes/voice match but don't enhance content very much

   Slight tears if sad—mild congruence

   Therapist is conventionally present but does not seem intently involved.

   Normal amplitude in voice and face

   Tone and prosody socially appropriate

   Routinely restrained congruence

   Mild congruence/connection between paraverbal behavior and affective content

   Arms/hands, smiles and other facial expressions, mildly congruent with the evident affect, most of the time

   Paraverbal Message: "My body language does reflect what I'm really feeling, but it gives off little deeper information about those affects."

5. Quite Congruent

   Eyes/hands/face match shifts in affect, for client or therapist

   Stronger congruence makes affect a little more real

   Body open when expressing intimate feeling

   Fairly strong match in eyes/body posture/voice tone/prosody

   Strong match in at least one of these areas just above

   Prosody, tone, amplitude of speech tells us more about how the subject really feels, enhances the message—the therapist reveals more about his true feelings

   Possible (spontaneous, broad, full) Duchênne smiles, active facial responses for either client or therapist

Very noticeable congruence some of the time for either therapist or client, and then it stops

Couples often touch

Paraverbal Message from Therapist: "I'm nonverbally reactive to your real concerns."

Paraverbal Message from Client: "My congruence feels strong enough that you can usually tell which affect and which content are really important to me."

6. Congruence Strong

Beyond social range in congruence

In most systems (posture, tone, prosody and amplitude of speech, eyes, face, arms) affect and paraverbal clues match

Arms open

Eyes direct

Palms up

Letting go in congruence; it isn't planned

It happens spontaneously

Upright posture when angry

Eyes revealing

Loud tone when angry

Two or three laughs when situation is truly funny

At least two or three Duchênne smiles for either client or counselor or both

Emotional release in the segment. These affects feel for real.

Couples touch and look directly at each other

Paraverbal Message for both Client and Therapist: "I'm present and strongly congruent in my speech. I'm verbally and paraverbally attentive to the other."

Expressiveness and affect match

7. Congruence Very Strong

Open body, face powerfully reflects content of speech

Tears when sad or dear/tender

Reaching out to partner (if couple)

Shouting, flailing arms if angry

Couples lean toward each other, initiate and maintain eye and hand contact

Client leans toward therapist or therapist leans toward client or both

Direct eye content when revealing something important

Strong match in body language between content and affect. All systems (eyes, postures, hands, face, arms, speech tones, prosody, amplitude) strongly enhance expression and meaning of verbal communication

Several sincere Duchênne smiles from either counselor or client or both

Both spontaneously transparent

Paraverbal strongly influences the power of the verbal content and strongly enhances the affective message, well beyond the social range of congruence

Paraverbal Message client: "You can see me at my core—my body language powerfully, authentically represents and enhances my affective expression and the content of my speech."

Paraverbal Message therapist: "I'm sincerely involved paraverbally as well as verbally. I'm resonating with you."

Appendix E

Control Mastery Scale

Adapted from Sampson and Weiss, 1986, p. 372; reprinted with the permission of Guilford Publications.

Patient tests therapist to disconfirm the pathogenic belief.

Part A: In peer consultation, the judges specify the pathogenic belief and the test that the therapist must pass. For example, a young woman wants a free, egalitarian, caring relationship with a man, but she is afraid she will never have it and that she won't achieve it with this male therapist either. Without this open relationship experience, the client risks becoming overwhelmed by the pathogenic belief: "I'm convinced I'm a second-class citizen not worthy of true male regard." Therefore, the therapist must offer her this freeing equal interchange that she so badly needs.

Part B: The therapist fails or passes the test: score 1–7. (The three judges make consensus rating.)

1. The therapist's response represents a clear-cut example of failing the test that is, he has no idea she needs an egalitarian relationship and reacts coldly when she pulls to initiate one between them.
2. Fails test but more subtly than #1.
3. Therapist mildly fails test.
4. Ambiguous position, midway between passing and failing the test, elements of both. For example, the therapist reacts supportively and openly to the client but doesn't understand her need for him to behave in an egalitarian fashion.
5. Mildly passing test, not explicit or clear.
6. Example of passing test, less clear than #7.

7. Excellent clear-cut example of passing test. Therapist may or may not directly enunciate that the patient wants an equal relationship with a man, but he actively unambiguously behaves in an open, direct, respectful, democratic way toward the client. He clearly does not repeat earlier, disrespectful, male relationships that the client has had.

References

Allen, J. G. (2013). *Restoring mentalizing in attachment relationships*. Washington, D.C.: American Psychiatric Publishing.

Amen, D. G. (1998). *Change your brain, change your life*. New York: Three Rivers Press.

Aron, L. (1996). *A meeting of the minds: Mutuality in psychoanalysis*. Hillside, NJ: Analytic Press.

Alexander, F. and French, T. M. (1946). *Psychoanalytic therapy: Principles and applications*. New York: Ronald Press.

Balint, M. (1968). *The basic fault: Therapeutic aspects of regression*. London: Tavistock Publications.

Balint, M., Ornstein, P. H., and Balint, E. (1972). *Focal psychotherapy*. London: Tavistock Publications.

Beebe, B. and Lachmann, F. (2002). *Infant research and adult treatment: Co-constructing interactions*. Hillside, NJ: Analytic Press.

Beebe, B., Knoblauch, S., Rustin, J. et al. (2005). *Forms of intersubjectivity in infant development and adult treatment*. New York: Other Press.

Bhatia, M. et al. (2009). Desensitization of conflicted feelings: Using the ATOS to measure early changes in a single-case affect phobia therapy treatment. *Archives of Psychiatry and Psychotherapy*, 1, p. 31–38.

Blatt, S. & Behrends, R, (1987). *Internalization, separation-individuation and the nature of therapeutic action*. Int. J of Psychoanal., 68, 279–297.

Blume-Marcovici, A. C., Stolberg, R. A., and Khademi, M. (2013). Do therapists cry in therapy? The Role of experience and other factors. *Psychotherapy*, 50, p. 224–234.

Birdwhistell, R. (1970). *Kinesics and context*. Philadelphia: University of Pennsylvania Press.

Bohart, A. C. and Tallman, K. (1999), *How clients make psychotherapy work*, Washington, D.C.: American Psychological Association.

Boston Change Process Study Group. (2002). Report 3. Explicating the implicit: The local level and the micro process of change in the analytic situation. *International Journal of Psychoanalysis*, 83, p. 1051–1062.

Boston Change Process Study Group. (2005). The something more than interpretation revisited: Sloppiness and co-creativity in the psychoanalytic encounter. *Journal of the American Psychoanalytic Association*, 53, p. 693–729.

Boston Change Process Study Group. (2010). *Change in psychotherapy: A unifying paradigm*. New York: W.W. Norton.

Budman, S. H. and Gurman, A. S. (1988). *Theory and practice of brief therapy*. New York: Guilford Press.

Caldwell, G. (2009). *Let's take the long way home*. New York: Random House.

Casement, P. (1985). *Learning from the patient*. New York: Guilford Press.

Cohn, j, Campbell, S & Ross, S.(1991). Infant response in the still-face paraddigm at 6 monts predicts avoidant and secure attachment at 12 months, *Developmental Psychology*, 26, 367–376.

Cozolino, L. (2014). *The neuroscience of human relationships: Attachment and the developing brain* (2nd Edition). New York: W. W. Norton.

Darwin, C. (1872). *The expression of emotions in man and animals*. London: John Murray. (also Filliquarian Paperbacks, Chicago, IL.)

Derogatis, L. R., and Lazarus, L. (1994). SCL-90-R: Brief symptom inventory and matching clinical scales. In M, E. Maruish, (Ed.), *The use of psychological testing for treatment planning and outcome assessment*. Hillside, NJ: Laurence Erlbaum, p. 217–248.

Diamond, D., Stoval-McClough, C., Clarkin, J. F., et al. (2003). Patient-therapist and attachment in the treatment of borderline personality disorder. *Bulletin Menninger Clinic*. 67, p. 227–259.

Dicks, H. V. (1967). *Marital tensions*. London: Karnac Books.

Donovan, J. M. (1989). Characterologic intervention and the physical position of the patient. *Psychiatry*, 52, p. 167–183.

Donovan, J. M. (2003). *Short term object relations couples therapy*. New York: Taylor and Frances.

Donovan, J. M., Osborn, K. A. R., and Rice, S. R. (2009). *The Accessibility and the Congruence scales – unpublished (available from the first author)*.

Dostoyevsky, F. (1864). *Notes from the underground*. London: Epoch and New York: Vintage reprint editions.

Ehrenberg, D. B. (1992). Psychoanalytic engagement. *Contemporary Psychoanalysis*. 18, p. 535–555.

Ekman, P. and Friesen, W. V. (1978). *Facial action coding system: A technique for the measurement of facial movement*. Palo Alto, CA: Consulting Psychologists Press.

Ekman, P. (2001). *Telling lies*. New York: W.W. Norton.

Ekman, P. (2003). *Emotions revealed*. New York: Henry Holt and Co., 2nd Edition.

Emerson, D. (2015). *Trauma sensitive yoga in therapy: Bringing the body into treatment*. New York: W.W. Norton.

Fairbairn, W. R. D. (1952). *An object relations theory of the personality*. New York: Basic Books.

Ferenczi, S. (1931). Child analysis in the analysis of adults. *International Journal of Psychoanalysis*. 12, p. 468.

Fonagy, P. (2001). *Attachment theory and psychoanalysis*. New York: Other Press.

Fonagy, P., Gergely, G., Jurist, E. L., et al. (2002). *Affect regulation mentalization and the development of the self*. New York: Other Press.

Fonagy, P. and Allison E. (2014). The role of mentalizing and epistemic trust in the therapeutic relationship. *Psychotherapy*. 51, p. 372–380.

Freedman, N. and Hoffman, S, P. (1967). Kinetic behavior in altered clinical states. *Perceptual and Motor Skills*, 24, p. 239–258.

Freedman, N. and Grand, S. (1984). Shielding: An associative organizer. In G. Stricker and R. H. Keisman (Eds.), *From research to clinical practice*. New York: Plenum Press.

Freedman, N., Blass, T., Rifkin, A. et al (1973). Body movement and the encoding of aggressive affect. *Journal of Personality and Social Psychology*. 26, p. 72–85.

Freud, S. (1912). Recommendations for physicians on the psychoanalytic method of treatment. In *Freud, Therapy and Technique*. P. Rieff (Ed.), New York: Colher, 1963.

Gaston, L., Piper, W. E., Debbane, E. G., et al. (1994). Alliance and technique for predicting outcome in short – and long – term psychotherapy. *Psychotherapy Research*, 4, p. 121–135.

Gay, P. (1988). *Freud: A life for our time*. New York: W. W. Norton.

Gedo, J. (1979). *Beyond interpretation: Toward a revised theory for psychoanalysis*. New York: International Universities Press.

Geller, S,M, & Porges, S,W.(2014). J of Psychotherapy Integration. Vol 24, No 3, 178–192.

Gladwell, M. (2005*). Blink: The process of thinking without thinking*. New York: Little Brown.

Goldbeck, T., Tolkmitt, F. and Scherer, K. R. (1988). Experimental studies on vocal affect communication. In *Facets of emotion*. Scherer, K. R. (Ed). Hillsdale, NJ: Lawrence Erlbaum.

Greenberg, J. R. and Mitchell, S. A. (1983). *Object relations in psychoanalytic theory*. Cambridge, MA: Harvard University Press.

Greenberg, L. S., Rice, L. N., and Elliott, R. (1993). *Facilitating emotional change: The moment-by-moment process*. New York: Guilford Press.

Greenson, R. (1967). *The technique and practice of psychoanalysis*. New York: International Universities Press.

Guntrip, H. (1969). *Schizoid phenomena, object relations and the self*. New York: International Universities Press.

Guntrip, H. (1975). My experience of analysis with Fairbairn and Winnicott. *International Review of Psychoanalysis*. 2, p. 145–156.

Gustafson, J.G. 1986. *The Complex Secret of Brief Psychotherapy*. New York: Guilford Press.

Gustafson, J. P. (1981). The complex secret of brief psychotherapy in the works of Malan and Balint. In S. H. Budman (Ed.), *Forms of Brief Therapy*. New York: Guilford Press, p. 83–128.

Gustafson J. P. (1984). An integration of brief dynamic psychotherapy. *American Journal of Psychiatry*, 141, p. 935–944.

Gustafson J. P. (1995). *Brief versus long term psychotherapy.* Northvale, NJ: Jason Aronson.

Hassin, R. R., Uleman, J. S. and Bargh, J. A. (2005). *The new unconscious.* New York: Oxford University Press.

Heller, M. and Haynal, V. (1997). A doctors face: A mirror of his patient's suicidal projects. In J. Guimon (Ed.), *The Body in psychotherapy.* Basel, Switzerland: Karger.

Hendrix, H. (1988). *Getting the love you want.* New York: Harper & Row.

Hendrix, H. (2008). *Getting the love you want: 20th anniversary edition.* New York: Harper & Row.

Hendrix, H. (2014). *Introduction to clinical training in imago relationship therapy – training manual text.* Lexington, KY: Imago Relationships International.

Hertenstein, M. (2013). *The tell,* New York: Basic Books.

Horowitz, L, M., Alden, L, E., Wiggins, J, S. (2000). *Inventory of interpersonal problems.* London: Psychological Corporation.

Jacobs, T, J. (1991). *The use of the self: Countertransference and communication in the analytic situation.* Madison, CT: International Universities Press.

Jaffe.J., Beebe,B. Feldstein, S. et al (2001). *Rythms of dialogue in early infancy.* Monographs of the society for research in child development, 66, Serial No. 264, pp 1–132.

Johnson, S. M. (1998). Emotionally focused couple therapy, in F. M. Datilio (Ed.), *Case studies in family and couple therapy,* New York: Guilford Press, p. 450–472.

Johnson, S. M. (1999). *Emotionally focused couple therapy: Straight to the heart.* New York: Guilford Press.

Kernberg, O, F. (1975). *Borderline conditions and pathological narcissism.* New York: Jason Aronson.

Khan, M. (1974). *The privacy of the self.* London: Hogarth Press.

Kohut, H. (1971). *The analysis of the self.* New York: International Universities Press.

Lambert, M, J. and Ogles, B, M. (2004). The efficacy and effectiveness of psychotherapy. In Lambert, M, J. (Ed). *Bergin and Garfield's, Handbook of psychotherapy and behavior change.* (5th Ed.). New York: Wiley, p. 307–390.

Levenson, H. (1995). *Time limited dynamic psychotherapy.* New York: Basic Books.

Linehan, M. N. (1993). *Cognitive behavioral treatment of borderline personality disorder.* New York: Guilford Press.

Lyons-Ruth, K. (1998). Implicit relational knowing: It's role in development and psychoanalytic treatment. *Infant Mental Health Journal,* 19, p. 272–289.

Lyons-Ruth, K., Yellen, C., Melnick, S. et al. (2005). Expanding the concept of unresolved mental states: Hostile/helpless states of mind on the adult attachment interview are associated with disruptive mother-infant communication and infant disorganization. *Developmental Psychopathology,* 17, p. 1–23.

Malan, D. (1979). *Individual psychotherapy and the science of psychodynamics.* London: Butterworths.

Maltsberger, J. T. and Buie, D. H. (1974). Countertransference hate in the treatment of suicidal patients. *Archives of General Psychiatry,* 30. 625–633.

Mann, J. (1981). The core of time-limited psychotherapy: Time and the central issue, in S. H. Budman (Ed.), *Forms of brief therapy*. New York: Guilford Press, p. 25–43.

Maroda, K. J. (1991). *The Power of countertransference*. Chichester, UK: Wiley.

Maroda, K. J. (1999). *Seduction, surrender and transformation: Emotional engagement in the analytic process*. Hillsdale, NJ: Analytic Press.

Maroda, K. J. (2010). *Psychodynamic techniques*. New York: Guilford Press.

McCullough, L. (Vaillant). (1997). *Changing character*. New York: Basic Books.

McCullough, L., Kuhn, M., Andrews, S. et al. (2003). *Treating affect phobia: A manual for short term dynamic psychotherapy*. New York: Guilford Press.

McCullough, L. (2003). The reliability of the achievement of therapeutic objectives scale. *Journal of brief psychotherapy*, 2, p. 75–90.

Mitchell, S. A. (1988). *Relational concepts in psychoanalysis*. Cambridge, MA: Harvard University Press.

Mitchell, S. A. (1993). *Hope and dread in psychoanalysis*. New York: Basic Books.

Mitchell, S. A. (1997). *Influence and autonomy in psychoanalysis*. Hillsdale, NJ: The Analytic Press.

Mitchell, S. A. and Black, M. (1995). *Freud and beyond*. New York: Basic Books.

Norcross, J. (Ed.), (2002). *Psychotherapy relationships that work: Therapist contributions and responsiveness to patients*. New York: Oxford University Press.

Norcross, J. C. and Lambert, M. J. (2014). Relationship science and practice in psychotherapy: Closing commentary. *Psychotherapy*. 51, p. 398–403.

Loewald, H. W. (1960). *On the therapeutic action of psychoanalysis*. Int. J. Psychoanal. 58, 463–472.

Ogden, P. and Fisher, J. (2015). *Sensorimotor psychotherapy: Interventions for trauma and attachment*. New York: W. W. Norton.

Ogden, T. H. (1994). The analytic third: Implications for psychoanalytic theory and technique. *The Psychoanalytic Quarterly*, 23, p. 167–195.

Osborn, K. et al (2014), *Creating Change through Focusing on Affect: Affect Phobia Therapy*. In N. Thoma & D. McKay (Eds.). Working with Emotions in Cognitive Behavioral Therapy: Techniques for Clinical Practice, (pp. 146–174). New York: Guilford Press

Osborn, K. A. R. (2009). *The ATOS Therapist Scale*. (unpublished – available from the author).

Pally, R. (2000). *The mind brain relationship*. New York: Other Press.

Racker, H. (1968). *Transference and countertransference*. New York: International Universities Press.

Reik, T. (1948). *Listening with the third ear*. New York: Farrar, Strauss and Young.

Rogalis, D. and Lazarus, (1994). SCL 90 and Inventory of Interpersonal Problems IIP Horowitz.

Rogers, C. R. (1951). *Client Centered Psychotherapy*, Boston: Houghton-Mifflin.

Rosenberg, M. (1965). *Society and adolescent self-image*. Princeton, NJ: Princeton University Press.

Safran, J.D & Muran J.C. (2000). *Negotiating the therapeutic alliance: A treatment guide*. New York: Guilford Press.

Scharff, D. E. and Scharff, J. S. (1991). *Object relations couples therapy*. Northvale, NJ: Jason Aronson.

Schore, A. N. (2003a). *Affect dysregulation and disorders of the self*. New York: W.W. Norton.

Schore, A. N. (2003b). *Affect regulation and the repair of the self*. New York: W.W. Norton.

Schore, A. N. (2014). The right brain is dominant in psychotherapy. *Psychotherapy*, 51, p. 388–397.

Schwartz, R. (2004). The larger self. *The Psychotherapy networker*, May/June, p. 1–9.

Searles, H. F. (1965). *Collected papers on schizophrenia and related subjects*. New York: International Universities Press.

Shapiro, F. (1995). *Eye movement desensitization: Basic principles, protocols and procedures*. New York: Guilford Press.

Siegel, D. J. (1999). *The developing mind: Toward a neurobiology of interpersonal experience*. New York: Guilford Press.

Siegel, D. J. (2012). *The developing mind: Toward a neurobiology of interpersonal experience*. (2nd Ed.). New York: Guilford Press.

Siegman, A. W., and Pope, B. (Eds). (1972). *Studies in dyadic communication*. Elmsford, NY: Pergaman Press.

Silberschatz, G. and Curtis, J. (1986). Measuring the therapist's impact on the patient's therapeutic progress in *Journal of Consulting and Clinical Psychology*.

Slade, A. (2008). The implications of attachment theory and research for adult psychotherapy: Research and clinical perspectives, in *Handbook of Attachment: Theory, Research and Clinical Applications*, 2nd Edition, Cassidy, J. and Shever, P. R. (Eds). New York: Guilford Press. P. 762–782.

Stark, M. (1994). *Working with resistance*. New York: Jason Aronson.

Stark, M. (1999). *Modes of therapeutic action*. Northvale, NJ: Jason Aronson.

Stern, D. N. (1985). *The interpersonal world of the infant*. New York: Basic Books.

Stern, D. N., Sander, L., Nahum, J., et al. (1998). Non-interpretive mechanisms in psychoanalytic therapy: The "something more" than interpretation. *International Journal of Psychoanalysis*, 79, p. 908–921.

Stiles, W. B. (1992). *Describing talk*. Newbury Park, CA: Sage Publications.

Stolorow, R. D., Brandschaft, B., and Atwood, G. E. (1987). *Psychoanalytic treatment: An intersubjective approach*. Hillsdale, NJ: Analytic Press.

Stone, M. H. (1990). *The fate of borderline patients*. New York: Guilford Press.

Stone, M. H. (2006). *Personality disordered patients: Treatable and untreatable*. Washington, DC: American Psychiatric Publishing.

Strupp, H.H. (Forward 1X) in Levenson. H. (1975). New York: Basic Books.

Tansey, M. J. and Burke, W. F. (1989). *Understanding countertransference*. New York: The Analytic Press.

Tronick, E. Z. (2007). *The neurobehavioral and social emotional development of infants and children*. New York: W.W. Norton.

Tronick, E. Z. (2007). The Still Face Experiment - YouTube.

Wachtel, P. L. (1977). *Psychoanalysis and behavior therapy: Toward an integration*. New York: Basic Books.

Wachtel, P. L. (1993). *Therapeutic communication: Principles and effective practice.* New York: Guilford Press.

Wachtel, P. L. (2007). *Integrative relational psychotherapy. American Psychological Association videotape, Systems of Psychotherapy*, Series 1.

Wachtel, P. L. (2008). *Relational theory and the practice of psychotherapy.* New York: Guilford Press.

Wachtel, P. L. (2010). Beyond "ESTs": Problematic assumptions in the pursuit of evidence based practice. *Psychoanalytic Psychology*, 27, p. 251–272.

Wachtel, P. L. (2011). *Inside the session.* Washington, D.C.: American Psychological Association.

Wachtel, P. L. (2014). An integrative relational point of view. *Psychotherapy*, 51, p. 342–349.

Wallin, D.J. (2007). *Attachment in psychotherapy.* New York: Guilford Press.

Wampold, B. (2001). *The great psychotherapy debate: Models, methods and findings.* Mahwah, NJ: Lawrence Erlbaum.

Weiss, J., Sampson, H., and The Mt. Zion Psychotherapy Research Group. (1986). *The psychoanalytic process.* New York: Guilford Press.

Weiss, J. (1993). *How psychotherapy works.* New York: Guilford Press.

Winnicott, D. W. (1965). *The maturational processes and the facilitating environment.* New York: International Universities Press.

Winnicott, D. W. (1971). *Playing and reality.* New York: Basic Books.

Wishnie, H. H. (2005). *Working in the countertransference: Necessary entanglements.* Lanham, MD: Rowman and Littlefield (originally published by Jason Aronson, 2002).

Index